The Mastering Engineer's Handbook

by Bobby Owsinski

Edited by Sally Engelfried

236 Georgia Street, Suite 100
Vallejo, CA 94590

Library of Congress Catalog Card Number: 00-100263

Art Director: Stephen Ramirez
Cover design: Linda Gough, Stephen Ramirez
Cover photo: Susana Millman
Special thanks to Fantasy Studios and mastering engineer George Horn
for appearing in the cover photo.
Production Staff: Mike Lawson, publisher; Glenn Meadows, technical editor;
Patrick Runkle, editorial director; Sally Engelfried, editor; Jessica Westcott, associate editor

MixBooks is an imprint of artistpro.com, LLC
236 Georgia Street, Suite 100
Vallejo, CA 94590
707-554-1935

Also from MixBooks:

The AudioPro Home Recording Course, Volumes I, II, and III
I Hate the Man Who Runs This Bar!
How to Make Money Scoring Soundtracks and Jingles
The Art of Mixing: A Visual Guide to Recording, Engineering, and Production
500 Songwriting Ideas (For Brave and Passionate People)
Music Publishing: The Real Road to Music Business Success, Rev. and Exp. 5th Ed.
How to Run a Recording Session
Mix Reference Disc, Deluxe Ed.
The Songwriter's Guide to Collaboration, Rev. and Exp. 2nd Ed.
Critical Listening and Auditory Perception
Modular Digital Multitracks: The Power User's Guide, Rev. and Exp. 2nd Ed.
The Dictionary of Music Business Terms
Professional Microphone Techniques
Sound for Picture, 2nd Ed.
Music Producers, 2nd Ed.
Live Sound Reinforcement

Also from EMBooks:

The Independent Working Musician
Making the Ultimate Demo, 2nd Ed.
Making Music with Your Computer, 2nd Ed.
Anatomy of a Home Studio
The EM Guide to the Roland VS-880

Printed in Auburn Hills, MI
ISBN 0-87288-741-3

CONTENTS

Foreword

When the subject of mastering comes up it quickly becomes apparent that most people, even people in the music business, aren't really clear on what it means. The best way to eliminate any confusion on the subject would probably be to read this book.

A lot of people confuse mastering with mixing. After all, the end product of a mixing session is a master, isn't it? And nowadays there are many software packages that allow someone to transfer material to a CD, and all of these packages refer to this as mastering, so it's reasonable to assume that just slapping something onto a CD is mastering, right?

In common music-business usage, we might refer to several different things as a master. If a project starts with a multitrack recording it is routine to refer to that tape as a master, or maybe as a multitrack master. After the mixdown we have a stereo (or multi-channel surround) master. Then at the mastering session a master is made for the replication plant, and then at the plant a couple of different things may be called masters. So what gives? I'm not going to argue against common usage, but it's worth remembering one time-honored definition: a master is the one from which many copies are made.

In that sense the multitrack tape is not the master, i.e. it doesn't contain the balances and the reverbs, etc. that come in at the mixing stage. The mixdown tape is closer, but there may still be adjustments at the mastering lab.

At the plant something called a glass master is made, and indirectly from the final CD or DVD is replicated. For this reason some people started to call the craft long known as mastering by a new name: pre-mastering. The new term has not totally caught on, at least in the US, and it's for good reason. The thing that the mastering engineer makes for the plant is often a tape, so clearly it isn't a disc until the glass master is made. But the mastering session is the last stage where any adjustments can be made. After that it's the plant's job to replicate it exactly, to change nothing other than the physical form. For this reason the mastering session is where everything about the sound of the recording is finally locked in. Most people still refer to this step as mastering.

For a long time the tools for mastering were not widely available. Back when I started, in the LP era, you had to have a lathe. In the beginning of the CD era you had to have a 1630. Both of these were pretty expensive pieces. Nowadays not only are there low cost tools available everywhere, but also it is even technically feasible to skip the step of mastering entirely. That's right, if you can somehow get your songs onto a DAT and get them into the right order, you can send that off to the plant and get CDs back.

Yet you may notice that all of your favorite CDs, and certainly any CD that even gets close to the charts, will have a mastering credit. Wonder why? It's not such a mystery. Artists, producers and engineers insist that their precious project gets to a good mastering engineer, and the reason has nothing to do with anyone controlling a technological chokepoint on the process. They want what the mastering process can bring to the project.

As you read the mastering engineers' comments throughout this book you will begin to see how sensitive they are to the factors that make music come across well in a recording. Sure, the job is part technical. You do have to make a master that the plant can use, and the specs are pretty strict. But it should become apparent that there's another side to the job, the aesthetic side. And I'd bet that every one of these engineers would tell you that the aesthetic side is really the main part of the gig. It is certainly their skills and talents in this realm that make the customers seek them out, and what keeps them coming back.

So, young prospective mastering engineers-in-training, can these aesthetic skills be learned from a book? Will reading this book make you an instant mastering engineer? Certainly not, but it's a heckuva good first step. Reading the comments from these masters of the craft can get you started toward being able to recognize these same things in recordings that you work on. It's also highly recommended for anyone producing or engineering music recordings. It will give you a much better idea of what to expect out of the mastering process, and it will teach you valuable information about preparing your recordings before you get there.

Paul Stubblebine – Mastering Engineer
www.paulstubblebine.com

Introduction

First of all, I want to say that I'm not a mastering engineer. I know the process pretty well because I have hung out in mastering studios for many years (both as a client and socially), have some very good friends that are great mastering engineers, and have taught some college courses on mastering. But never in my wildest dreams would I consider myself a mastering engineer.

Why not? Because, more so than any other job in audio, mastering is more than just knowing the process and owning the equipment. Yes, more than any other job in audio, mastering is about the long, hard grind of experience. It's about the cumulative knowledge gained from 12-hour days of listening to both great and terrible mixes, working on all types of music (not just the type you like), saving the clients' butts without them ever knowing it, and doing ten times more work than the client ever sees.

But even though I'm not a mastering engineer, I want to give you an insider's look at the process, not so much from my eyes, but from those of the legends and greats and near-greats of the business. No, I'm not a mastering engineer but I can tell you about it from the perspective of someone who greatly appreciates those who do it so well every day.

My goal with this book is a simple one: to keep the people who want to do their own mastering out of trouble and help them do a better job. I also want to show you that there's a lot more to a professional mastering job then meets the eye.

For those of you who have read my previous book *The Mixing Engineer's Handbook* (also from MixBooks), you'll notice that the format for this book is identical. It's divided into three sections:

Part One: Mastering in Stereo gives an overview of the tools, rules, and tricks used by the best mastering engineers in the business.

Part Two: Mastering in Surround gives an overview of what mastering is about to become with the emergence of surround sound.

Part Three: The Interviews is comprised of interviews with some of the finest (and, in some cases, legendary) mastering engineers in the world. You might have read some excerpts of these interviews previously in *EQ Magazine,* but the entire contents of the interviews are contained in Part Three of this book.

Meet the Mastering Engineers

As a matter of fact, here's a list of the engineers who contributed to this book, along with some of their credits. I've tried to include not only the most notable names in the business from the main media centers, but also engineers who deal with specialty clients. I'll be quoting them from time to time, so I want to introduce them to you now so you have some idea of their backgrounds when they pop up.

Doug Sax—Perhaps the godfather of all mastering engineers, Doug became the first independent one by starting his famous Mastering Lab in Los Angeles in 1967. Since then he has worked his magic with such diverse talents as The Who, Pink Floyd, the Rolling Stones, The Eagles, Kenny Rogers, Barbra Streisand, Neil Diamond, Earth, Wind and Fire, Rod Stewart, Jackson Brown, and many more.

Bernie Grundman—One of the most widely respected names in the recording industry, Bernie Grundman has mastered literally hundreds of platinum and gold albums, including some of the most successful landmark recordings of all time such as Michael Jackson's *Thriller*, Steely Dan's *Aja*, and Carole King's *Tapestry*. A mainstay at A&M Records for 15 years before starting his own facility (Bernie Grundman Mastering) in 1984, Bernie is certainly one of the most celebrated mastering engineers of our time.

Bob Ludwig—After having worked on literally hundreds of platinum and gold records and mastered projects that have been nominated for scores of Grammies, Bob Ludwig certainly stands among the giants in the mastering business. After leaving New York City to open his own Gateway Mastering in Portland, Maine, in 1993, Bob proved that you can still be in the center of the media without being in a media center.

Greg Calbi—Greg started his career as a mastering engineer at the Record Plant New York in 1973 before moving over to Sterling Sound in 1976. After a brief stint at Masterdisk from 1994 to 1998, Greg returned to Sterling as an owner, where he remains today. Greg's credits are numerous, ranging from working with Bob Dylan, John Lennon, U2, David Bowie, Paul Simon, Paul McCartney, Blues Traveler, and Sarah McLachlan, among many others.

Glenn Meadows—Glenn is a two-time Grammy winner and a multi-TEC award nominee who has owned the Nashville-based Masterfonics (recently purchased by Emerald Entertainment) since the '70s. He has worked on scores of gold and platinum records for a diverse array of artists including Shania Twain, LeAnn Rimes, Randy Travis, Delbert McClinton, Widespread Panic, and Bananarama, as well as for producers and engineers such as Tony Brown, Jimmy Bowen, and Mutt Lange.

Eddy Schreyer—Eddy opened Oasis Mastering in 1996 after mastering stints at Capitol, MCA, and Future Disc. With a list of chart-topping clients who span the various musical genres such as Babyface, Eric Clapton, Christina Aguilera, Fiona Apple, Hootie and the

Blowfish, Tracy Chapman, Offspring, Take 6, and Tupac, as well as soundtracks from movies like Howard Stern's *Private Parts, Phenomena,* and *Pleasantville,* Eddy's work is heard and respected worldwide.

Bob Olhsson—After cutting his first number one record (Stevie Wonder's "Uptight") at age 18, Bob worked on an amazing 80 Top Ten records while working for Motown in Detroit. Now located in San Francisco and mastering primarily for the new age label Hearts of Space, Bob's insightful account of the history of the industry makes for a truly fascinating read.

Dave Collins—Dave has been a mainstay at Hollywood's A&M Mastering (recently purchased by Jim Henson Productions) since 1988. In that time, he has brought his unique approach to a host of clients such as Sting, Madonna, Bruce Springsteen, and Soundgarden.

David Cheppa—David began cutting vinyl in 1974 and since that time has cut almost 32,000 sides. He is the founder of Better Quality Sound, which is currently one of the few remaining mastering houses dedicated strictly to vinyl. Thanks to his intense interest and design engineering background, David brought a medium once given up for dead to new, unsurpassed heights of quality.

Bob Katz—Co-owner of Orlando, Florida–based Digital Domain, Bob specializes in mastering audiophile recordings of acoustic music, from folk music to classical. The former technical director of the widely acclaimed Chesky Records, Bob's recordings have been named Disc of the Month in *Stereophile* and other magazines numerous times, and his recording of *Portraits of Cuba* by Paquito D'Rivera won the 1997 Grammy for Best Latin-jazz Recording. Bob's mastering clients include major labels EMI, WEA-Latina, BMG, and Sony classical, as well as numerous independent labels.

PART ONE: MASTERING IN STEREO

What Exactly Is Mastering?

Technically speaking, mastering is, quite simply, the intermediate step between taking a tape fresh from mixdown from a studio and preparing it for replication. But it is also much more than that.

> **Mastering is the process of turning a collection of songs into a record by making them sound like they belong together in tone, volume, and timing (spacing between songs).**

Mastering is not a set of tools or a device that music is run through to come out mastered. It's an art form that, when done conscientiously, relies most on an individual's skill, experience with various genres of music, and good taste.

BERNIE GRUNDMAN: *I think that mastering is a way of maximizing music to make it more effective for the listener, as well as maybe maximizing it in a competitive way for the industry. It's the final creative step and the last chance to do any modifications that might take the song to the next level.*

GLENN MEADOWS: *I think that mastering is, and always has been, the real bridge between the pro audio industry and the hi-fi industry. We're the ones that have to take this stuff that sounds hopefully good or great on a big professional monitor system and make sure it also translates well to the home systems. We're the last link to get it right or the last chance to really screw it up and make it bad, and I think we're all guilty at times of doing both.*

In the early days of vinyl, mastering was a black art practiced by technical curmudgeons who mysteriously made the transfer from the electronic medium of tape to the physical medium of vinyl. There was a high degree of difficulty in this process because the level applied to the vinyl lacquer was so crucial; too low a level and you got a noisy disc. Hit it too hard and you destroyed the disc and maybe the cutting stylus too.

Along the way, mastering (back then sometimes called "transfer") engineers found ways to make the discs louder (and therefore less noisy) by applying equalization and compression. Producers and artists began to notice that certain records actually sounded louder on the radio. If it sounded louder, the general public usually thought it sounded better, so maybe, they speculated, the disc would sell better as a result. Hence, a new breed of mastering engineer was born: a mastering engineer with some creative control and the ability to influence the final sound of a record rather than just being a transfer jock from medium to medium.

Today's mastering engineers practice less of the black art of disc cutting but are no less the wizard as they continue to subtley shape and mold the variations of frequencies and dynamics of a project.

From Vinyl to the CD and Beyond

Until 1948, there was no distinction between audio engineers because everything was recorded directly onto vinyl (all records were 10-inch and played at 78 rpm). In 1948, however, the age of the "transfer" engineer began when Ampex introduced its first commercial tape recorder. With most recording now being done to tape, a transfer had to be made to a vinyl master for delivery to the pressing plant; hence, the first incarnation of the "mastering engineer" was born.

In 1955, Ampex released "Sel-Sync" (Selective Synchronous Recording), which gave the multitrack recorder the ability to overdub. The recording industry was forever changed, and so began the real distinction between the recording and mastering engineer.

In 1957, the stereo record became commercially available and really pushed the industry to new sonic heights. At that point, the mastering engineer became more influential, thanks to judicious and creative use of equalization and compression.

With the introduction of the CD in 1982, the mastering engineer was forced into the digital age while still using tools from the vinyl past. But with the 1989 introduction of the Sonic Solutions workstation with premastering software, mastering gradually developed into its current digital state.

In 1999, 5.1 surround sound, high sample rates and 24-bit word lengths took the mastering engineer into new, uncharted, and highly creative territory.

WHY MASTER ANYWAY?

In Europe, mastering is looked upon as the first stage of the manufacturing process because it is the place where the electronic impressions on tape get transferred to either a mechanical medium (such as vinyl) or another electronic medium better suited for mass production (like CDs or cassettes). In the United States, however, mastering is considered the final step in the creative process since it's the last chance to polish and fix a project. Although both of these views are true, it's a shame to overlook the creative aspect.

A project that has been mastered (especially at a top flight-mastering house) simply sounds better. It sounds complete, polished, and finished. The project that might have sounded like a demo before now sounds like a "record." This is because the mastering engineer added judicious amounts of EQ and compression to make the project bigger, fatter, richer, and louder. He matched the levels of each song so they all have the same apparent level. He fixed the fades so that they're smooth. He inserted the spreads (the time between each song) so the songs now flow seamlessly together. He sequenced the songs so they fall in the correct order. He edited out bad parts so well you didn't even notice. He made all the songs blend together into a cohesive unit. He proofed your master before you sent it to the replicator to make sure it's free of any glitches or noise. He also made and stored a backup clone in case anything should happen to your cherished master, and he took care of all of the shipping to the desired duplication facility. And all this went so quickly and smoothly that you hardly knew it was happening.

WHY IS IT SO GOOD WHEN THE PROS DO IT?

There are a lot of reasons why a commercial mastering house produces a better product than "home" mastering. First of all, the mastering house is better equipped. They have many things available that you probably won't find in a simple DAW (digital audio workstation) room, such as multiple tweaked half-inch and quarter-inch two-tracks, Dolbys, high quality digital transfer consoles and A/D and D/A converters, ultra-smooth compressors and equalizers, and an exceptional monitoring system. They also have provisions to make media for the replicator such as industry standard 1630 machines, DDP, or PMCDs (more on these in Chapter 3, "Tools for Mastering.").

The monitor system at these facilities sometimes costs far more than entire home studios. But cost isn't the point here; quality is, since you can rarely hear what you need to hear on near-fields in order to make the adjustments that you need to make.

GLENN MEADOWS: *The reason people come to a mastering engineer is to gain that mastering engineer's anchor into what they hear and how they hear it and the ability to get that stuff sounding right to the outside world.*

EDDY SCHREYER: *Then you have the environmental issue. You can't make a move or create a fix if you can't hear it, so obviously the mastering environment is extremely important. A great facility to me means both client services and a comfortable place that's able to facilitate both large and small sessions. I am assuming my studio is somewhat the norm. I can seat about five*

The Mastering Engineer's Handbook

to six people in my room very comfortably, and I believe that is probably somewhat common. I think a mastering room that's too small is not a good thing. At times there are more than two or three people who want to show up at a mastering session, so that part of the client relationship is very important to me. So the facility sort of dictates what your goal is in terms of the client/engineer relationship and just how comfortable you want these people to be.

EXPERIENCE IS THE KEY

But the mastering engineer is the real key to the process. This is all he does day in and day out. He has big ears because he does it for at least eight hours every day and knows his monitors the way you know your favorite pair of shoes. Also, his reference point of what constitutes a good sounding mix is finely honed thanks to working hours and hours on the best and worst sounding mixes of each genre of music.

DAVE COLLINS: *I personally think experience is as valuable as equipment in a large sense because after you've done it for 10 or 20 years, you've heard almost everything that can possibly go wrong—and go right—on a mix. So you can, in one respect, quickly address people's problems.*
When a guy writes a book, he doesn't edit the book himself. He sends it off to an editor, and the editor reads it with a fresh set of eyes, just like a mastering engineer hears it with a fresh set of ears.

GLENN MEADOWS: *I don't mean to be arrogant, but it has to do with the experience of the engineer working in his environment. He's in the same room every day for years. I can walk into this room in the morning and know if my monitors are right or wrong just by listening to a track from yesterday. To me, that's the value of a mastering engineer. What they bring to the table is the cross section of their experience and their ability to say, "No, you really don't want to do that."*

GREG CALBI: *As far as the person who might be trying to learn how to do his own mastering, or understand mastering in general, the main thing is that all you need is one experience of hearing somebody else master something. Your one experience at having it sound so incredibly different makes you then realize just how intricate mastering can be and just how much you could add to or subtract from a final mix.*

BERNIE GRUNDMAN: *Most people need a mastering engineer to bring a certain amount of objectivity to their mix, plus a certain amount of experience. If you (the mastering engineer) have been in the business a while, you've listened to a lot of material, and you've probably heard what really great recordings of any type of music sound like. So in your mind you immediately compare it to the best ones you've ever heard. You know, the ones that really got you excited and created the kind of effect that producers are looking for. If it doesn't meet that ideal, you try to manipulate the sound in such a way as to make it as exciting and effective a musical experience as you've ever had with that kind of music.*

BOB OLHSSON: *To me it's a matter of trying to figure out what people were trying to do, and then do what they would do if they had the listening situation and experience that I have.*

GLENN MEADOWS: *I find that the real value of a mainstream mastering facility versus trying to do it yourself or doing it in a small backwoods-type place or a basement place is that the experience of the engineer comes into play and it can save you money and time.*

Finally, if mastering were so easy, don't you think that every big-time engineer or producer (or record company for that matter) would do it themselves? They don't, and mastering houses are busier than ever, which tells you something.

DAVE COLLINS: *Every so often, I'll have a client whose budget is gone by the time he's ready to master. And so he says, "Well, I'll go in the studio and I'll hook up a Massenburg EQ to my two-track, and I'll do a little equalization, and I'll put a compressor of some type on the output of it." But he'll ultimately call back and say, "Well, I don't know what I'm doing here. I'm just making it sound worse."*
And that's kind of analogous to some guy trying to edit his own writing. It is the impartial ear that you get from your mastering engineer that is valuable. All this equipment and new technology that we've got is a great thing, but you're really asking for someone who has never heard the record before to hear it for the first time fresh.

BERNIE GRUNDMAN: *Mastering is more than just knowing how to manipulate the sound to get it to where somebody wants it to go. I think that a lot of it is this willingness to enter into another person's world and get to know it and actually help that person express what he is trying to express, only better.*

While all of the above might seem like I'm trying to discourage you, the reader, from doing your own mastering, that's really not the case. In fact, what I'm trying to do is give you a reference point, and that reference point is how the pros operate and why they are so successful. From there, you can determine whether you're better served by doing it yourself or using a pro.

But the reason that you're reading this book is because you want to learn about all the tricks, techniques, and nuances of a major mastering facility, right? Read on, and I'll show you the how and why of these operations in detail.

The Mechanics of Mastering

The actual mechanics of mastering can be broken down into a few functions, namely maximizing the level, maintaining the frequency balance, and using the main functions of the DAW such as editing, fades, and spreads. What really separates the upper echelon mastering engineers from the rest is the ability to make the music (any kind of music) as big and loud and tonally balanced as possible but *with the taste to know how far to take those operations.* The DAW functions, on the other hand, are somewhat mechanical, and although there are tricks involved, they don't usually get the same amount of attention as the former.

LEVEL

The amount of level on a CD without distortion is one of the things that many top mastering engineers pride themselves on. Notice the qualifying words *without distortion,* since that is indeed the trick: to the make the music as loud as possible (and thereby competitive with other product) while still sounding natural. Be aware that this generally applies to modern pop/rock/R&B genres and not at all to classical or jazz, whose listeners much prefer a wider dynamic range where maximum level is not a factor.

As I stated before, the volume/level wars really began way back in the vinyl era of the '50s when it was discovered that if a record played louder than the others on the radio, the listeners would perceive it to be better and therefore make it a hit. Since then, it has been the charge of the mastering engineer to make any song intended for radio as loud as possible in any way possible.

And of course, this also applies to situations other than the radio. Take, for instance, the CD changer or record jukebox. Most artists, producers, and labels certainly don't want one of their releases to play softer than their competitors. Therefore, they squeeze every ounce of level out of the track that they can.

This practice has come under fire as of late since we've just about hit the loudness limit, thanks to the digital sales medium (CDs and DVDs) that we now use. Still, engineers try to cram more and more level onto the disc only to find that they end up with either a distorted or overcompressed product (listen to the Red Hot Chili Peppers' "Californification" for an example). While this might be the sound that the producer/artist is looking for, it does violate the mastering engineer's unwritten code of keeping things as natural sounding and unaltered as possible while performing his level magic.

EDDY SCHREYER: *What I am hearing is that various houses are really overcompressing, trying to get more apparent level. The tradeoff with excessive compression to me is the blurring of not only the stereo image, but the highs too. An overcompressed program sounds pretty muddy to me. In the quest to get the level, they end up EQing the heck out of these tracks, which of course induces even more distortion between the EQ and the compression.*

BOB LUDWIG: *When digital first came out, people knew that every time the light went into the red that you were clipping, and that hasn't changed. We're all afraid of the over levels, so people started inventing these digital domain compressors where you could just start cranking the level up. I always tell people, "Thank God these things weren't invented when the Beatles were around because for sure they would've put it on their music and would've destroyed its longevity." I'm totally convinced that overcompression destroys the longevity of a piece. Now, when someone's insisting on hot levels where it's not really appropriate, I find I can barely make it through the mastering session. I suppose that's well and good when it's a single for radio, but when you give that treatment to an entire album's worth of material, it's just exhausting. It's a very unnatural situation. Never in the history of mankind has man listened to such compressed music as we listen to now.*

BERNIE GRUNDMAN: *That's one of the unfortunate things about the industry, and it was even that way with vinyl. What* *happens is everybody is right at that ceiling level as high as you can go, so now guys without a lot of experience try to make things loud, and the stuff starts to sound god-awful. It's all smashed and smeared and distorted and pumping. You can hear some pretty bad CDs out there.*

BOB OLHSSON: *We can do things beyond anything we were ever able to do before, like turn the signal into a square wave, even. The other thing is that people are commonly going too far with compression during mixing so much that an awful lot of mixes can't be helped. I average a couple of mastering jobs a year where I can't do anything to it. If you switch anything in at all, it just absolutely turns to dust. All you can do is hope that the stations that play it won't destroy it too much more.*

DAVE COLLINS: *I never would've thought that we would be cutting CDs at this level. It's to the point where a large amount of our day is optimizing the gain structure in the console and checking what kind of limiter you're going to use and how you're going to use it just to get the CD as loud as you possibly can. I don't get it. I have to play the game because if you want to stay in business, you've got to compete on absolute level, but it's really a horrible trend. I wish all mastering engineers would speak out about this because it sucks.*
I buy records that I really want to listen to, and they are so fatiguing. It's impossible to get that amount of density and volume on a CD and not make you want to turn it off after three songs. I don't know how to put it in print in a diplomatic way, but when you get mastering engineers together and you get a couple of beers in them, they'll all agree that CDs are too loud. We hate it and wish we didn't have to do it, then it's right back to work on Monday and squeeze the shit out of it all over again.

GLENN MEADOWS: *The level wars? We had level wars in vinyl right near the end of it, where everybody was trying to get the vinyl hotter and hotter and hotter. And at least in vinyl you had this situation where when the record skipped, the record label would say, "Well, it's too loud and you're gonna have returns." We origi-nally thought we had that type of limitation on digital, but what ended up happening is there's so many tools out now for doing the dynamic range squash that you can literally get tracks now where you put them in a workstation and it looks like a 2 x 4. It comes on* at the quietest passage on the beginning of the intro and it's full level. You get into what I call "dynamics inversion." Spots in the record that should get louder actually get softer because they're hitting the compressor/limiter too hard. I don't think that the record companies and the producers at this point have enough insight or understanding about what radio has learned a long time ago, which is the tune-out factor for distortion.

GREG CALBI: *It's gotten so insane. I'm a huge music fan and I listen to CDs constantly at home. I have to say that the CDs that always please me the most sonically are not the real hot ones when I bring them in here and look at them on the meters. I tell people, "If you want yours to be hot, I know how to do it, and I'll make it as hot as we can possibly make it and still be musical. But I just want to tell you that you may find that it's not as pleasing to you if you get it too hot."*

BERNIE GRUNDMAN: *I just don't think that you should do anything that draws attention to itself. Like if you're going to use a compressor or limiter on the bus, if you use it to the point where you really hear a change in the sound, you're going a little too far. Some of the automatic settings in these devices really aren't as good as they make them out to be. And when you use them, you have to realize that you're going to degrade the sound, because compressors and limiters will do that. If you put a compressor in the circuit, not even compressing, you will hear a difference and it will sound worse.*

But getting the most level onto the disc is not the only level adjustment that the mastering engineer must practice. Just as important is the fact that every song on the disc must be perceived to be as loud as the next. *Perceived* is the key word since this is something that can't be directly measured and must be done by ear.

How to Get Hot Levels
The bulk of the level work today is done by a combination of two of the mastering engineer's primary tools; the compressor and the limiter, which in mastering, contrary to recording where one box can do either job (depending on the settings), are actually two different boxes. The compressor is used to increase the small and medium level signals, while the limiter controls the instantaneous peaks.

Limiting

In order to understand how a limiter works in mastering, you have to understand the composition of a typical music program first. In general, the highest peak of the source program determines the maximum level that can be achieved from a digital signal. But because many of these upper peaks are of very short duration, they can usually be reduced in level by several dB with minimal audible side effects. By controlling these peaks, the entire level of the program can be raised several dB, resulting in a higher average signal level.

Most digital limiters used in mastering are set as "brick wall" limiters. This means that no matter what happens, the signal will not exceed a certain predetermined level and there will be no digital "overs." With the latest generation of digital limiters, louder levels are easier to achieve than ever before because of more efficient peak control. This is thanks to the "look-ahead" function that just about all digital limiters now employ. Look-ahead delays the signal a small amount (about two milliseconds or so) so that the limiter can anticipate the peaks in such a way that it catches the peak before it gets by. Analog limiters don't work nearly as well since an analog input can't predict its input like a digital limiter with look-ahead can. Since there is no possibility of overshoot, the limiter then becomes known as a brick wall limiter.

By setting a digital limiter correctly, the mastering engineer can gain at least several dB of apparent level just by the simple fact that the peaks in the program are now controlled.

EDDY SCHREYER: *When a program is mixed with a hot snare, for example, I can use a digital limiter that will sort of clip the peak off so that I can back off the dynamics of that particular instrument in the mix without EQing it out. Because if I go for the snare with EQ, I'm going to be pulling down the vocals and possibly the guitars as well. If I go for a kick that's mixed too hot, adjusting 80, 60, 40 cycles or something to pull a kick down, it will really sacrifice the bottom quite a bit, so I'll tend to use digital limiting to peak limit excessive dynamics in those particular cases.*

Compression

As the name implies, compression actually increases the lower level signals while a limiter decreases the loud ones.

The key to getting the most out of a compressor are the Attack and Release (sometimes called Recovery) controls. These controls have a tremendous overall effect on a mix and are important to understand. Generally speaking, transient response and percussive sounds are affected by the Attack control setting. Release is the time it takes for the gain to return to normal or zero gain reduction.

In a typical pop style mix, a fast Attack setting will react to the drums and reduce the overall gain. If the Release is set very fast, the gain will return to normal quickly but can have an audible effect of reducing some of the overall program level and attack of the drums in the mix. If the Release is set slower, the gain changes that the drums cause might be heard as "pumping," which means that the level of the mix will increase and then decrease noticeably. Each time the dominant instrument starts or stops, it "pumps" the level of the mix up and down. Compressors that work best on full program material generally have very smooth release curves and slow release times to minimize this pumping effect.

Compressor Tips and Tricks

• Gain changes on the compressor caused by the drums can pull down the level of the vocals and bass and cause overall volume changes in the program.

• Slower Release settings will usually keep the gain changes more inaudible but will also lower the perceived volume.

• A slow Attack setting will tend to ignore drums and other fast signals but will still react to the vocals and bass.

• A slow Attack setting might also allow a transient to distort the next piece of equipment in the chain.
If the source is too percussive or has loud drums in the mix, try adjusting the Attack and Release controls.

• Sometimes fast Attack and medium Release helps tame drums.

• Fast Attack and Release settings tend to reduce transients.

• Usually only the fastest settings can make a unit pump.

• Slower Release settings tend to be the most inaudible.

• The more bouncy the meter seems, the more likely that the compression will be audible.

• Generally speaking, the trick with compression in mastering is to use a slow Release and less (usually way less) than 5dB of compression.

• Quiet passages that are too loud and noisy are usually a giveaway that you are seriously overcompressing.

GLENN MEADOWS: *My typical approach is to use a 1.15:1 compression ratio and stick it down at −20 or −25 so you get into the compressor real early and don't notice it going from linear to compressed and basically just pack it a little bit tighter over that range. I'll get maybe 3dB of compression, but I've brought the average level up 3 or 4dB and it just makes it bigger and fatter. People think that they have to be heavily compressed to sound loud on the radio, and they don't.*

Three Rules for Hot Levels

- Set a digital limiter as above to contain peaks.

- Set a compressor as above to gain apparent level.

- Set your master fader to −.2dB to avoid digital overs.

EDDY SCHREYER: *You go as loud as you can and you begin listening for digital clipping, analog grittiness, and things that begin to happen as you start to exceed the thresholds of what that mix will allow you to do, in terms of level. Again, just spanking as much gain as you can, be it in the analog or digital world, doesn't matter. You go for the level and properly control it with compression, then you start to EQ to achieve this balance. Of course, it all depends on the type of mix, how it was mixed, the kind of equipment that was used, how many tracks, the number of instruments, and the arrangement.*

GREG CALBI: *What I do in general is try to use three or four different devices to a point where each one is just a little past the point of overload. I overdrive two, sometimes three and even four pieces of gear, one of them being an A/D converter and the other ones being digital level controls. I find that if I spread the load out among a couple of different units and add them together, I'm able to get it as loud as I can.*

To Normalize or Not to Normalize

Professional mastering engineers do *not* use the normalization function of a DAW to adjust level. Normalization looks for the highest peak of the audio file and adjusts all the levels of the file upward to match that level. Although that seems like a very simple and easy way to adjust levels, it is seldom, if ever, used.

Even the smallest adjustment inside the DAW causes some massive DSP recalculations, all to the detriment of the ultimate sound quality. The biggest problem of normalizing is that it just looks at the digital numbers involved and not at the content of the music. As a result you end up with some songs (ballads, for example) that are way too loud because of the way that they're electronically boosted.

The reason that normalization or plug-ins aren't used is strictly a sonic one; it doesn't sound good, and it really doesn't do as good a job at creating average levels in between songs as the human ear. Ultimately, you're not looking for equal electronic loudness, you're looking for equal *perceived* loudness between songs. This is something that normalization can't achieve.

BOB KATZ: *I'll give you two reasons [why I don't normalize]. The first one has to do with just good old-fashioned signal deterioration. Every DSP operation costs something in terms of sound quality. It gets grainier, colder, narrower, and harsher. Adding a generation of normalization is just taking the signal down one generation.*
The second reason is that normalization doesn't accomplish anything. The ear responds to average level and not peak levels, and there is no machine that can read peak levels and judge when something is equally loud.

FREQUENCY BALANCE

One of the most important charges of the mastering engineer is fixing the frequency balance of a project (if it's needed). This is done with an equalizer, but the type used and the way it's driven is generally much different from during recording or mixing. Where in recording you might use large amounts of EQ (from 3 to 15dB) at a certain frequency, mastering is almost always in very small increments (usually in tenths of a dB to 2 or 3 at the very most).

What you will see is a lot of small shots of EQ along the audio frequency band, again in very small amounts.

For example, these might be something like +1 at 30Hz, +.5 at 60Hz, .2 at 120Hz, –.5 at 800Hz, -.7 at 2500Hz, +.6 at 8kHz, and +1 at 12. Notice that there's a little happening in a lot of places.

Frequency Feathering

Another technique that's used frequently is known as "feathering." This means that rather than applying a large amount of EQ at a single frequency, you add small amounts at the frequencies adjoining the main one. An example of this is instead of adding +3dB at 100Hz, you add +1.5dB at 100Hz and +.5dB at 80 and 120Hz. This lowers the phase shift brought about when using analog equalizers and results in a smoother sound.

Four Rules for Frequency Balancing

- Know the sound you're going for.

- Use a little EQ at a time—a little goes a long way.

- Feather the frequencies.

- A/B against the original.

BERNIE GRUNDMAN: *One of the things that is really hard is when the recording isn't uniform. What I mean by uniform is that all of the elements don't have a similar character in the frequency spectrum. In others words, if a whole bunch of elements are dull and then just a couple of elements are bright, it's not uniform. And that's the hardest thing to EQ because sometimes you'll have just one element, like a hi-hat, that's nice and bright and crisp and clean, and everything else is muffled. That is a terrible situation because it's very hard to do anything with the rest of the recording without affecting the hi-hat. You find yourself dipping and boosting and trying to simulate air and openness and clarity and all the things that high end can give you, and so you have to* *start modifying the bottom a lot. You do the best you can in that situation, but it's usually a pretty big compromise.*

DAVE COLLINS: *I guess when we were talking about the philosophy of mastering, what I should have added was one of the hardest things—and it took me forever to get this—is knowing when to not do anything and leave the tape alone. As I have gained more experience, I am more likely to not EQ the tape, or just do tiny, tiny amounts of equalization.*

EDDY SCHREYER: *Frequency balance is making adjustments with compression, EQ, and such so that it maintains the integrity of the mix, yet achieves balance in the highs, mids, and low frequencies. I go for a balance that it is pleasing in any playback medium that the program may be heard in. And, obviously, I try to make the program as loud as I can. That still always applies.*
But there are also limiting factors on what balance can be achieved. Some mixes just cannot be forced at the mastering stage because of certain ingredients in a mix. If something is a little bottom-light, you may not be able to get the bottom to where you would really like it. You have to leave it alone so it remains thinner because it distorts too easily.

PROCESSING ON LOAD-IN

Contrary to popular belief, the majority of the elite mastering engineers do most of their level adjustments and equalizing before going into the workstation and do *not* use the processing functions of the DAW or plug-ins to do the job. As mentioned previously, this is mostly a sonic issue, since the dedicated outboard devices sound better than what can be offered within the DAW. But the issue of major number crunching causing a degradation in signal quality equivalent to a generation loss is also a concern (see the section "The Signal Path" in Chapter 3, "Tools for Mastering").

GREG CALBI: *The only time I ever do anything is if there's like a thump on the tape and you want to do a quick rollout at 80 cycles or something. Or if there's an extra hard snare hit that just sounds too loud and you just want to take a little 4k off of it. Outside of that, I never use anything in the Sonics. It just doesn't compare to anything else that I have.*

BOB KATZ: *Most of the time I take the signal through the Sonic Solutions desk at 24 bits with the Sonic set for unity gain so that it doesn't do any calculations. I don't like the EQs in Sonic. I'll use them for certain patches if I have to, but even the high-pass filter in Sonic has its own characteristic sound on the high end.*

EDITING

Editing during mastering has gone through a complete metamorphosis in just a few short years. Until the mid-1980s when most mastering entered the digital age, most editing was still done by hand using a razor blade and splicing tape on an analog two-track recorder. But as the demand for CDs began to rise, razor blade editing quickly gave way to electronic editing in the digital domain using a Sony DAE-3000, which was basically a modified video editor, and two BVU-800 (and later DMR 4000) 3/4-inch video decks which carried the digital audio. Today, virtually all editing is done on a digital audio workstation (DAW), which is a hardware/software package using a personal computer as the engine.

While the speed and capability varies from unit to unit, the main operations required from the mastering engineer remain the same. The mastering engineer must supply fades (both fade-ins and fade-outs), spreads (the time between songs), and basic additions/subtractions to the song with cut and paste techniques. As with most mastering operations, what may seem easy can be enormously difficult without the proper knowledge of how to apply the proper tools.

Fades

Just about anyone with a workstation knows how to apply fades, but does that mean that they are the right fades? Another one of the main elements of professional mastering is making sure that the fade not only happens but sounds good as well. As a result, the mastering engineer is frequently called upon to either do the fade entirely, or to help it out. Even in these days of automated mixing, many mix engineers still actually leave the fade completely up to the mastering engineer.

Fade-Ins

There are two schools of thought on the fade-ins or head-fades; one uses a sharp "butt cut," and the other a more gradual algorithmic fade. Regardless of which type of fade is chosen, the principle is to get rid of count-offs, coughs, and noises left on the recording before the song begins. Although this seems as if it would be an easy procedure, care must be used in order to maintain the naturalness of the downbeat.

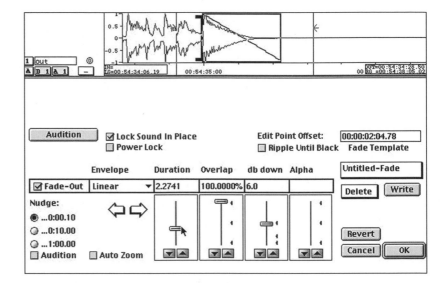

Figure 1
A linear fade

BOB KATZ: *At the head of things, it's not as easy. The biggest problem with the head-fades is that people just cut it off. The breath at the beginning of a vocal is sometimes very important. But if you cut something, not just the breath but something which I guess we would call the air around the instruments prior to the downbeat, it doesn't sound natural.*

Fade-Outs

Which fade selection used can make a big difference, as you'll see. The temptation is to use a linear curve to make a fade, as in *Figure 1*. However, an exponential curve *(Figure 2)* is sometimes smoother and much more realistic sounding.

BOB KATZ: *If you're good at editing, you can supply artificial decays at the end of songs with a little reverb and a careful Sonic Solutions crossfade that's indistinguishable from real life.*

BOB LUDWIG: *Oh yeah, it happens often enough. A lot of people assemble mixes on ProTools, and they don't listen to it carefully enough when they're compiling their mix, and they actually cut off the tails of their own mixes. You can't believe how that*

The Mastering Engineer's Handbook

happens. So a lot of times we'll use a little 480L to just fade out their chopped off endings and extend it naturally.

EDDY SCHREYER: *I've had some projects where they clipped intros, and I've had to grab beats from other places and put them on the top, so I prefer it if you don't cut the program too tight.*

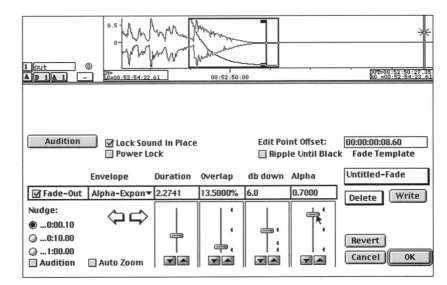

*Figure 2
Exponential curve*

Even when a fade is made during the mix, it sometimes needs some help due to some inconsistencies. The term "following the fade" means drawing a curve that approximates the one on the mix, only smoother *(see Figure 3)*.

Spreads

The spread is the time between each song. While this might seem to be quite arbitrary in many cases, the savvy mastering engineer usually times the spread to correspond with the tempo of the previous song. In other words, if the tempo of the first song was at 123 beats per minute, the mastering engineer times the very last beat of the first song to stay in tempo with the downbeat of the next. The number of beats in between depends upon the flow of the album.

Please note that this might not be appropriate in all cases since each project is unique. It is a place to start, however. Many times a smooth flow between songs is not desirable and a longer space is far more appropriate. The spread in that case is replaced with a two-, three-, or four-second area in between songs to keep them disconnected.

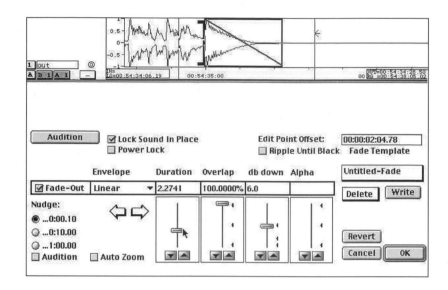

Figure 3
Following the fade

EDLs

Instead of using cut and paste operations to determine the song sequence and spreads, most professional workstations used for mastering use the Edit Decision List (EDL) instead. The EDL, which was originally developed for video editing, makes it easy to change the order of songs at any time. The EDL is the list of all the elements that make up the final result and the position those elements will take in the final sequence (*see Figure 4*). Those elements are usually songs and will also be described in some fashion, usually by the name of the song.

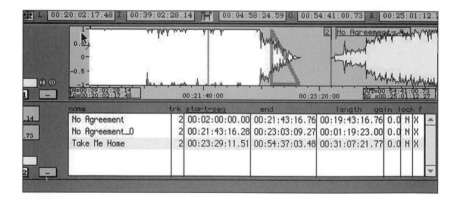

Figure 4
A sample EDL

EFFECTS

Although mastering engineers were occasionally asked to add effects in the past, it is now far more commonplace. This is partly due to the proliferation of the digital audio workstation, especially when a poorly chosen fade was used prior to mastering. And then there's the fact that many artists and producers are sometimes horrified to find that the amount of reverb is suddenly less than they remember during the mix.

Most mastering engineers prefer to add any effects in the digital domain, both from an ease-of-use and a sonic standpoint. This is usually done by sending the output of the workstation into the effects device, then recording the result back into the workstation on two different tracks. The resulting effects tracks are then mixed in the proper proportions in the workstation.

Because this processing is done in the digital domain, an effects device with digital I/O is essential. Among the devices used are the Lexicon PCM91 and 300, Sony V77, and the TC Electronics M5000 and 3000, although any high quality processor that operates in the digital domain will do.

BOB KATZ: *A reverb chamber is used surprisingly a lot in mastering to help unify the sound between things. I might use it on 5 percent of all my jobs. I discovered the Sony V77, which is already obsolete (in Sony's typical way). After you spend a couple of hours fine-tuning it, it can sound just like an EMT.*

BOB LUDWIG: *I do a fair amount of classical music mastering, and very often a little bit of reverb is needed on those projects. Sometimes if there's an edit that for some reason just won't work, you can smear it with a bit of echo at the right point and get past it. Sometimes mixes come in that are just dry as a bone and a small amount of judicious reverb can really help that out. We definitely need it often enough that we've got a 480L in our place, and it gets used probably once every week.*

DAVE COLLINS: *We've done a lot of soundtrack mastering at A&M, and it's very common to add a touch of reverb at the final stage. Generally, you won't want to add reverb to a whole pop mix because it gets too washy. But five times a year, I bring up an Eventide DSP4000 because I want to flange the whole mix like you hear on that Lenny Kravitz track ["Are You Gonna Go My Way"], where the whole thing goes through a flange and you cut it back into the regular track. And sometimes we'll go to the telephone-limited bandwidth kind of sound for a measure or two and back again, or something like that.*

CHAPTER 3

Tools for Mastering

Someone once said that mastering is about 30 percent tools and 70 percent ears. That said, the tools that are required are very unique to the genre; in the analog days, they were often custom made. Even today there are custom mastering versions of some very popular recording units (again, mostly analog). These units vary mostly in their need to have very precise repeatable settings; therefore many of the most-used controls are detented and selectable, which becomes a rather expensive feature.

BERNIE GRUNDMAN: *We build our own equipment. It's built mostly as an integrated system to avoid a lot of extra electronics and isolation devices and so forth. We have all separate power to each one of our rooms and a very elaborate grounding setup, and we've proven to ourselves that it helps time and time again. We have all custom wire in the console. We build our own power supplies as well as everything else; the equalizers, everything.*

COMMON ELEMENTS

All tools for mastering, regardless of whether analog or digital, have two major features in common: extremely high sonic quality and repeatability. The sonic quality is a must, and any device in either the monitor or signal chain should have the least effect possible on the signal. The repeatability is important (although less so now than in the days of vinyl) because the exact settings must be repeated in the event that a project must be redone (as in the case of additional parts or changes being called for weeks later). While this feature isn't much of a problem in the digital domain because the settings can be memorized, a great many analog mastering devices are still used, so these devices require special "Mastering" versions that have 1dB or less segment selections on the controls (***see Figures 5 and 6***). These additions add seriously to the cost of the device.

Figure 5
GML 9500
mastering equalizer

Figure 6
Avalon AD2077
mastering version equalizer

The Signal Path

Most major mastering facilities have both analog and digital signal paths (*see Figures 7 and 8*) because so many of the tools and source materials exist in both domains. In either case, the overall signal path is kept as short as possible, with any unneeded item removed so the signal remains unaffected.

GREG CALBI: *On the analog side, what I try to do is combine light and dark, solid-state and tube. So I have a bunch of tube equipment. I have the EAR compressors and the EAR EQs; the MEQ and the regular one, like the old Pultec. And I have an Avalon compressor and Avalon equalizer, which is a little bit more specific. I also have a Manley tube limiter/compressor, one of those Vari-Mu's, and one of Doug Sax's level amplifiers, which I'll use sometimes in-between my console.*

DAVE COLLINS: *The analog signal path is a Studer 820 used just as a transport. We use a Flux-Magnetics playback head that's connected to the outboard tape playback electronics that we talked about before that is a half tube, half solid-state. That feeds an all-custom analog console. Basically, the tape machine feeds some passive attenuation and from there I've got a custom EQ that we* *use. I've got a Prism analog EQ, a Manley Vari-Mu compressor, and a heavily modified SSL console compressor. And we've got a Waves L2 limiter (serial number 0) and a dB Technology A/D converter. I also use a TC dB Max.*

Figure 7
The analog signal path

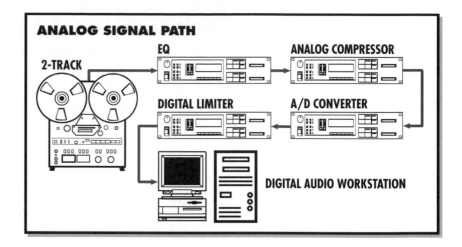

DOUG SAX: *As a point of interest, whether the source is analog or digital, if it needs EQ, I EQ it as an analog. That makes sense because if you come in with 96/24, I just look at it as good sounding analog. I do what I want with it, then I'll get it down to 44.1 and 16-bit in the best way possible. So whether it's half-inch or quarter-inch analog or digital, it goes into good converters and comes up as analog. Then the EQ is passive with the same equalizer I've had since 1968. The limiters are all tubes, and they're transformerless. Ninety-nine percent of what I do is done between those two devices.*

GLENN MEADOWS: *It can be a combination, but my path is typically 99 percent digital because 99 percent of what I am getting is digital. For example, with this one-inch two-track that I am working with, if I decide I need an analog EQ, I will come through a Millenium Dual (the mastering version with the detents on it), then run into my Prism AD2 converter, and then come into the rest of the mastering chain 24-bit digital. Then we will store it 24-bit digital and do anything else that we have to do at 24 bits internally. Then on the way back out the door, I can now loop out and back in and pick up my Z-Sys equalizer, using the power of POW-r word length reduction if I need to. The SADiE has the Apogee UV22 built-in, if I decide to use that. So I have got the ability to handle it whichever way is most appropriate for the music. But the* *processing gear at the moment on the digital side is the Z-Systems six-channel EQ and Weiss EQ and compressor/limiters.*

Figure 8
The digital signal path

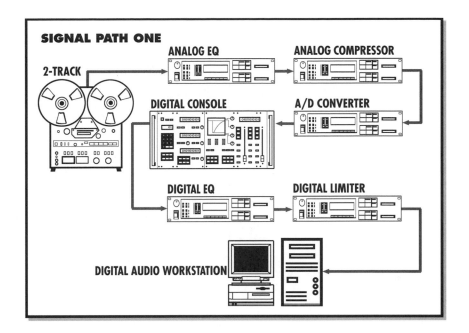

BOB LUDWIG: *In the analog domain, it goes from the tape machine into George Massenburg/Sony electronics that are as minimal and audiophile as one can get. The output of that goes into either a dCS, Pacific Microsonics, or sometimes Apogee analog-to-digital converter. When I need other outboard gear, we've got Neumann EQs and NTP and Manley compressors. Between the Manley, NTP, and digital domain compressors, that normally fills the bill for me, but I do have some Aphex Compellors. In the digital domain, I have all the Weiss 96/24 stuff. The bw102, which has the 96kHz de-esser in it as well, is complete with a mixer, compressor, and equalization.*

As you can see, the analog path is somewhat of a hybrid, in that it starts out in the analog domain but eventually enters the digital. Also, just because a source tape starts out in the digital domain (such as a DAT), it doesn't necessarily mean that it will remain there. It's not uncommon for the mastering engineer to come back to analog in order to insert a specific equalizer or compressor then return to digital (***see Figure 9***). This domain jumping is sometimes called "signal jacking" and is generally avoided if possible.

Figure 9
Signal jacking

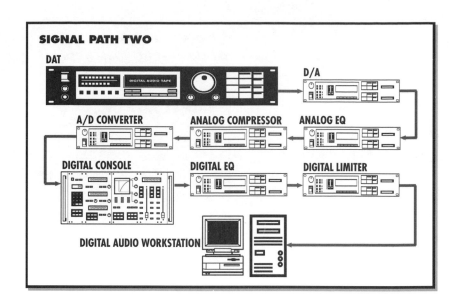

The Digital Detangler

One of the few tools that seems to be universal among major mastering studios is a Z-Systems Detangler. This is essentially a digital router that allows patching one digital device to another (or many others) at the push of a button. The unit functions as a digital audio patchbay, a distribution amplifier, a router, a format converter, and a channel switcher, all in one box (*see Figure 10*). For more information on the Detangler, go to **www.z-sys.com**.

Figure 10
Z-Systems 32.32r
Digital Detangler

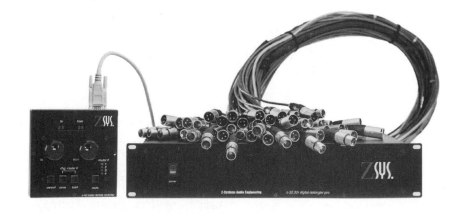

THE MONITOR SYSTEM

The heart and soul of the mastering signal chain are the loudspeakers you choose. More than any one device, these are the mastering engineer's link to both the reference point of the outside world and the possible deficiencies of the source material. More great pains go into the monitoring system than just about any other piece of gear in the studio.

BERNIE GRUNDMAN: *Probably the one biggest and most important piece of equipment that a mastering engineer can have is his monitor, and he has to understand that monitor and really know when it's where it should be. If you know the monitor and you've lived with it for a long time, you're probably going to be able to make good recordings.*

GLENN MEADOWS: *My mastering room has an in-wall Kinoshita monitoring system. It's about an 80 or 90 thousand-dollar speaker system when you include the amplification. What we found is that when you have it sounding really great on that, it sounds good on everything else you play it on. Yeah, it's a different characteristic than a home system without the dome tweeters and that thin, ethereal top end that comes out of there, but if the components in the big system are in good shape and they've been maintained properly, you're going to get that same perspective. It also doesn't rip my head back and forth trying to go to different monitoring systems.*

The Acoustic Environment
Having the finest reproduction equipment is all for naught unless the acoustic environment in which they are placed is sound. Because of this, more time, attention, and expense are initially spent on the acoustic space then virtually any other aspect of mastering.

BOB KATZ: *A great monitor in a bad room does absolutely nothing for you, so if you don't start with a terrific room and a plan for how it will integrate with the monitors, you can forget about it. No matter what you do, they will still suck and you will still have problems.*

BOB LUDWIG: *To tell you the truth, I think a lot of people have heard about the effort we've gone through to make our room as acoustically perfect as possible. So many times people come into the room and they go, "Oh, my God!" or something like that. I felt that if I stayed in New York, I'd never be able to have a room that was acoustically as perfect as we knew how to make it. But in order to get as near perfect a situation as possible, you actually* *need a fairly large shell that's at least 30 feet long and accommodates a 17- or 18-foot high ceiling.*

Since the room design is beyond the scope of this book, here's a list of references for more information.

Francis Manzella Design Limited–**www.fmdesign.com**

Waterland Design–**www.waterland.com**

Wavespace–**www.wave-space.com**

Russ Berger Design Group–**www.rbdg.com**

BOTO Design–**www.BOTO.com**

Walters/Storyk Design–**www.wsdg.com**

Rosati Acoustics and Multimedia–**www.rosatiacoustics.com**

Bob Hodas Acoustical Analysis–**www.bobhodas.com**

Chips Davis Designs–**www.chips-davis.com**

Jeff Cooper Architects—**www.jeffcooper.com**

TMH Corporation–**www.tmhlabs.com**

Monitors

The key to a mastering monitor is wide and flat frequency response. Wide frequency response is especially important on the bottom end of the frequency spectrum, which means that a rather large monitor is required, perhaps with a subwoofer as well. This means that many of the common monitors used in recording and mixing, especially near-fields, will not provide the frequency response required for mastering.

Smooth frequency response is important for a number of reasons. First, an inaccurate response will result in inaccurate equalization in order to compensate. It will also probably mean you'll overuse the EQ in an unconscious attempt to overcome the deficiencies of the monitors themselves.

Although the selection of monitoring is a very subjective and personal issue (just as in recording), there are some brand names that repeatedly pop up in major mastering houses. These include Tannoy (**www.tannoy.com**), Dunlevy, B&W (**www.bwspeakers.com**), and Duntech (**www.duntech .com.au**).

BOB LUDWIG: *One reason I've always tried to get the very best speaker I can is I've found that when something sounds really right on an accurate speaker, it tends to sound right on a wide variety of speakers. I've never been a big fan of trying to get things to sound only right on an NS-10Ms.*

EDDY SCHREYER: *I've been using Tannoys since about 1984 or '85. I'm a big fan of the dual concentrics. I think the phase coherency is unsurpassed. Once you get used to listening to these boxes, it's very difficult to listen to spread drivers again. In this particular case, my Dual 15s have been custom modified for the room to some degree, and using them is just a great treat. I think they are one of the easier speakers to listen to, and they certainly don't sound like the big brash monitor that they might look to be. A typical comment made about the monitors here at Oasis is that they sound like the best big stereo system they've ever heard, which is a terrifically flattering compliment. I also have some little Tannoy System 600s for near-fields, and now I've added some dual 15 subs to the mains.*

BERNIE GRUNDMAN: *We build our own boxes and crossovers, and we use all Tannoy components. We have it all mixed in with different elements that we feel are going to give us the best sound. It's not that we're going for the biggest or the most powerful sound— we're going for neutral because we really want to hear how one tune compares to the other in an album. We want to hear what we're doing when we add just a half dB at 5k or 10k. A lot of speakers nowadays have a lot of coloration and they're kind of fun to listen to, but boy, it's hard to hear those subtle little differences. We just use a two-way speaker system with just one woofer and one tweeter so it really puts us in-between near-fields and big soffited monitors.*

On the Bottom

Getting a project to have enough low end so that it translates well to speaker systems of all sizes is one of the things that mastering engineers pride themselves in, and one of the reasons that near-field or even popular soffit-mounted large monitors are inadequate for mastering. The only way that you can properly tune the low end of a track is if you can hear it; therefore, a monitor with a frequency response to at least 40Hz is definitely required.

Subwoofers

In order to hear that last octave on the bottom, many mastering engineers are now resorting to subwoofers. A great debate rages as to whether a single subwoofer or stereo subwoofers are required for this purpose. Those that say stereo subs are a must insist that enough directional response occurs at lower frequencies to require a stereo pair. There is also a sense of envelopment that better approximates the realism of a live event with stereo subs. Either way, the placement of the subwoofer(s) is of vital importance due to the standing waves of the control room at low frequencies.

Subwoofer Placement and Adjustment Tips

Though there is a totally scientific way to place the subwoofer, it is beyond the means of all but the largest facilities. Fortunately, there's a method that will get you in the ballpark, although you'll have to tweak a bit by experimenting from there. Keep in mind that this method is for single subwoofer use.

For Best Subwoofer Placement

1. Place the subwoofer in the engineer's listening position behind the console.

2. Feed pink noise only into the subwoofer at the desired reference level (85dB SPL should do it, but the level isn't critical).

3. Walk around the room near your main monitor speakers until you find the spot where the bass is the loudest. That's the spot to place the sub. For more level, move it toward the back wall or corner, but be careful because this could provide a peak at only one frequency. You're looking for the smoothest response possible (which may not be possible without the aid of a qualified acoustic consultant).

To Calibrate the Subwoofer

1. Using only one main speaker, feed pink noise in at a desired level (80dB, for example) with the subwoofer disconnected.

2. Listening only to the subwoofer, set its level 6dB less than the main speaker (74dB). This applies if you're using an SPL meter such as a Radio Shack. If you're using a Real Time Analyzer, the level of each band is the same as your reference level (80dB, in this case).

3. Adjust the phase of the subwoofer to the position with the most bass. This can be done by adjusting the phase control on the unit or by simply reversing the wires on the input connector.

4. Adjust the crossover point until the transition between subwoofer and satellite is the most seamless.

Amplifiers

While the trend for most recording-style monitors is toward self-powered units, most speakers in the mastering environment still require an outboard amplifier, and a rather large one at that. It is not uncommon to see amplifiers of well over 1000 watts per channel in a mastering situation. This is not for level (since most mastering engineers don't listen all that loudly) but for headroom so that the peaks of the music don't induce distortion. Since many speakers used in a mastering situation are rather inefficient as well, this extra amount of power can compensate for the difference.

Although many power amps that are standard in professional recording such as Manley (**www.manleylabs.com**), Bryston (**www.bryston.ca**), and Hafler (**www.rockfordcorp .com/hafler/**) are frequently used, it's not uncommon to see audiophile units such as Cello, Threshold, Krell (**www.krellonline.com**), and Chevin (**www.chevin-research .com**).

BOB LUDWIG: *When I started Gateway, I got another pair of Duntech Sovereigns and a new pair of Cello Performance Mark II amplifiers this time. These are the amps that will put out 6,000-watt peaks. One never listens that loudly, but when you listen it sounds as though there's an unlimited source of power attached to the speakers. You're never straining the amp, ever.*

CONVERTERS

With the coming of the digital age, mastering studios were forced to add a new set of tools to their arsenal: analog-to-digital (A/D) and digital-to-analog (D/A) converters. Since each brand has a slightly different sound (just like most other pieces of gear), most mastering facilities have numerous versions of each type available for a particular type of music.

Among the current popular converters are dB Technologies, Prism, dCS, Apogee, and Pacific Microsonics.

GREG CALBI: *I usually work with two different A/D converters. I have a dB Technologies converter, and I have one that the guys at JVC were fooling around with for a while, which is excellent. I try to have two different converters at all times, one that maybe has a deeper bottom and better imaging and another one that's maybe a little more exciting in the midrange.*

EQUALIZERS

One of the bread-and-butter tools of the mastering engineer, the equalizer, or more accurately a set of equalizers, is used more than almost any other device with the exception of the compressor. Mastering equalizers differ from their recording counterparts in that they usually feature stepped rather than continuously variable controls in order to be able to repeat the settings.

Popular analog equalizers include the GML 8200 (*see Figure 11*) and 9500, Avalon 2055 (*see Figure 12*) and 2077, Sontec MFS 432, and the Manley Massive Passive (*see Figure 13*). Some of the more popular digital equalizers are the Weiss EQ-1 (*see Figure 14*) and the Z-Sys Z-Q1.

Figure 11
GML 8200 equalizer

Figure 12
Avalon 2055 equalizer

Figure 13
Manley Massive Passive
equalizer

Figure 14
Weiss EQ-1
digital equalizer

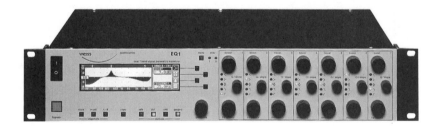

COMPRESSORS AND LIMITERS

The other major bread-and-butter tools of the master engineer are the compressor and limiter. Although during recording this is usually one unit that can function either way, mastering requires two separate units. Generally speaking, the compressor is used to shape the dynamics of a song by adding punch and strength, while the limiter is used to raise the apparent level of the song by controlling the musical peaks.

Compressors that are often found in major mastering facilities include the analog Manley Vari-Mu (*see Figure 15*) and Tube Tech LCA-2B and the digital Junger d01 (*see Figure 16*), Waves L2 (*see Figure 17*), and TC M5000.

Figure 15
Manley
Vari-Mu compressor

Figure 16
Junger d01 limiter

Figure 17
Waves L2 limiter

TAPE MACHINES

With the source tapes being sent to most mastering facilities currently running about 60/40 percent analog-to-digital and the delivery formats to the replicator taking many different digital formats, the complete mastering facility must have a wide variety of both analog and digital tape machines on hand for any eventuality.

Analog Tape Machines

Far and away the workhorse of the analog world is the half-inch two-track tape machine, although this usually has a quarter-inch headstack available as well. The most widely sought-after machine for this purpose is the Ampex ATR-102, although many facilities have Studer 827s as well. It is not uncommon for the electronics of these machines to be highly modified to improve the signal path. It should be noted that neither machine is currently in production, so they draw premium prices on the used market.

The Mastering Engineer's Handbook

A new format that seems to be slowly catching on is the one-inch two-track. Again, this is a one-inch headstack mounted on an Ampex or Studer transport.

At one point in time, cassette decks were an important part of the mastering facility. These days, their importance has been minimized with the proliferation of the CD-R.

BOB KATZ: *My analog path starts with a custom-built set of Ampex MR70 electronics, which in my opinion is the best playback electronics that Ampex ever invented. I have that connected to a Studer C37 classic 1964 vintage transport with the extended low-frequency heads that John French put in made by Flux Magnetics. It's just real transparent and not tubey sounding at all, just open and clean.*

BOB LUDWIG: *We've got six different ways of playing back analog tape. We've got a stock Studer A820. We've got a Studer that's got Cello class A audiophile electronics. We've got a stock ATR, a tube ATR, and an unbalanced ATR. We also have one of the Tim de Paravicini one-inch two-track machines with his fantastic tube electronics. When you record with his custom EQ curve at 15 ips, it's basically flat from 8 cycles up to 28kHz.*

GREG CALBI: *I have an ATR analog deck with tube electronics and one with solid-state electronics. I also have a Studer 820. Most of the time at the beginning of an analog session, I'll play it off each of those three machines and see which one sounds the best.*

Digital Tape Machines

DAT

The DAT machine is still king of the mastering studio, and the Panasonic 3700/3800 is the most widely used transport. In virtually all cases though, the A/D and D/A converters are bypassed for ones of higher quality. The limiting factor of the typical DAT is still the fact that it is a 16-bit medium.

24-bit DAT

In order to overcome the 16-bit limitation of the DAT medium and improve the resolution up to 24 bits, many mixers are resorting to several methods of packing those additional bits on tape. The first is to use the Tascam DA-45HR 24-bit DAT recorder *(see Figure 18)*, which doubles the tape speed in order to record the additional bits. This machine also runs in standard speed mode in order to play and record standard 16-bit DATs.

Bit-Split Masters

Another popular method of increasing the resolution up to 24 is by using a method known as "bit-splitting." This method uses an eight-track unit such as an ADAT or DA-88 and prints the last eight bits to an additional pair of tracks. The most widely used method for this uses a Prism Sound MR-2024T unit using their MRX bit-splitting technology and a Tascam DA-88 Hi-8 machine. Although this can give up to four tracks at full 24-bit resolution, obviously two tracks (with two additional data tracks) are only used for stereo.

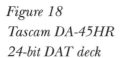

Figure 18
Tascam DA-45HR
24-bit DAT deck

COURTESY TASCAM

BOB LUDWIG: *We primarily get bit-split tapes. It used to be the Prism and the Paqrat boxes, but nowadays it's almost all Apogee PSX-100 or the AD-8000. Lately we've been getting more and more CD-ROMs that have ProTools 24-bit mixes. And of course, we've been getting 24-bit Sonic Solutions mixes for years. ProTools is still far away from catching up with Sonic Solutions' ability to handle 192kHz/24-bit files.*

DAVE COLLINS: *We're seeing much more bit-split DA-88s right now, and I just did some stuff off Genex 24-bit MO format. Those things really sound great. We worked on that Santana [Supernatural] record and they mixed to half-inch and bit-split DA-88 and the bit-split DA-88 beat the half-inch soundly. It was better in every way. So I think when you get to these 20- or 24-bit formats, then it really can compete with the best analog.*

DOUG SAX: *I get a lot of 96/24 stuff in. It's cheap, it's here, it's now. So any comment that I make about a Sony 1610 from 1985 that was absolutely just horrible then, is true. And when I say that a 96/24* *recording done with dB Technology converters sounds terrific, that's also true. The new Apogee PSX-100 has a bit-splitter in it so you can go into that thing, come out of the bit-splitter onto a DA-88, and you've got 96/24 on ten bucks worth of tape. If you come in with 96/24, I just look at it as good sounding analog.*

EDDY SCHREYER: *I would suspect that this year there'll be far more dumping to 24-bit. It's a big improvement over 44.1/16-bit. We've gotten a couple in at 88.2kHz that were very happening. The 88.2kHz through some good converters is as close to analog as I've heard, as a matter of fact. Yeah, the higher sampling rate is just really, really superb.*

Sony PCM-1630

One of the staples of the mastering scene is the Sony PCM-1630, which is a digital processor connected to either a Sony DMR 4000 or BVU-800 ¾-inch U-matic video machine. Since the beginning of the CD, this has been the standard format for the mastering facility to deliver to the replicator, and every facility still uses them. Another machine not currently being manufactured and therefore drawing premium prices, the 1630 is noted for its low error count and is still frequently used where other media fails. (See also Chapter 4, "Mastering for CD.")

DDP

DDP (Disc Description Protocol) is a propriety format from Doug Carson Associates based on the 8mm Exabyte format. It is the delivery standard to the replicator preferred by the labels of the Universal Music Group (see also Chapter 4).

CONSOLES

Although mastering consoles at one time were much more sophisticated, these days mastering consoles are basically a piece of wire with relays in the middle to connect the various pieces of gear and control the monitors. A mastering console differs from a normal recording console in that there are only two inputs (four at most for manual crossfades between songs) and no channel or track assignment switches. And since most of the processing, such as EQ and compression/limiting, comes from specialized outboard devices, the console can be the virtual "straight wire with gain."

Due to the unique nature and relative small size of the mastering market, few companies currently manufacture consoles. Manley Labs designs custom-built analog-based consoles while Weiss (with their now-standard 102 modules—*see Figure 19*) and the upstart Crookwood manufactures console modules for the digital domain.

Figure 19
Weiss bw102 console

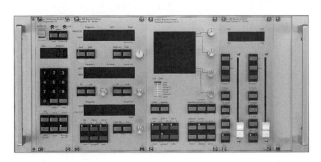

THE DIGITAL AUDIO WORKSTATION (DAW)

In a relatively short amount of time (five years or so), the digital audio workstation (DAW) has become the heart and soul of the mastering studio, allowing the engineer to complete tasks such as editing and sequencing with far greater ease than was ever thought possible. The DAW also allows new tasks to be carried out that were not possible before.

The Big Players

By far the biggest player in the mastering DAW game is the Mac-based Sonic Solutions with its SonicStudio. Although quite deep in features, which means a steep learning curve Sonic (as it has come to be known) has several features that put it heads and tails above the average DAW for mastering. These include a powerful editor, a wide variety of fade algorithms, PQ code placement, and creation of a premastered CD (PMCD—see Chapter 4).

About the only other DAW to make a serious dent in the Sonic stranglehold of the market is the English PC-based SADiE. While SADiE has most of the features of Sonic and is widely used in Europe, it is a relative latecomer to the U.S. and must therefore take on the heavily entrenched Sonic marketplace.

Other popular DAWs, such as ProTools, Digital Performer, and Sound Forge, are very good editors but lack the neces-

The Mastering Engineer's Handbook

sary tools that a mastering engineer routinely uses such as PQ code editing and elegant and powerful fade options.

THE NETWORK

One of the most widely used features of the Sonic system is the network feature known as MediaNet. MediaNet gives the ability for multiple DAWs to share project files throughout the facility *(see Figure 20)*. This means that the main mastering engineer can start a project in Room A for EQing and loading, hand it off to an assistant in Room B for editing, then hand it off again to a production engineer in Room C for parts creation and copy burns. All this takes place without ever leaving the computer or physically moving files with a tape or hard drive. The network is an essential time saver in a busy facility and eliminates data or pilot errors by keeping the files always in the same place.

Figure 20
A networked facility

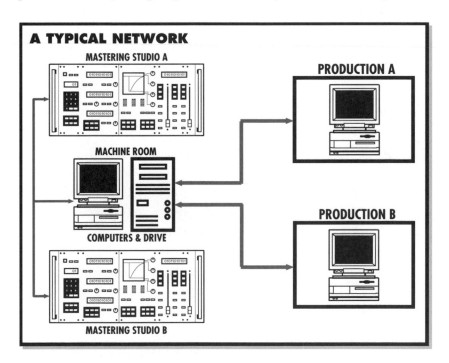

BACKUP

Since a DAW networked system at a major facility may have more than 50 hard drives totaling nearly a terabyte (that's a thousand gigabytes) of information, backup is important. Actually, backup takes two forms: network backup and project backup. Most facilities will usually make a backup of a project on a CD-R or PMCD well after the project is approved and completed. This backup is then put into the facility vault on-site. The record company is usually charged for this service.

System backup is usually determined by the size of the system or network as this determines the type of backup system required. In general, backup options fall into several categories, which differ primarily in speed and capacity:

DDS (Digital Data Storage) is a 4mm, two-reel tape cartridge sometimes known as a dataDAT that stores as much as 12GB at a speed of up to 60MB per minute. DDS differs from standard audio DAT in that the tape is taken from the center of the roll and certified to be error free. Computer grade tape has a lower BLER (block error rate) rate than standard audiotape and is significantly more reliable. DDS uses hardware data compression, which is faster and more efficient than software compression.

AIT (Advanced Intelligent Tape) is an 8mm Exabyte cartridge, developed by Sony for computer data storage, that stores up to 25GB at a speed of up to 180MB per minute. AIT's unique characteristic is memory-in-cassette (MIC), a computer chip on the tape itself which remembers where specific pieces of information are stored. AIT II currently stores 50GB of uncompressed data (100GB compressed) at rates up to 6MB per second.

DLT (Digital Linear Tape) is a half-inch tape cartridge that stores up to 35GB at a speed of up to 300MB per minute. Originally invented by Digital Equipment Corporation and bought by Quantum, DLT has become the standard master format for DVD replication, as well as for high-end server and network systems backup. DLT has continually led the other tape technologies in terms of speed and capacity. DLT 7000, the latest incarnation, holds up to 35GB native (70GB compressed). DLT 7000 offers transfer speeds of up to 5MB per second and uses hardware data compression.

The UV-1000

Most mastering facilities have a unit made by Apogee Electronics known as the UV-1000 (*see Figure 21*). This is a unique box that serves a number of mastering functions from digital source selection to providing a digital oscillator, precision clock and automatic black (insertion of digital silence), to selecting copy protect modes. But the primary use of the unit is for its UV22 Super CD encoding process, which is a high quality dither system designed to

Figure 21
Apogee UV-1000

capture high resolution signal (20- to 24-bit) onto a standard 16-bit CD. While there are now many types of dither available to the mastering engineer (they all sound different) besides the UV22 process, the UV-1000 still provides many additional features vital to everyday mastering operations. Unfortunately, the unit is no longer manufactured (probably because most mastering facilities already have one).

Metering

Precise and accurate metering is essential for the mastering engineer, so in many cases an outboard device is added. Although the modern mastering studio is loaded with peak reading digital meters, most mastering engineers still like to use a good old-fashioned VU meter as well. This is because the VU gives a more accurate indication of the relative loudness than a peak meter does. The classic example of this is the human voice where a very quiet voice can have an extremely high peak level. It *looks* loud on a digital meter, but it *sounds* quiet. Because of its mechanical properties and ballistics, a VU meter displays the signal closer to the way we hear than a peak meter does.

A VU meter doesn't have the precision necessary for modern mastering, however, because the mastering engineer is constantly concerned about peaks and digital overs. That's why most mastering facilities use precision metering from manufacturers like Durrough, Mytek, Logitek, and RTW.

Sampler Rate Converters

It is not uncommon for a DAT to be delivered at a sample rate other than the standard 44.1kHz used for CD, and therefore the need for a sample rate converter (SRC) is sometimes necessary. Although this function is sometimes available within the DAW, this is a complicated DSP task requiring massive calculations that tend to change the sound. Therefore, most mastering engineers prefer to use a dedicated system for this task. Popular models include the Z-Systems 2-src and Weiss SFC2. With the oncoming high sample rate formats of 96 and 88.2kHz, SRCs will be increasingly called into use in the future.

De-essers

One of the most important tools of the mastering engineer is the de-esser *(see Figure 22)*. As the name implies, a de-esser limits the amount of *s* sounds or high-frequency content that might occur in a track. Excessive high-frequency content is

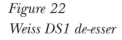

Figure 22
Weiss DS1 de-esser

sometimes a byproduct of compression and is known as sibilance. A de-esser is a frequency-dependent compressor that only triggers when excessive high-frequency content is present. Although sibilance control is a somewhat greater concern when cutting vinyl (see Chapter 6, "Mastering for Vinyl"), it's still of utmost importance to the mastering engineer as sibilance can have a very negative effect on the quality of the program.

The Alesis Masterlink ML-9600

The Alesis Masterlink may very well soon become a staple of both the recording and mastering studio alike due to its unique ability to create and play back a high-resolution

Figure 23
Alesis ML-9600
Masterlink

(up to 96kHz/24-bit) CD known as a "CD24." This allows the mixing engineer to bypass laying the mix to analog tape, DAT, or any of the more unwieldy bit-split formats, and to record directly to the unit and then burn either a standard red book (44.1kHz/16-bit) or CD24. With the increasing demand for easily transportable high-resolution audio coupled with the steady industry-wide movement away from tape, Masterlink will be increasingly seen in mastering facilities in the future.

CD-ROM Files

More and more mastering engineers are receiving 24-bit AIFF or WAV files burned to a CD-ROM in an effort to gain better resolution without the hassle of either tape or bit-splitting. When a CD-ROM is received, the mastering engineer must import the files into the DAW. From there, processing can occur either in the digital domain using software plug-ins, or through the desired outboard processing by playing the imported files back through the appropriate analog or digital signal path.

BOB KATZ: *Many of the customers that used to send me DATs are now using cheap digital mixing consoles and bringing the signal into the computer at 24 bits and cutting me a CD-ROM. So as a result, it's become more like 40 percent DAT, 30 percent 24-bit files, and the other 30 percent half-inch analog.*

BOB LUDWIG: *Lately, we've been getting more and more CD-ROMs that have ProTools 24-bit mixes. And of course, we've been getting 24-bit Sonic Solutions mixes for years.*

Mastering for CD

Mastering for CD requires that the mastering engineer know far more than the basics of EQ, dynamics, and editing. In fact, a proper and efficient job entails awareness of everything from dealing with word lengths to the different choices for the master medium to checking that master medium for errors.

DITHER

Dither is a low-level noise signal that is added to the program in order to trim a large digital word into a smaller one. Since the Red Book (see the section "The Books" in Chapter 5, "CDs—How They Work and How They're Made") specifies that the word length for an audio CD must be 16 bits, a program with a longer word length (say, 24 bits) must eventually be decreased. Just lopping off the last 8 bits (called "truncation") sounds horrible, so the dither signal is used to gently accomplish this task. Since word lengths generally expand when a signal undergoes digital signal processing (up to as many as 64 bits), eventually it must be reduced to 16 bits to fit on a CD.

All dither is not created equally. There are currently many different algorithms which accomplish this task. Among the most popular are Apogee's UV22 process (they say it's a new process, but it does the same thing as dither), as well as processes by Meridian, Pacific Microsonics (their HDCD is widely used), and Weiss, among others. One of the most popular is the POW-r dithering technique that has been produced by the POW-r consortium. This consortium is comprised of a number of digital audio powerhouses, including Weiss, SADiE, Millennia Media, Z-Systems, and Lake DSP.

For a more in-depth look at dither, check out the dither discussion on Bob Katz's Digital Domain Web site at **www .digido.com/ditheressay.html**.

ISRC

ISRC stands for International Standard Recording Code and was developed by ISO (International Organization for Standardization) to identify sound and audio-visual recordings. It is officially known as International Standard ISO 3901. ISRC is a unique identifier of each recording that makes up the album. If a recording is changed in any way, it requires a new ISRC, but otherwise it will always retain the same ISRC, independent of the company or format it is in. An ISRC code may not be reused.

The ISRC is contained in the subcode (Q-channel) of a CD (see the section "CD Subcodes") and is unique to each track. Each ISRC is comprised of 12 characters, as follows:

Length (chars)	Description
2	Country
3	First owner (allocated by the RIAA)
2	Year of recording (actually the last two digits)
5	Designation code (assigned by first owner)

CD SUBCODES

When the CD was first developed, data known as a subcode was included along with the main data channel as a means of placing control data on the disc. The main channel was originally intended entirely for audio, not any other form of data, although it has been used for other things since.

In addition to the main data channel of a CD (which contains audio or other data), there are eight subcode channels labeled P to W that are interleaved with the main channel on the disc and available for use by CD audio and CD-ROM players. The subcodes are as follows:

P-channel indicates the start and end of each track and was intended for simple audio players that did not have full Q-channel decoding.

Q-channel contains the time codes (minutes, seconds, and frames), the Table of Contents or TOC (in the lead-in), track type, and catalog number.

Channels R to W are for subcode graphics known as CD+G and CD text that accompany the main audio data.

Except in the very special circumstances where the rare CD+G disc is being made, all subcodes except the P and Q are ignored. However, the PQ codes must be supplied with every master sent to the replicator, and therefore must be added and/or edited. Among the items that might require editing are general offsets of track ID numbers to help with universal playability (some old players take a few frames to unmute the outputs when starting to play a new track, so you need to have the ID mark happen several frames ahead of the first frame of audio), changing song times, and ISRCs. One of the reasons the Sonic Solutions' DAW is so popular for mastering is because it has a built-in PQ editor.

Usually a PQ log is printed out and sent with the master to the replicator as a check to ensure that the correct songs and ISRCs have been provided. Also, when making a master (1630, DDP, PMCD), the PQ info is put on the master somewhere separate from the audio so the plant can read it, check it against the PQ log you provide, and use it to cut the glass master (*see Figure 24*).

THE SONY PCM-1630

One of the staples of the mastering scene is the Sony 1630 (*see Figure 25*), which is a digital processor connected to a Sony DMR 4000 or BVU-800 3/4-inch U-matic video machine. Since the beginning of the CD, this has been the standard format that mastering facilities have used to deliver to the replicator, and every facility still uses them. Another machine not currently in manufacture and therefore drawing premium prices, the 1630 is noted for its low error count and is still frequently used where other media fails.

The PCM-1630 (its predecessor was the 1610) is a modulation format recorded to 3/4-inch videotape. It was, for many years, the only way one could deliver a digital program and the ancillary PQ information to the factory for pressing and is still widely used for CD production. At the replicator, glass mastering from U-matic can only be done at single speed so it's usual to transfer the audio data to another media (like

Figure 24: PQ log

PQ LOG

Client : Test Records
Project: Sample
Title : Sample
Date : March 6, 2000
Studio : Test Mastering

Disc Type: Audio
Time Format: 30/NDF

PQ Track 1 Offset: 00:00:00:10	PQ StartOffset: 00:00:00:10
PQ SpliceOffset: 00:00:00:06	PQ EndOffset: 00:00:00:02
PQ MinIndex0Width: 00:00:01:00	UPC/EAN CODE: 0000000000000

PQ Track/Index Information:

T-X TITLE/ISRC COPY EMPH D/A NO OFFSET OFFSET OFFSET CD
TIME TIME DURATION TIME
hh:mm:ss:ff hh:mm:ss:ff hh:mm:ss:ff mm:ss:ff

---

0 Pause	00:01:58:00 00:01:57:20 00:00:02:00 00:00:00
1 Suffering & Smiling—Part 1&2	00:02:00:00 00:01:59:20 00:21:31:02 00:02:00
TOTAL:	00:21:33:02

---

2 GBCNP7780130 OFF OFF A	
0 Pause	00:23:30:20 00:23:30:22 00:00:02:08 21:33:05
1 No Agreement—Album	00:23:33:10 00:23:33:00 00:15:30:00 21:35:25
TOTAL:	00:15:32:08

---

3 GBCNP7780140 OFF OFF A	
0 Pause	00:39:02:28 00:39:03:00 00:00:01:18 37:05:25
1 Dog Eat Dog— Album	00:39:04:28 00:39:04:18 00:15:32:18 37:06:70
TOTAL:	00:15:34:06

Lead-out	00:54:37:04 00:54:37:06 52:39:40

Total 00:52:39:16

DDP Exabyte) for higher speed cutting (which is not necessarily a good thing to do from an audio standpoint).

When directly mastering from U-matic tape, the audio must be recorded at 44.1kHz to the Sony 1610/1630 format, and the PQ code recorded on channel 1 so that the title can be mastered directly from the U-matic tape. This "PQ burst" (which sounds similar to a modem tone) is basically just a data file placed on the tape before starting audio.

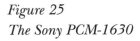

Figure 25
The Sony PCM-1630

BOB LUDWIG: *We're still doing mostly 1630s. When the 1630 was invented, I remember all the guys on the West Coast screaming about how awful it was. And now that plants are doing 4X cutting and glass mastering off of CD-Rs, that 1630 is like the Holy Grail of professional audio. The fact is that the error rate is very low on it and you can computer verify it with a DTA 2000 to make sure that everything is precisely just as you want. And if you send it to a replicator that still has a 1630 and insist on doing it single speed, you might get a CD back that sounds something like what you sent to the plant.*

BERNIE GRUNDMAN: *I'm not sure, but I think we might do 60 percent 1630s and 40 percent CD-Rs. We're doing a lot more CDs lately because the factories don't want to mess with 1630s because they're just a headache.*

DAVE COLLINS: *I would say the majority of our releases still go out on 1630. What they get transferred to at the CD plant I don't know. I'm actually warming up to DDP. I've heard some CDs that came back that we did off DDP that sound fine. They're not significantly different from the master.*

DOUG SAX: *Without question, the best results are still from a 1630. It's the least amount of transfer. You don't have to go into computer because you can assemble right to it. It's one generation from the source and you can cut glass from it. So for the most part I either do 1630 or PMCD.*

GLENN MEADOWS: *On major label projects, it's probably mostly all 1630 and DDP. It's mostly the smaller guys that are doing CD-R. MCA wants all DDPs. Capitol wants 1630s in their vaults, but they'll run DDP to the plant. BMG Nashville/RCA Records will go one way or the other depending on the project; sometimes they do 1630, sometimes they do DDPs.*

1630 Mastering Setup

- Digital audio is recorded at 44.1kHz on the video track.

- Audio begins at two minutes (to eliminate tape-induced errors).

- PQ code burst is recorded on audio track 1 before the digital audio begins.

- 30-frame nondrop SMPTE time code recorded on audio track 2.

THE PMCD

PMCD stands for pre-mastered CD and is a proprietary format jointly owned by Sonic Solutions and Sony. PMCD was originally an effort to replace the Sony PCM-1630 as the standard media delivered to the replicator. It differs from a normal CD-R in that a PQ log is written into the lead-out of the disc (see Chapter 5). At readback, this log is used to generate the PQ data set during glass mastering, which eliminates a step during replication. A PMCD can only be written from a Sonic Solutions DAW.

Although a great idea at the time, PMCD never quite lived up to its intentions due to the fact that most masters are now digitally copied to DDP format (see the next section) at the replicator for high-speed glass master cutting. Even though this high-speed cut is faster and more efficient for the replicator, most mastering engineers agree that the end result is an inferior end product thanks to the jitter induced in the process.

EDDY SCHREYER: *PMCDs are probably still the most common. 1630s are dwindling. Exabyte DDPs, maybe 5 percent. But PMCDs are really taking over now.*

DDP

DDP (Disc Description Protocol) is a propriety format from Doug Carson Associates based on the 8mm Exabyte format tape that is used as a master medium to send to the replicator as well as an internal medium used by the replicator to cut the glass master. DDP has quickly become a master medium of choice and there are many reasons for this:

DDP Exabyte has the fewest errors of any master medium, thanks to computer data quality error correction. CD-Rs and PMCDs have a lot less robust error correction and will output data whether it's bad or not. It's therefore possible to get different data each time you play it, and it requires a diligent plant to get an error-free transfer from a CD-R.

It's easier and safer to go past the 74-minute boundary with DDP. Long CD-Rs are less reliable, although that does not mean they won't work.

Many plants will transfer a CD-R to DDP before sending it to the glass cutter so that they can cut the glass master at high speed (either 2X or 4X). Although this is better for the plant, it usually doesn't sound as good as a single-speed cut.

It's impossible to play back a DDP without the right equipment, which isn't readily available. This means that there's less chance for an accidental playback of the master. A CD-R can get smudged and scratched, but the DDP will stay in its baggie until it hits the plant.

BOB OLHSSON: *I find I get the best results with a DDP tape. We did a bunch of studies doing different methods of cutting some years ago, and we found that our own DDP tapes consistently resulted in pressings that sound like our own CD-Rs. That wasn't necessarily the case if we sent out a CD-R.*

CD-R BURNERS

Now that CD recorders are relatively inexpensive and widespread, it's possible to cut a master disc to send to the replicator even without the help of an expensive workstation or piece of software. Most plants now accept regular CD-Rs, Exabyte tapes, or even DATs for pressing, but the danger here is that some users may think that they can prepare their own masters without the slightest understanding of what the technical specifications are. Therefore, it's important that we discuss some areas of concern.

Disc-at-Once

In order to create a disc suitable for pressing, it's important to use what's known as "disc-at-once" mode. This means that the CD-R is cut in one complete pass with no stops where the laser is turned off. Using the other cutting mode, "track-at-once," is not permitted because it stops the laser in between songs, which creates unreadable frames that will cause the disc to be rejected at the plant.

Recorder Speed

High-speed (2X, 4X, 8X, meaning the recorder is cutting at two, four, or eight times real-time) CD-R recording is far less desirable than 1X recording. This is because high-speed recording generally results in greater disc errors and increased jitter. Also, recording power does not increase linearly with speed, therefore higher speed recording can reduce the total energy required for recording.

It's also generally acknowledged that discs cut at 1X usually *sound* better. Although there are many theories as to why this is true, it's widely accepted that the jitter begins to rise with the speed of the cut.

ERROR CHECKING

Errors on any media are extremely critical; they can make the difference between making a good cut on the glass master or a reject. These errors can be in many forms, from tape dropouts to scratches or dust on tape or disc to just plain bad media. Therefore, most major mastering facilities use several ways to check if errors have occurred. On the 1630, the Sony DTA-2000 is normally used. For CD-R and PMCD, a measurement unit like the StageTech EC2 is used.

Error rate measurements such as the E series (E11, E21, E31, E12, E22, E32) and BLER provide vital information as to the general condition of a tape or disc. BLER (block error rate) represents frame error rate and is one of the most widely used error measurements. One frame represents the smallest integral data package on a disc and contains 24 bytes of data along with sync, subcode, Q parity, and P parity. Data is read from a CD-ROM at the rate of 7350 frames per second in a 1X player. BLER measures the rate of bad frames that contain one or more read errors. If 1 percent of the frames contain errors, then BLER will be 73.5 per second at 1X. It is required that a disc have a frame error rate less than 3 percent, or a 1X BLER of 220 per second. High quality discs have much lower frame error rates than this, usually in the range of 20 to 30.

CHAPTER 5

CDs – How They Work and How They're Made

It behooves engineers to know the most they can about the ultimate medium on which their art and craft resides. So here it is, everything you ever wanted to know about CDs, plus a reference list at the end to find out even more.

THE BOOKS

When it comes to the technical talk about CDs, sooner or later the matter of "Books" comes up. The Books are simply a set of technical specifications that CDs must follow in order to be compatible with each other and, therefore, any CD player. Since quite a number of books exist, it's easy to get overwhelmed and confused, but they're really quite simple once you get rid of the technical jargon.

Red Book

Red Book is the prerecorded CD audio standard that you find in music stores today. Because of this standard, any audio CD will play in any audio compact disc player, and this has been a major factor in the growth of the CD industry. Specified are the sample rate (44.1Khz), bit depth (16), type of error detection and correction, and how the data is stored on the disc among other things.

Also defined is a way to add graphics information to the CD for a CD+G (CD plus graphics) disc, which was weakly tried by the major record labels in the mid-1980s and is not generally available today. Approximately 16MB of graphics data can be stored on a disc. Each Red Book disc can have up to 99 audio tracks and be 74:33 minutes in length (although it's possible to reach 80 minutes under special circumstances).

Orange Book

The Orange Book defines the standard for writable or recordable media such as CD-Rs and magneto-optical

(MO) discs. It defines where the data can be written and, in the case of the MO, how it is erased and rewritten.

Blue Book

This is a hybrid disc that is part Red Book and part Yellow Book. A Blue Book CD is also sometimes referred to as CD Plus or CD Extra.

An offshoot of a Blue Book/CD Extra disc is an "enhanced CD." The difference is the order in which the files are written, which is data first (the Yellow Book info), then audio in the CD Extra.

Green Book

A precursor to DVD in terms of flexibility, the Compact Disc Interactive (CD-I) standard was released by Phillips in 1987 and allowed for full motion video on a standard five-inch disc. Now defunct, it requires a dedicated CD-I player and is not compatible with a standard audio CD player.

Yellow Book

This is the CD-ROM standard for computer data. It also adds two additional track types that differ from the Red Book audio disc: Mode 1, which is usually computer data, and Mode 2, which is usually compressed audio data or video/picture data.

White Book

Sometimes known as Karaoke CD, White Book CDs are used in applications where the combination of limited full-motion video and audio is needed. These were originally called Video CDs but soon renamed due to their more widespread use in karaoke applications. White Book CDs utilize MPEG 1 and 2 compression schemes in order to compress audio and video down to a usable size. The format was originally written by Philips in conjunction with the Japanese Victor Company (JVC) and is also supported by Sony and Matsushita.

Photo CD

Developed by Eastman Kodak and Philips, Photo CD is a way of cataloging photographs on a CD. The photos can be read in a number of ways: from dedicated photo CD players, CD-I players (now obsolete), computers with a Photo CD driver set, and 3DO players.

HOW CDS WORK

A CD is a plastic disc, 1.2mm thick and five inches in diameter that consists of several layers. First, to protect the microscopically small pits (more than eight trillion of them) against dirt and damage, the CD has a plastic protective layer on which the label is printed. Then there is an aluminum coating that contains the ridges and reflects laser light. Finally, the disc has a transparent carrier through which the actual reading of the disc takes place. This plastic forms a part of the optical system *(see Figure 26)*.

Mechanically, the CD is less vulnerable than the record, but that does not mean that it shouldn't be treated with care. Since the protective layer on the label side is very thin (only one ten thousandth of an inch), careless treatment or granular dust can cause small scratches or hair cracks, enabling the air to penetrate the evaporated aluminum coating. If this occurs, the coating will begin to oxidize.

Figure 26
The CD has several layers. Notice how the ridges contain binary information.

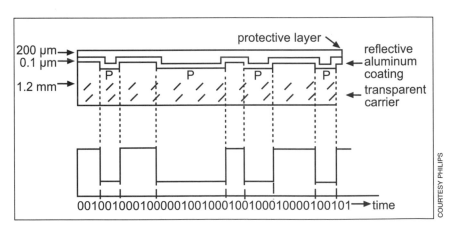

The reflecting side of the CD is the side that is read. People tend to set the CD down with the reflecting side up. However, the more vulnerable side is not the reflecting side but the label side. On the label side, the reflecting layer with its ridges has been evaporated. The sensitive layer on the reflecting side has been protected better than the one on the label side. It is therefore better to store

The Mastering Engineer's Handbook

CDs with the reflecting side down. It is best to store the CD back in the jewel case, where it is safely held by its inside edge.

Never write on the label side, even with a felt-tipped pen. The ink may penetrate the thin protective coating and affect the aluminum layer *(see Figure 27)*.

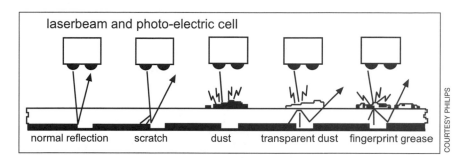

CDs are easily scratched and should never be cleaned with just any cloth. CDs should be cleaned radially: not along the grooves, but at right angles to the direction of the grooves. If a smear, however small, should remain on the CD running along the direction of the grooves, much information could be lost. It is advisable to use a special CD cleaner that operates with a rotating brush at right angles to the direction of the grooves.

The area of the disc that contains data is divided into three areas *(see Figure 28)*:

The lead-in contains the Table of Contents in the subcode Q-channel and allows the laser pickup head to follow the pits and synchronize to the audio or computer data before the start of the program area. The length of the lead-in is determined by the number of tracks stored in the Table of Contents.

The program area contains up to about 76 minutes of data divided into 99 tracks maximum.

The lead-out contains digital silence or zero data and defines the end of the CD program area.

Figure 28
The CD Layout

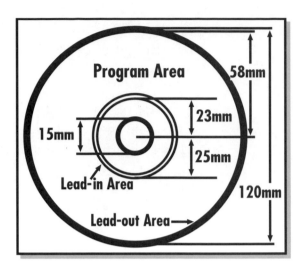

Scanning the Disc

Like vinyl records, the information on optical discs is recorded on a spiral track in the form of minute indentations called "pits." These pits are scanned from the reverse side of the disc (this makes them appear as ridges to the laser) by a microscopically thin laser beam during playback. The scanning begins at the inside of the back of the disc and proceeds outwards. During playback, the number of revolutions of the disc decreases from 500 to 200 rpm (revolutions per minute) in order to maintain a constant scanning speed. The disc data is converted into electrical pulses (the bit stream) by reflections of the laser beam from a photoelectric cell. When the beam strikes a land, the beam is reflected onto a photoelectric cell. When it strikes a ridge, the photocell will receive only a weak reflection. A D/A converter (digital-to-analog converter) converts these series of pulses to binary coding, then to decimal values, and then back to an analog waveform *(see Figure 29)*.

It should be noted that the ends of the ridges seen by the laser are 1s and all lands and ridges are 0s; thus turning on and off the reflection is 1, while a steady state is a string of 0s.

Thanks to this optical scanning system, there is no friction between the laser beam and the disc. As a result, the discs don't wear regardless how often they're played. Discs must be treated carefully, however, since scratches, grease

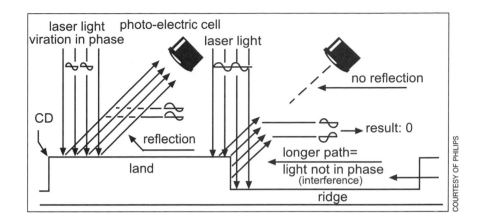

Figure 29
The disc data is converted into electrical pulses (the bit stream) by reflections of the laser beam off a photo-electric cell.

stains, and dust can diffract the light and cause some data to be skipped or distorted. This problem is solved by an error correction system that automatically inserts any lost or damaged information. Without this error correction system, optical disc players could not exist, as even the slightest vibration causes sound and image distortions.

The scanning must be very accurate because the track of ridges is 30 times narrower than a single human hair. There are 20,000 tracks on one compact disc *(see Figure 30)*. The lens which focuses the laser beam on the disc has a depth of field of about one micron (micrometer = one-millionth of a meter). It is quite normal for the disc to move back and forth 1mm during playback. A flexible regulator keeps the lens at a distance of +/-2 microns from the rotating disc. For the same reason, a perfect tracking system is required. The complex task of following the track is controlled by an electronic servo system. The servo system ensures the track is followed accurately by measuring the signal output. If the output decreases, the system recognizes this as being "off-track" and returns the tracking system to its optimum state.

Figure 30
There are 20,000 tracks like this one on one CD.

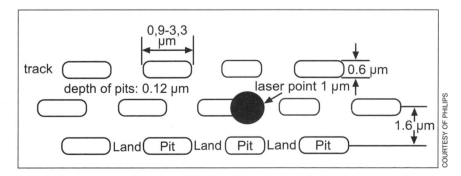

Many CD players use three-beam scanning for correct tracking. The three beams come from one laser. A polarized prism projects three spots of light on the track. It shines the middle one exactly on the track, and the two other "control" beams generate a signal to correct the laser beam immediately, should it deflect from the middle track.

Courtesy Philips—Inventors of the CD

HOW CDS ARE MADE

Data is copied onto the CD in a "pit-and-land" pattern that begins at the inner hub of the disc and spirals toward the outer edge in a counter-clockwise direction. For 650MB of data, the continuous track is over four miles long ***(see Figure 31)***.

Figure 31
CD pits and lands

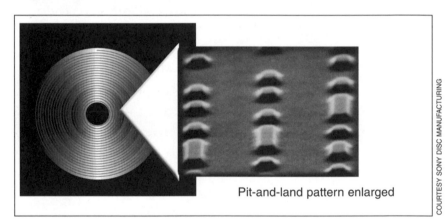

Pit-and-land pattern enlarged

COURTESY SONY DISC MANUFACTURING

Data on a CD, represented by a series of pits and lands, are so small that the width of a human hair would cover over 40 tracks. Over 60 CD tracks could be placed within a single LP groove ***(see Figure 32)***.

Step 1

Glass mastering is comprised of a number of stages that are required to create a metallized glass master from which CD stampers are produced. All of the processes are carried out in a clean room, where the mastering technicians must wear special clothing such as face masks and footwear to minimize any stray particles.

The eight-inch diameter, 6mm thick glass blanks can be recycled, so glass master preparation begins by stripping

The Mastering Engineer's Handbook

Figure 32
Pit size

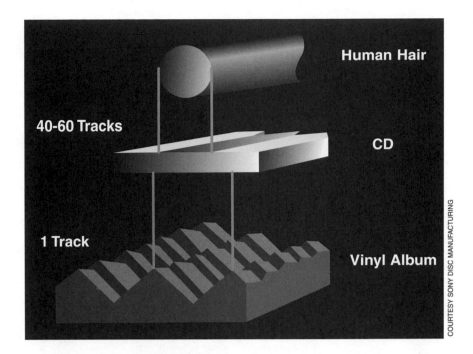

the old photo-resist from its surface, which is then followed by a washing with deionized water and a careful drying. The surface of the clean glass master is then coated with a photo-resist layer a scant 150 microns thick with the uniformity of the layer measured with an infrared laser. The photo-resist coated glass master is then baked at about 176 degrees for 30 minutes, which hardens the photo-resist layer and makes it ready for exposing by laser light.

Laser beam recording is where the photo-resist layer is exposed to a blue gas laser fed directly from the source audio of either a 1630, PMCD, or DDP master tape. The photo-resist is exposed where pits are to be pressed in the final disc. The photo-resist surface is then chemically developed to remove the photo-resist exposed by the laser and therefore create pits in the surface. These pits then extend right through the photo-resist to the glass underneath to achieve the right pit geometry. The glass itself is unaffected by this process *(see Figure 33)*.

Step 2

The surface of this glass master, which is called the "metal master" or "father," is then coated with either a silver or nickel metal layer. The glass master is then played on a disc master player (DMP) to check for any errors. Audio masters are actually listened to at this stage.

Figure 33
The glass master

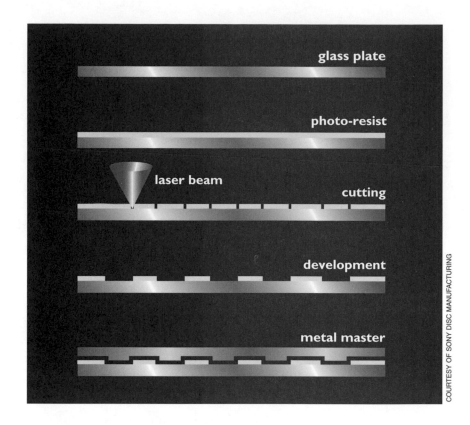

Figure 34
Making the stamper

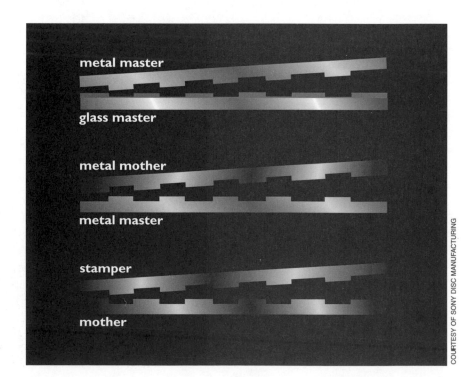

The Mastering Engineer's Handbook

Step 3

The next stage is to make the reverse image stamper or "mother" (a positive image of the final disc pit and land orientation). The mother is then form pressed onto the extruded "children" membranes, which ultimately contain all the binary information used to play the disc.

Step 4

Stampers are then made from the mother and secured into the molding machines that actually stamp the CD discs *(see Figure 34)*.

Step 5

After a CD disc has been molded from clear polycarbonate, a thin layer of reflective metal is bonded onto the pit and land surface and a clear protective coating is applied.

Figure 35
The final product

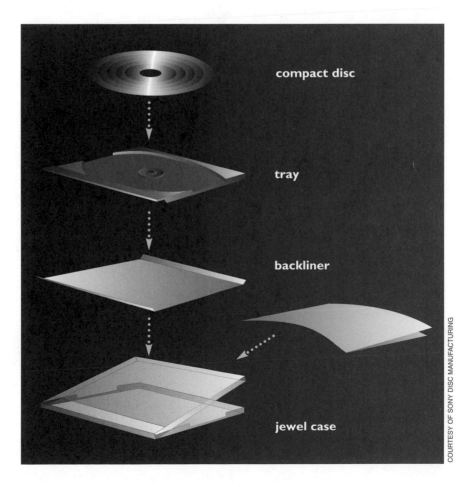

compact disc

tray

backliner

jewel case

Step 6

The disc label is printed on the nonread surface of the disc, and the CD is inserted into a package such as a jewel case with a tray, booklet, and backliner *(see Figure 35)*.

A single unit called a "monoliner" *(see Figure 36)* is actually used to replicate CDs after the stamper has been created. The monoliner consists of a complete replication line comprised of a molding machine, metaliser, lacquer unit, printer (normally three-color), and inspection. Good and bad discs are transferred to different spindles. Finished discs are removed on spindles for packing. It's also possible for the monoliner to not include a printer so a new job can continue without being stopped while the printer is being set up.

A duoline is a replication line comprising two molding machines, metaliser, lacquer unit, and inspection. Each molding machine can run different titles, with the discs being separated after inspection and placed on different spindles.

Figure 36
A monoliner

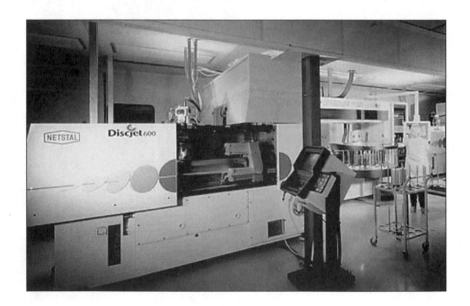

The Mastering Engineer's Handbook

CD Pressing Plants

Sonopress
108 Monticello
Weaverville, NC 28787
www.Sonopress.com/

Allied
15 Gilpin Avenue
Hauppauge, NY 11788

Specialty
1400 Lackawanna Avenue
Olyphant, PA 18448
www.Wamodvd.com/

Cinram
1600 Rich Road
Richmond, IN 47374
www.Cinram.com/

Cinram
4905 Moores Mill Road
Huntsville, AL 35811-1511

Cinram
3400 East La Palma Avenue
Anaheim, CA 92806

JVC
3443 Laguna Boulevard
Elk Grove, CA 95758

JVC
2 JVC Road
Tuscaloosa, AL 35405

Denon
1380 Monticello Road
Madison, GA 30650

www.americdisc.com/

www.sdm.sony.com/

www.amtechdisc.com/

www.discusa.com/

Of Additional Interest

Andy McFadden's CD Recordable FAQ
www.fadden.com/CD-Rfaq/

Glenn Meadows' CD-R Test Results
www.digido.com/meadows.html

www.cd-info.com/

Doug Carson Associates
www.dcainc.com/

Mastering for Vinyl

Although it seems like almost an ancient technology in these days of 1s and 0s, the vinyl record seems to be at least holding its own in the marketplace and even making a bit of a resurgence. This is partly because of the high demand from DJs and also from an audiophile community that still insists that vinyl packs a sonic punch second to none.

While it's pretty certain that most new mastering houses won't be getting the gear to do vinyl anytime soon, it's still pretty important to know what makes the format tick so you can get the best performance when the order comes to make some records along with the CDs. But before we get into the mastering requirements for vinyl, let's take a look at the system itself and the physics required to make a record. While this is by no means a complete description of the entire process of cutting a record, it is a pretty good overview.

DAVID CHEPPA: *If you just want to cut a mediocre record, you don't need to know a lot of anything. If you want to cut a better record, it's good to know something. If you want to cut an incredible record, you need to have an understanding of the physical world and the physical laws that govern it. You have to know what the limits really are, physically and electronically. So I think it's a balance of art, science, and technology.*

A BRIEF HISTORY OF VINYL

It's important to look at the history of the record because in some ways it is the history of mastering itself. Until 1948, all records were 10-inch and played at 78 rpm. When Columbia Records introduced the 12-inch 33-1/3 rpm in 1948, the age of high-fidelity actually began, and sonic quality took a quantum leap over the previous generation of disc. However, records of that time had a severe limitation of only about ten minutes of playing time per side since the grooves were all relatively wide in order to fit the low frequencies on the record.

To overcome this time limitation, two refinements occurred. First, the Record Industry Association of America (RIAA) instituted an equalization curve in 1953 that narrowed the grooves, thereby allowing more grooves to be cut on the record, which increased the playing time and decreased the noise. This was done by boosting the high frequencies by about 17dB at 15kHz and cutting the lows by 17dB at 50Hz when the record was cut. The opposite curve is then applied during playback. This is what's known as the RIAA curve. It's also the reason your turntable sounds so bad when you plug it directly into a mic or line input of a console. Without the RIAA curve, the resulting sound is thin and tinny due to the overemphasized high frequencies and attenuated low frequencies.

The second refinement was the implementation of "variable pitch," which allowed the mastering engineer to change the number of grooves per inch according to the program material. In cutting parlance, pitch is the rate at which the cutter head and stylus travel across the disc. By varying this velocity, the number of grooves can be varied as well. These two advances increased the playing time to the current 25 minutes or so (more on this later) per side.

In 1957, the stereo record became commercially available and really pushed the industry to the sonic heights that it has reached today.

THE PHYSICS OF VINYL

To understand how a record works you must understand what happens within a groove. If you were to cut a mono 1kHz tone, the cutting stylus would swing side to side in the groove 1000 times per second (*see Figures 37–50*). The louder you want the signal, the deeper you have to cut the groove.

While this works great in mono, it doesn't do a thing in stereo and, in fact, this was a problem for many years. As stated before, stereo records were introduced in 1957, but the stereo record cutting technique was actually proposed in 1931 by famed audio scientist Alfred Blumlein. His technique, called the 45/45 system, was revisited some 25 years later by the Westrex Corporation (who were the big guns in record equipment manufacturing at the time) and resulted in the eventual introduction of the stereo disc.

Essentially, a stereo disc combines the side-to-side (lateral) motion of the stylus with an up-and-down (vertical) motion. The 45/45 system rotated the axis 45 degrees to the plane of the cut. This method actually has several advantages. First, mono and stereo discs and players become totally compatible and second, the rumble (low-frequency noise from the turntable) is decreased by 3dB.

Figures 37 through 50 and their accompanying information are courtesy of Clete Baker at Studio B in Lincoln, Nebraska; they detail what record grooves can look like under different signal conditions.

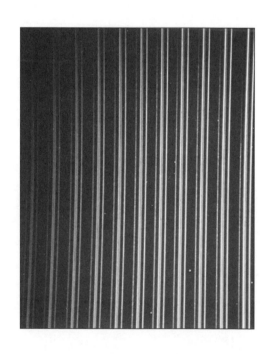

Figure 37
A silent groove with no audio information. The groove width across the top of the "vee" from land to land is two mils (.002 inch) as measured with the microscope's graticule, which had to be removed for the camera mount. Groove depth is approximately the same as the width for this particular stylus (Capps).

The Mastering Engineer's Handbook

Figure 38

From the outside diameter in: a low-frequency sine wave, a mid-frequency sine wave, and a high-frequency sine wave, all in mono (lateral excursion). All frequencies were at the same level at the head end of the system (i.e., prior to application of the RIAA curve). This demonstrates that for any given level, a lower frequency will create a greater excursion than a high frequency, and thus will require greater pitch to avoid intercuts.

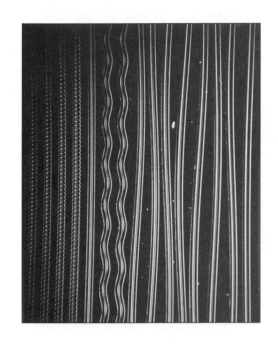

Figure 39

This is a sine wave applied to left channel only toward the outer part of the record, summed to mono in the center of the view, and applied to the right channel only toward the inner part of the record. You can easily see the difference between the purely lateral modulation of the mono signal and the vertical of the left and right channel signals.

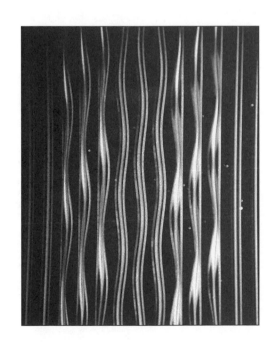

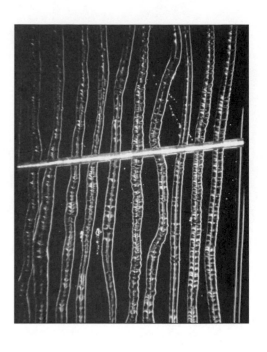

Figure 40
A human hair laid across the groove offers a point of reference for size.

Figure 41
Again, lower frequency and higher frequency sine waves demonstrate that more land is required to accommodate the excursion of lows than of highs.

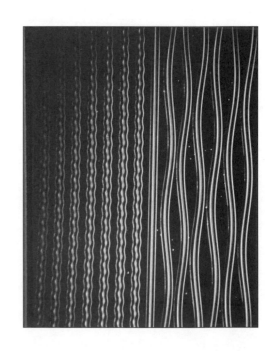

The Mastering Engineer's Handbook

Figure 42
To allow for the accommodation of low-frequency excursions without wasting vast amounts of disc real estate, variable pitch is employed to spread the groove in anticipation of large excursions and to narrow the groove in the absence of material that doesn't require it. This figure shows variable pitch in action on program audio.

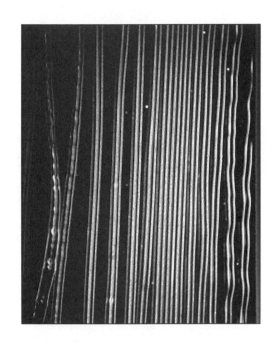

Figure 43
When variable pitch goes bad. Oops... a lateral intercut caused by insufficient application of variable pitch for a wide lateral excursion. Toward the bottom center of the slide, the outside wall of the loud low frequency has "kissed" the adjacent wall of the previous revolution, but the wall has not broken down; at least two mils of depth separate the two, which is a safe margin. However, on the next revolution a chance excursion toward the outside of the disc has all but overwritten its earlier neighbor; less than half a mil separates the bottom of the grooves there, which is certain to cause mistracking down the line.

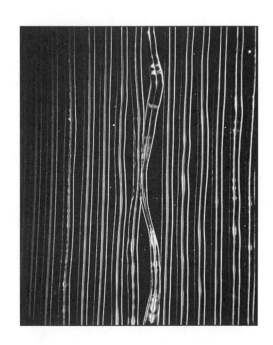

Figure 44
Lateral excursions aren't the only source of intercuts.
This figure shows a large low-frequency vertical excur-
sion caused by out-of-phase information, which has
been encroached upon by its neighbor during the next
revolution. The wall of the later revolution is compro-
mised down to about .5 mil. This is not severe enough
to cause mistracking, but some distortion will be
heard from the deformity.
Since this type of problem arises exclusively from out-
of-phase low frequency information that would be
acoustically cancelled upon playback anyway, mono
summing is generally performed at low frequencies to
eliminate such large vertical excursions.

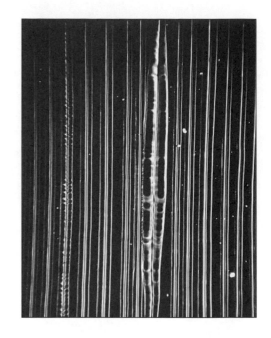

Figure 45
Large vertical excursions can cause problems not only
by carving out deep and, consequently, wide swaths
that result in intercuts, but by making the cutting
stylus literally lift right off the disc surface for the
other half of the waveform. Obviously, a lift such as
this would inevitably cause a record to skip and is
always unacceptable.

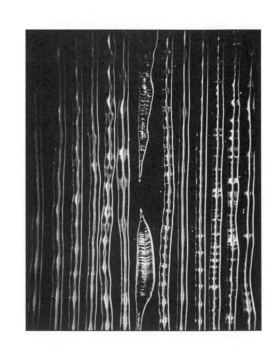

Figure 46

Here a near lift (only a tenth of a mil remains of the groove walls) is accompanied on the following revolutions by lateral intercut. The deformity along the inside wall of the new groove as the outside wall encounters the previous revolution is clearly visible opposite the breach. This will result in audible distortion. The mastering engineer has several tools at his disposal to solve problems such as these. Among them are increasing groove pitch and/or depth, lowering the overall level at which the record is cut, reducing low frequency information, summing low frequencies at a higher crossover point, or adding external processing such as a peak limiter. Each of these can be used alone or in combination to achieve a satisfactory master, but none can be employed without exacting a price.

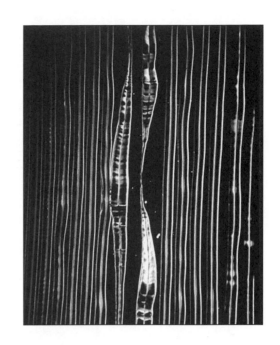

Figure 47

Here is the same audio viewed in Figure 46, after processing. In this case, a limiter was employed to reduce dynamic range (the surrounding material is noticeably louder as well) and rein in the peaks, which were causing intercuts and lifts. This section is cut more deeply, averaging perhaps three to four mils instead of the more common two mils, in order to give vertical excursions plenty of breathing room. Pitch, too, has had to be increased overall in order to accommodate the slightly wider groove, despite the reduced need for dramatic dynamic increases in pitch due to the reduction of peaks by the limiter.

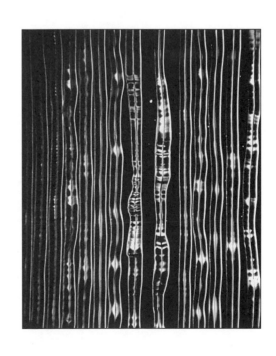

Figure 48
Among the truisms of disc cutting: high-frequency
information suffers terribly as the groove winds closer
to the inner diameter. Here is high-frequency rich
program material near the outer diameter of the disc.

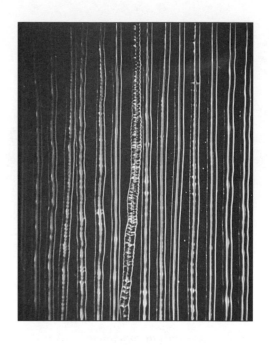

Figure 49
Here is the same audio information as in Figure 44,
but it's nearer the inside diameter of the disc.

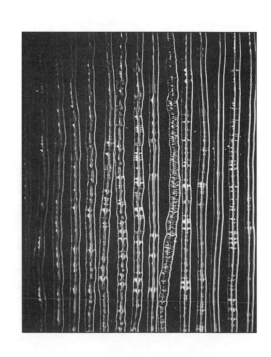

The Mastering Engineer's Handbook

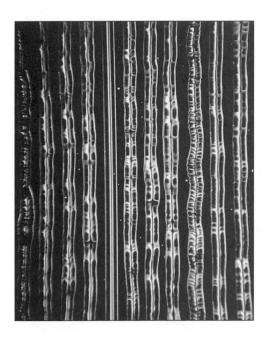

Figure 50
The ideal: normal, healthy-looking program audio.

THE VINYL SIGNAL CHAIN

While the signal chain for vinyl is similar to that of a CD, there are some important distinctions and unique pieces involved. Let's look at the chain from the master lacquer (the record that we cut to send to the pressing plant) on back.

The Master Lacquer

The master lacquer is the record that you cut to send to the pressing plant. It consists of a mirror-smooth substrate of aluminum coated with cellulose nitrate (a distant cousin to nitroglycerine), along with some resins and pigments to keep it soft and to help with visual inspection. The lacquer is extremely soft as compared to the finished record and can never be played after it is cut. In order to audition the mastering job before a lacquer is cut, a reference disc called a "ref" or "acetate" is made. Since this is made of the same soft material as the master lacquer, it can only be played five or six times (at most) before the quality has been significantly degraded. There is a separate lacquer master for each side of the record. The lacquer is always larger than the final record (a 12-inch record has a 14-inch lacquer), so repeated handling does not damage the grooves.

The Cutting Stylus and Cutter Head

The cutting stylus, which is made of sapphire, sits inside the cutter head, which consists of several large drive coils. The drive coils are powered by a set of very high-powered (typically 1000 to 3500 watts) amplifiers. The cutting stylus is heated for an easier and quieter cut.

The Lathe

The lathe contains a precision turntable and the carriage that holds the cutter head assembly as well as a microscope to inspect the grooves and adjustments that determine the number of grooves and the depth of cut. No lathes are currently being manufactured, but models by Scully and Neumann were once among the most desirable *(see Figure 51)*.

Figure 51
Neumann VMS-80 with SX 84 cutter head from 1984

COURTESY NEUMANN

DAVID CHEPPA: *We've actually developed it quite a lot. In the old days, way, way back in the '50s, the first cutting systems weren't very powerful. They only had maybe 10 or 12 watts of power. Then in the '60s, Neumann developed a system that brought it up to about 75 watts per channel, which was considered pretty cool. Then in the '70s, the high-powered cutting systems came into being, which was about 500 watts. That was pretty much it for a while. I mean, it made no sense beyond that because the cutter heads really weren't designed to handle that kind of power anyway. Even the last cutting system that came off the line in about 1990 at Neumann in Berlin hadn't really had changed other than it had newer panels and prettier electronics. It wasn't really a big difference.*

In the physical world with sound systems, all the energy is in the low end. But in cutting, it's the exact opposite. All of the energy is in the upper spectrum, so everything from about 5,000 cycles up begins to require a great amount of energy. This is why our cutting systems are so powerful. One lathe has 3,600 watts of power and our least powerful one is about 2,200 watts. It's devastating if something goes wrong at that power. If I get a master that's raw and hasn't been handled at all and there is something that just tweaks out of nowhere, it can take the cutter head out.

The Mastering Console

The mastering console for a disc system is equal to that used today for CD prep in sound quality and short signal path, but that's where the similarity ends. Because of the unique requirements of cutting a disc and the manual nature of the task (thanks to the lack of computerized gear at the time), there are several features on this type of desk that have fallen by the wayside in the modern era of CDs.

Figure 52
A Neumann SP-75 vinyl mastering console

The Preview System

Chief among those features is the preview system, which is an additional monitor path made necessary by the volatile nature of cutting a disc. Here's the problem: disc cutting is essentially a nonstop operation. Once you start to cut, you must make all your changes on the fly without stopping until the end of the side. If a portion of the program had excessive bass information, a loud peak, or something out-of-phase, the cutter head would cut right through the lacquer to the aluminum substrate. This would not only destroy the lacquer, but maybe an expensive stylus as well. Hence, the need for the mastering engineer to hear the problem and make the necessary adjustments before any harm came to the disc.

Enter the preview system. Essentially, the program going to the disc was delayed. Since digital delays weren't invented yet, an ingenious dedicated mastering tape machine with two separate head stacks (program and preview) and an extended tape path *(see Figures 53a and 53b)* was used. This gave the mastering engineer enough time to make the necessary adjustments before any damage was done to the disc or system.

Figure 53a
MCI tape machine with
preview head

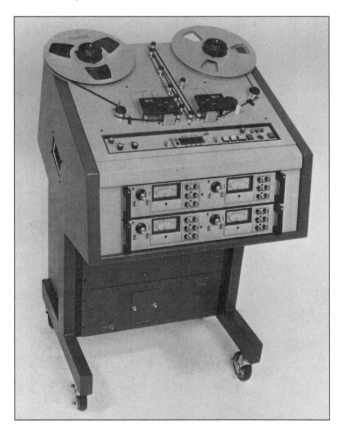

Equalization

Since a disc had to be cut on the fly and computer automation was still years away, a system had to be created in order to make EQ adjustments from song to song quickly, easily, and, most importantly, manually. This was accomplished by having two of each unit and having the controls of each stepped so that adjustments could be repeatable.

The Mastering Engineer's Handbook

Figure 53b
Studer tape machine with
preview head

The mastering engineer would then run down all the songs of a side (one side of the LP) and write down the EQ settings required. Then, as the first song was being cut through the A equalizer, he would preset the B equalizer. As song 2 was playing through the B equalizer, he would preset equalizer A for song 3, and so on.

Although this method was crude, it was effective. Naturally, today it's much easier now that all EQ and compression presets can be recalled with only a touch of a button.

Figure 54
Dual Equalizer
for vinyl mastering

EQ "A"

EQ "B"

The Elliptical Equalizer

One of the more interesting relics of the record days is the elliptical equalizer or low-frequency crossover. What this unit does is move all low frequencies below a preset frequency (usually 250, 150, 70 and 30Hz) to the center. This is done to stop excessive lateral movement of the cutting stylus because of too much low-frequency energy on one side only or excessive out-of-phase material. Obviously, use of this device could negatively affect the sound of a record and must be used judiciously.

HOW RECORDS ARE PRESSED

Pressing records is such a primitive process by today's standards that it's pretty amazing they sound as good as they do. This is a multistep operation that's virtually entirely mechanical and manual with a host of areas that could influence the end product in a mostly negative way.

Step 1

The master lacquer is used as the first of several metal molds from which the plastic records are pressed. The lacquer is first coated with a layer of tin and silver nitrate, then dropped in a nickel sulfamate bath and electroplated. The lacquer is removed from the bath, and the nickel coating is peeled away. The separated nickel is what's known as the metal master and is a negative of the lacquer.

Step 2

The metal master is dropped back into the nickel bath and electroplated again. The resultant separated metal part is known as the mother and is a positive copy that can be played since it has grooves (although it won't be because it will destroy the disc).

Step 3

The mother is dropped back into the nickel bath and electroplated again. The resultant separated metal part is known as the stamper and is a negative copy that is bolted into the record presser to actually stamp out the plastic records.

It should be noted that, just like tape, each resultant copy is a generation down and will result in 6dB worse signal-to-noise ratio. Also, great care must be used when peeling off the electroplating, since any material left behind will result in a pop or click on the finished product.

Step 4

The vinyl used to make records actually comes in a granulated form called "vinylite," and it isn't black, it's honey-colored. Before being pressed, it is heated into the form of modeling clay and colored with pigment. At this point it is known as a biscuit. The biscuit is then placed in the press, which resembles a large waffle iron and is heated to about 300 degrees. Temperature is important because if the press if too hot, the record will warp; if it's too cold, the noise will increase. After pressing, excess vinyl is trimmed with a hot knife, and the records are put on a spindle to cool at room temperature.

All of these metal parts wear out. A stamper will go dull after about 70,000 pressings. Because of that, several sets of metal parts have to be made for a large order, and in the case of a large-selling record, even several lacquers.

For some nice lathe pictures go to:

www.stratozoo.ch/cut/lathe.html

www.aardvark-mastering.com/history.htm

Parts Production

Although the more high profile and documented part of mastering lies in the studio with the mastering engineer, the real bread and butter of the business happens after the fact, during what's known as production. Production is the time when the various masters are made, verified, and sent to the replicator. While not a very glamorous portion of the business, it's one of the most important, since a problem there can negate a perfect job done beforehand.

MULTIPLE MASTERS

Generally speaking, every project will have a number of masters cut, depending upon the marketing plans and policy of the label *(see Figure 55)*. This usually breaks down as follows.

The CD Master
This is the master that the glass master will be cut from, which in turn will ultimately make the replicated CDs. If an artist is to have a worldwide release, a separate master for each world region is made.

The Cassette Master
If the label is going to make cassettes (which is less and less likely these days), a separate master is required since the song sequence is usually different from the CD due to the split sides of the cassette format. This master is sometimes just a DAT with 30 seconds of dead space to indicate a side switch.

The Vinyl Master
If a vinyl record is desired, a separate master is required due to the song sequence of the two-sided format.

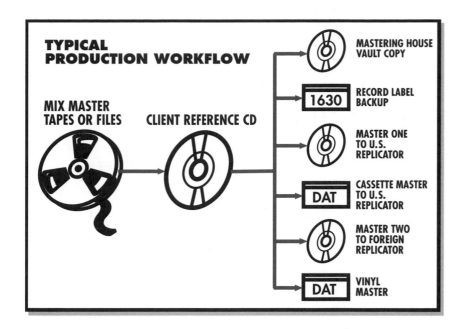

Figure 55
Mastering workflow

Backup Masters

Most major labels will ask for a backup master that they will store in the company vault. Many times the mastering facility will make a "house" backup as well to save time should a new master be required at a later time.

CLIENT REFS

Before production occurs, a reference, or "ref," is made for the client to approve. In the vinyl days, this was actually a record known as an acetate, but now it is more likely to be a CD-R thanks to the relatively cheap media. The client can then take the CD to an environment that they're comfortable with and approve the edits, fades, EQ, compression, sequencing, and general sound quality. Any changes will be relayed back to the mastering engineer, who will make those changes and cut another ref for the client to approve. As soon as the client is satisfied, the process of production begins.

MASTER VERIFICATION

Before a master is sent to the replicator, it is verified several different ways to ensure sonic integrity. When using a Sony 1630 3/4-inch U-matic, the tape is first electronically tested using a Sony DTA-2000 tape analyzer, which measures the number of data errors per second. If the error rate reaches 30 per second, the media is presumed faulty and the master is cut again.

If using a PMCD or a CD-R, the disc may be tested using a StageTech EC2. If the BLER rate (see Chapter 4, "Mastering for CD") exceeds 220, the disc must be rejected, although it is usually rejected far before that rate. Acceptable BLER rates usually range from 20 to 30 per second.

Most major facilities will also employ some type of audio verification as well, where a production engineer will listen to the entire contents of the master (sometimes with headphones) to ensure that it is free from pops, clicks, or glitches.

This attention to detail, as well as the large number of man hours required to create and verify a master, enables a mastering house to charge a premium for this service. A master sent to the replicator can range anywhere from $350 to $1000, depending on the mastering facility.

CHAPTER 8

Ten Recording Tips to Remember Before Mastering

1. Don't over-EQ when mixing. Better to be a bit dull and let your mastering engineer brighten things up. In general, mastering engineers have an easier time and can do a better job if the master is on the dull side rather than the bright side.

2. When using DAT, print your mixes hot, but not too hot. Printing too hot robs the mastering engineer of room to work. Also, some DAT machines' analog circuitry can actually distort before a digital overload occurs. Levels that peak at −3dBFS or so are usually sufficient.

3. Don't compress your mix too much. If you overcompress the whole mix, you'll rob the mastering engineer of a valuable tool. He might be able to reverse the effects of equalization in a mix, but there is no way for him to recover lost dynamics. A good rule of thumb for compression is, "If you can hear it, then it's too much."

4. Don't trim your mixes before hand. There is no way for the mastering engineer to recover lost material if you clip an intro or make a bad fade at the outro. You're potentially making a lot more work that will ultimately cost you money. It's best to leave all count-offs and tails alone and let the mastering engineer trim it.

5. Make sure you print tones. For analog tape, these should be done before mixdown on the same machine that you mix on rather than after the fact. Don't fudge these tones either. The mastering engineer couldn't care less if you had a perfect alignment or were 2dB down on the left channel. All he wants to do is set up his playback machine to be a mirror image of your recorder so it plays back exactly the same. You must print 30 seconds or so of 1Khz for channel balance, 10Khz for azimuth adjust, and 50Hz for low-frequency compensation. The last frequency is particularly important. The oscillator on many older consoles can only output 100Hz, but this is usually way higher than the head bump of the recorder, and any small adjustment at this frequency will mean a huge adjustment in the head bump area. 50Hz will provide a far more accurate alignment.

Print any Dolby alignment tones if Dolby was used.

For digital (such as DAT), a 1kHz tone at any of the popular standard levels (depending who you talk to, –12, –14, –16 or –20dBFS is used) can be printed but is not absolutely necessary.

6. Check your phase when mixing. It can be a real shock when you get to the mastering studio and the engineer begins to check for mono compatibility and the lead singer disappears. Even though this was more of a problem in the days of vinyl and AM radio, mono is still important since many so called stereo sources (such as television) are either pseudo-stereo or only stereo some of the time. Check it, and fix it if necessary before you get to mastering.

7. Be careful when using Dolby® Noise Reduction. Dolby (A, B, C, S, or SR) can be a godsend or it can be trouble if you're not careful. Don't double encode if you can help it. For instance, don't use Dolby for multitrack recording, then for mixing as well. This can cause some very distinctive phase anomalies that you will hear emphasized in the mastering studio. If you must mix with Dolby, it helps if you bring the original Dolby encoders with you since there are subtle calibration changes that are hard to duplicate from unit to unit.

8. Use caution when using DATs as a master. Make sure that all songs have IDs written and logged. Ideally, you want to be able to tell the mastering engineer to go to ID 3, 7, 14, etc., for example. Nothing is more unprofessional than when a DAT has no IDs and the producer is unsure which take is the right one or where it is on the tape.

Also, it's usually best to not record on a DAT master for the first couple of minutes since if any major errors do occur, this is where they're likely to be. This is the reason some manufacturers have 32-, 62-, 92-, and 122-minute tapes instead of the standard 30, 60, 90, and 120s.

It goes without saying, but you recorded simultaneously on a second DAT for backup, didn't you?

9. Come prepared. Make sure all documentation, shipping instructions and sequencing is complete before you get there.

Always bring the most original material (earliest mixdown generation) to the session, even if you're going to work from copies or compiled copies. In fact, bring every version of every song you have just in case a fix is required.

Knowing the order of songs (sequencing) beforehand will save you a bunch of money in mastering time. This is especially important if you will be releasing in multiple formats such as CD and cassette or vinyl since they will probably require a different song order due to the two sides of cassettes and records.

Other things that should be documented include any tape flaws, digital errors, distortions, bad edits, fades, shipping instructions, and matrix (record company identification) numbers. Don't be afraid to put down any glitches, channel imbalances, or distortions. The mastering engineer won't think less of you if something got away (you wouldn't believe the number of times it happens to everybody), and it's a whole lot easier than wasting a billable hour trying to track down an equipment problem when the problem is actually on the tape itself.

10. Have your songs timed out. This is important for a couple of reasons. First, you have to know how long a master tape or CD-R to use. CDs have a total time of just under 80 minutes (74:33 to be exact) and 3/4-inch U-matics come in either 60- or 80-minute lengths, while CD-Rs are available in 63 or 74 minute lengths.

Bonus Tips

Records may be around for a while (but in limited quantities) so the following applies if you intend to cut vinyl:

•   Cumulative time is important because the mastering engineer must know the total time per side before he starts cutting due to the physical limitations of the disc. You are limited to a maximum of about 25 minutes per side (although it's better if you use less) if you want the record to be nice and loud.

•   Your sequencing for a record will be different from the CD because it's split into two sides. Prepare for this ahead of time.

PART TWO: MASTERING IN SURROUND

CHAPTER 9

The Future Is Here

With surround sound production beginning to ramp up, producers now find they need the same finishing touches in mastering in surround that they've long been accustomed to in stereo. As a result, mastering facilities worldwide now face the daunting task of upgrading to the brave new world of multichannel. Perhaps even more than in recording and mixing studios, mastering houses now find that entry into this environment requires greater thought, planning, and skill than other audio facilities face. In surround mastering, it's not just a question of adding four channels of additional equipment and carrying on as before. The question really is, are there other services that will be expected by the client as well?

Here are some of the concerns faced by the mastering engineer contemplating surround.

FIRST, A BIT OF HISTORY

Surround sound in one form or another has actually been with us for more than 50 years. Film has always used the three-channel "curtain of sound" developed by Bell Labs in the early '30s. This was because it was discovered that a center channel provided the significant benefits of anchoring the center by eliminating phantom images (in stereo, the center images shift as you move around the room) and better frequency response matching across the sound field.

The addition of a rear effects channel to the front three channels dates as far back as 1941 with the Fantasound four-channel system utilized by Disney for the film *Fantasia* and the '50s with Fox's Cinemascope. Still, the rear channel didn't come into widespread use until the '60s when Dolby Stereo became the surround de facto standard. This popular film format uses four channels (left, center, right, and a mono surround, sometimes called LCRS) and is encoded onto two tracks. Almost all major shows and films currently produced for theatrical release and broadcast television are presented in Dolby Stereo since it has the added advantage of playing back properly in stereo or mono if no decoder is present.

With the advent of digital delivery formats capable of supplying more channels in the '80s, the number of surround channels was increased to two and the low-frequency effects channel was added to make up the six-channel 5.1, which soon became the modern standard for most films, music, and DTV. *Star Wars Episode 1: The Phantom Menace* (1999) introduced the Dolby Digital Surround-EX 6.1 format in which a center rear channel is used (DTS soon followed with their ES version). And Sony Dynamic Digital Sound (SDDS) offers a 7.1 with the

Figure 56
A 5.1 surround system

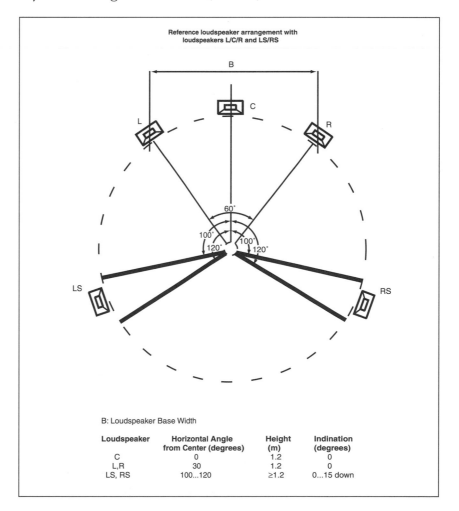

Reference loudspeaker arrangement with
loudspeakers L/C/R and LS/RS

B: Loudspeaker Base Width

Loudspeaker	Horizontal Angle from Center (degrees)	Height (m)	Indination (degrees)
C	0	1.2	0
L,R	30	1.2	0
LS, RS	100...120	≥1.2	0...15 down

addition of two additional screen channels called left center and right center.

And of course, there's always quad from the '70s, the music industry's attempt at multichannel music that killed itself as a result of two noncompatible competing systems (a preview of the Beta vs. VHS war) and a poor psychoacoustic rendering that suffered from an extremely small sweet spot.

TYPES OF SURROUND SOUND

The format known as 5.1 is the mostly widely used surround format today, being used in motion picture, music, and digital television. The format consists of six discrete speaker sources; three across the front (left, center, and right) and two in the rear (left surround, right surround) plus a subwoofer (known as the low frequency effects channel or LFE), which is the .1 of the 5.1 *(see Figure 56)*. This is the same configuration that you hear in most movie theaters, because 5.1 is the speaker specification used not only by THX but in popular motion picture release formats such as Dolby Digital and DTS.

Figure 57
Bass management

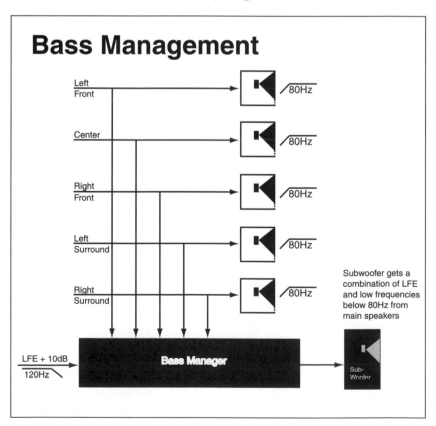

The Mastering Engineer's Handbook

The LFE Channel

LFE stands for low frequency effects and is sometimes referred to in film production circles as the "boom channel" because that's what it's there for: to enhance the low frequencies of a film so you get the extra boom out of an earthquake, plane crash, explosion, or other such dramatic scenes requiring lots of low frequencies.

The LFE, which has a frequency response from about 25Hz to 120Hz (although DTS cuts off the high end of the filter at 80Hz), is unique in that it has an additional 10dB of headroom built into it. This is needed to accommodate the extra power required to reproduce the low-frequency content without distortion.

Bass Management

The Bass Manager (sometimes called bass redirection) is a circuit that takes all the frequencies below 80Hz from the main channels (according to the Dolby spec) and the signal from the LFE channel and mixes them together into the subwoofer *(see Figure 57)*. This is done to make use of the subwoofer for more than the occasional low-frequency effect since it's in the system already. This enables the effective response of the system to be lowered to about 25Hz.

Since the overwhelming majority of consumer home theater systems (especially the average low-end ones) contain a Bass Management circuit, there's a school of thought that says you should use one in the studio so you can hear things the way the people at home hear it. Otherwise, consumers may actually be hearing things (like unwanted rumbles) that you can't hear since the Bass Manager gives a low-frequency extension below that of the vast majority of studio monitors.

Other Types of Surround

There are many other widely used surround formats. Three-channel (stereo front speakers with a mono surround), four-channel (three front speakers with a mono surround) such as Dolby Prologic, five-channel (three front speakers with a stereo surround but no LFE channel), and seven-channel (the Sony SDDS format with five front speakers) surround configurations all abound.

There are other nonstandard formats that use as many as ten channels for height and extra rear and side channels as well. The 6.1 Dolby Digital-EX and DTS-ES formats take film sound to a new level by adding a center rear channel, something that film mixers have been asking for more and more. And many amusement rides such as Universal Studio's *Back to the Future* ride use as many as 14 channels to enhance the surround experience.

THE DIFFERENCES BETWEEN SURROUND AND STEREO

When you listen to surround sound you'll notice quite a few differences (some might say improvements) over stereo:

• The **sonic clarity** is enhanced because the center channel anchors the sound and eliminates any phantom image shifts that you take for granted in stereo.

• **There is no sweet spot per se.** Actually, the whole room becomes a sweet spot in that you can move around freely and never lose the sense of clarity, dimension, and spatial continuity. One listener describes it perfectly as an "audio sculpture" in that, just as when you walk around a piece of artwork and get a different perspective of the art, when you walk around the 5.1 room you get a different perspective of the mix. You might get closer to the guitar player, for instance, if you walk to the left of the room. Walk to the right and you're closer to the piano. Indeed, you don't have to even be in the speaker field to get a sense of the depth of the mix. Even people sitting outside the soundscape often describe an enhanced experience.

• **Speaker placement is very forgiving.** Yes, there are standards for placement, but these tend to be noncritical. The sense of spaciousness remains the same regardless of how haphazardly the speakers are distributed around the room. In fact, stereo is far more critical placement-wise than surround sound.

The Mastering Engineer's Handbook

For the mastering engineer to know what to expect from a surround mix, it's important to discuss the various features, differences and philosophies that the mixing engineer must deal with in creating a surround mix.

Surround Mix Features

Here are several surprising features that a typical surround mix will have as opposed to a stereo mix:

• **Clarity of instruments**. Everything sounds much more distinct as a result of having more places to sit space-wise in the mix. This means that the mixer spends a lot less time EQing trying to get each instrument heard.

• **Added dimension**. Even mono tracks are big and dimensional in surround! No longer is there a need to stereoize a track by adding an effect. Simply spreading a mono source across the speakers with the pan pot makes it sound big.

• **The ambience is different.** When you mix in stereo, you usually must recreate depth by using effects. In surround, the depth is built-in. Because of the naturally increased clarity and dimension, the mixer no longer has to spend as much time trying to artificially add space with reverb, delays, etc. This is not to say that these effects won't be used at all, but the approach is different since surround automatically has a sense of depth that must be created artificially with stereo.

• **Mixes go faster**. It actually takes less time to do a mix because surround sound automatically has a depth of field that you normally have to work hard to create when you're mixing in stereo. Most mixers find they need less EQ and fewer effects because there's more room in the sound-scape to place things.

DIFFERENCES BETWEEN MIXES FOR PICTURES AND MUSIC

In the theater, usually all of the primary sound information comes from the front speakers, and the surround speakers are utilized only for ambience; this is to keep your attention on the screen. The LFE is intended for use with special effects such as explosions and earthquakes and is therefore used infrequently. One of the reasons that the surround speakers don't contain more source information is a phenomena known as the "exit sign effect," which means that your attention is drawn away from the screen to the exit sign when the information from the surrounds is too loud.

But music-only surround sound has no screen to focus on and therefore no exit sign effect to worry about. Take away the screen and it's possible to utilize the surround speakers for more creative purposes.

DIFFERENT PERSPECTIVES: AUDIENCE VS. ONSTAGE

There are two schools of thought about how surround sound for music should be mixed. The "audience" or classical perspective puts the music in the front speakers and the hall ambience in the surrounds, just as if you were sitting in the audience of a club or concert hall. This method may not utilize the LFE channel at all and is meant to reproduce an audience perspective of the musical experience.

In the "onstage" perspective, the band is spread all over the room via the five main speakers. This puts the listeners in the center of the band and envelops them with sound. This method usually results in a much more dramatic

Figure 58
Isolated elements in the
center channel

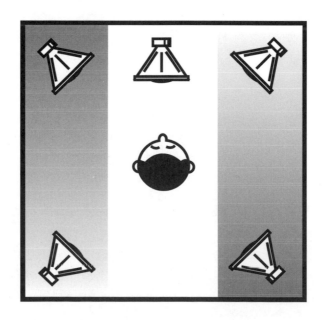

The Mastering Engineer's Handbook

soundstage that is far bigger sounding than the stereo that you're used to. This may not be as authentic a soundscape as some music (any kind of live music where the listeners' perspective is from the audience) might require, however.

THE CENTER CHANNEL

In film mixing, the center channel is used primarily for dialog so the listener doesn't get distracted by sonic movement. In music, however, its use prompts debate among mixers.

No Center Channel

Many veteran engineers who have mixed in stereo all their lives have trouble breaking the stereo paradigm to make use of the center channel. These mixers continue to use a phantom center from the left and right front speakers and prefer to use the center speaker as a height channel or not use it at all.

Isolated Elements in the Center Channel

Many mixers prefer to use the center channel to isolate certain elements such as lead vocals, solos, and bass. While this might work in some cases, many times the isolated elements seem disconnected from the rest of the sound-scape *(see Figure 58)*.

Figure 59
Integrated center channel

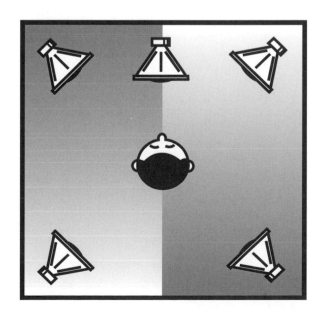

The Center as Part of the Whole

Mixers who use the center channel to its fullest find that it acts to anchor the sound and eliminates any drifting phantom images. In this case, all five speakers have equal importance, with the balance changing the sound elements placed in the soundscape. It's actually easiest to picture this *(see Figure 59)* with the soundscape cut in half from the middle of the center speaker.

THE LFE (SUBWOOFER) CHANNEL

Anything that requires some low-frequency bass extension can be put into the subwoofer via the LFE channel. Many mixers put a little kick and/or bass there if it's used at all. Remember that the frequency response only goes up to 120Hz, so the definition from the instrument actually comes from the main channels.

Surround Master Media Prep

Surround sound brings a new level of complexity to mastering not normally found in stereo. Therefore, it's imperative that as much information about the project is indicated as possible. Many potential problems can be avoided as long as the master is prepped and the steps in this chapter are followed.

These steps apply to the mastering engineer, but even more so to the mixing engineer. Therefore, it's important for the mastering engineer to communicate their importance to the mixer prior to getting a project.

1. SLATE THE MASTER

More than ever before, it's important to not only properly document the master tape or disc, but also to prep the master in order to make sure that there's no questions as to the actual track assignments. Even an engineer who's mixed the tracks sometimes has a hard time determining which is the center channel and which is the left surround, so it's necessary to take any guesswork out of the process.

The best way to avoid confusion is to go back to the admittedly low-tech but foolproof method of using an audio slate on each channel indicating the channel assignment (e.g., Channel One—Left Front, Channel Six—Right Surround).

Master Tape Track Assignments

Sooner or later, the question of channel assignment on the master recorder (be it tape or disc) always arises. What is the correct track assignment? There are several generally accepted channel assignment formats for surround, but the SMPTE/ITU standard channel assignment *(see Figure 60)* is fast becoming the de facto standard.

Figure 60
The SMPTE/ITU
standard channel
assignments

1	2	3	4	5	6
Left Front	Right Front	Center	LFE	Left Surround	Right Surround

A dedicated stereo mix, or Lt/Rt (Left Total/Right Total), or encoded AC3 can be recorded onto Tracks 7 and 8.

This format is the SMPTE and ITU standard, as well as the assignment matrix suggested by Dolby Labs. This method transfers easily to the corresponding four audio tracks (L, R, C, LFE) of the most widely used video formats today, such as DigiBeta or D5. This is also the recommended format by Dolby as it is the common pairing of channels in Dolby Digital encoding (although the AC-3 encoder can actually be configured to any track configuration). The surround products of Panasonic, Mackie, and Martinsound, to name just a few, now support this configuration as well.

The assignment methods shown in Figures 61 and 62 are also used, but this is becoming less common as the SMPTE/ITU standard becomes more widespread.

Figure 61
Preferred film channel
assignments

1	2	3	4	5	6
Left Front	Center	Right Front	Left Surround	Right Surround	LFE

The configuration shown here is what many film studios use and is seen in some music production as well. It seems to make sense in that it's a somewhat visual representation of the way the speakers are laid out, but it falls short when it comes to logical track pairings.

Figure 62
DTS standard channel
assignments

1	2	3	4	5	6
Left Front	Right Front	Left Surround	Right Surround	Center	LFE

The configuration shown here is preferred by DTS. Again, the pairings are logical, but the placement is different from the SMPTE /ITU standard. Tracks 7 and 8 usually contain the stereo version of the mix, if one is needed.

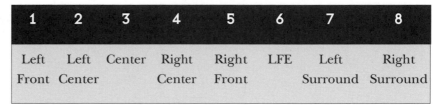

1	2	3	4	5	6	7	8
Left Front	Left Center	Center	Right Center	Right Front	LFE	Left Surround	Right Surround

Figure 63
SDDS channel
assignments

SDDS (Sony Dynamic Digital Sound) is a special case in that it's a 7.1 format. SDDS uses a track assignment that differs from the norm, as shown here, but it makes sense in that it gives you a visual representation of the way that the speakers are laid out.

There are other assignment permutations that are occasionally used, but they seem to be falling by the wayside quickly as the SMPTE/ITU track assignment method takes hold.

2. PRINT A TEST TONE

Print at least 30 seconds of 1kHz tone at −20dBFS, which is the SMPTE standard reference level, across all tracks. A 1kHz tone is a pretty good way to discover if there are any clock discrepancies because the purity of the signal will suffer as a result of clicks and warbles that might not be heard during the actual program material.

Also, keep in mind that any program on tape media should start no earlier than two minutes into the tape, since that's where most errors and dropouts usually occur.

3. PRINT TIME CODE

If the audio program is intended for DVD in any form, time code is necessary to maintain sync when it is authored. Generally speaking, it's safest to use 29.97-Drop Frame SMPTE on an audio-only program since it is the NTSC color television standard. If a music video is later added to the program (which can cause a multitude of additional problems), it's highly likely that the picture will be at that frame rate. *Audio that must be synched to existing picture must use the existing picture time code frame rate, however.*

4. SURROUND TO STEREO COMPATIBILITY

Although it's possible to have the surround mix automatically downmixed to stereo either with SMART Content downmixing inherent in a DVD-Audio disc or by selection of the downmix parameters on the Dolby Digital encoder, the results are often unpredictable and many times unsatisfactory. Since many surround mixes will default to stereo if only two speakers are present (such as when played in the DVD-ROM drive of a computer), it's as important to check the surround to stereo compatibility as it is to check the stereo to mono compatibility.

5. DOCUMENT THE DETAILS

Once again, the following details must be indicated to avoid confusion latter during the authoring process:

Is the LFE channel filtered and at what frequency?

This is important if for no other reason than it's easy to figure out which is the subwoofer channel if the assignment documentation is lost. The LFE should have a low-pass filter that cuts off at 120Hz.

What is the reference level in SPL?

This helps to better approximate what you were hearing if the program should require remastering. Typical reference levels are 85dB SPL (the film reference) or 79dB SPL (the television reference).

What is the sampling rate?

This helps to avoid any clock or sync issues that may arise during authoring. Depending on the ultimate distribution media, the sample rate can be any number of standard rates. For instance:

Legal Sampling Rates	
DTS Music Disc	44.1kHz
DVD-Video	48kHz multichannel, 96kHz stereo
DVD-Audio	44.1, 48, 88.2, 96, 176.4, or 192kHz

What is the bit resolution?

Once again, the type of distribution media will determine the bit resolution.

Legal Bit Resolution	
DTS Music Disc	20-bit
DVD-Video	16-to 24-bit
DVD-Audio	16-to 24-bit

What is the time code format?

As stated before, if the audio program is linked to picture or intended for DVD in any form, time code is necessary to maintain sync. The frame rate chosen must be indicated in order to avoid latter confusion.

Are the surround channels calibrated equal to the front channels or –3dB?

In film-style mixing, the surround channels are calibrated 3dB down from the screen channels. Music style mixing has the surrounds equal in level to the front speakers.

What is the media format and how many pieces are there?

The master elements may be on several pieces of media across several different formats. A warning here about which piece of media contains the audio master can eliminate the confusion of an incomplete authoring job later.

How long is the program?

This information is necessary because it determines whether data compression must be used during authoring and helps with managing the total bit budget for the entire DVD.

Surround Equipment

MONITORING

To a mastering facility, its monitor resolution is its major selling point. It is the gold standard, second only to its engineers, by which its clients perceive the facility. While the monitors used in mastering have long been largely a personal choice (even more so than in recording studios), more variables than ever lie ahead when choosing a surround system for the mastering studio.

But there are several questions to be asked when choosing surround monitors. Should the monitor choice be five identical direct radiators? Should the surrounds be dipoles? Or tripoles? Perhaps all of the above to cover all situations? Should the system be a totally integrated package that includes subwoofer and bass management or should those components be customized to the application? Should a typical consumer home theater system be included for comparison?

Of course, the type of program being mastered will determine the answers to many of these questions. For instance, if the typical program is mostly classical music, then dipole surrounds are required. If the program is pop music, then direct radiators are probably in order. It should be noted however, that the majority of the 30 million surround systems currently in the homes use dipoles, so mastering engineers should probably check their work against that type of system at some point regardless of the type of surround monitor the music was made on.

BASS MANAGEMENT

Bass Management is an area of both great importance and confusion. It's imperative that the mastering engineer not only hear at the highest resolution possible, but also know that what he's hearing will translate correctly to the consumer in the home. Once again, virtually all of the 30 million home surround systems currently employ some sort of Bass Manager. Therefore, Bass Management (sometimes also referred to as Bass Redirection) must be properly implemented in the mastering studio in order for low end compatibility to occur. If Bass Management isn't employed, it's entirely possible that the consumer with a high-quality home theater system will hear things in the subwoofer (because of the low-frequency extension of the system) that the mastering engineer cannot.

TEST EQUIPMENT

With speaker alignment more critical than ever, it is of utmost importance that the mastering facility have the proper test gear available to keep the system properly adjusted. Gone are the days when a Sonopulse or a Radio Shack SPL meter and some wide-band pink noise kept things merely close enough. A multichannel test disc (such as Tomlinson Holman's Test and Measurement Series distributed by Hollywood Edge) or a test tape (such as the TMH Studio Setup and Test Tape), along with a spectrum analyzer, is now a must in order to adjust the level of the subwoofer to the required precision.

THE CONSOLE

While most mastering consoles have always been a somewhat custom item, a surround mastering console requires features that are no trivial matter. Besides the minimum six channels, the major component of the surround console is monitor level control, which must be precisely calibrated to increase or decrease the volume level as needed without disturbing the balance between the main monitors and subwoofer, or front speakers from the surrounds. The ability to switch between several surround systems (A/B switching), listen through a decoder, listen to surround formats other than 5.1, as well as stereo and mono monitoring, is vital to the final product and must be included. Many after-market monitor control products are presently available as well, including the Martinsound Multimax, Baldwin Masterpot, and Otari Picmix.

At what point in the signal path the program treatment such as EQ and compression are added has a major effect on the console. If all treatment is intended to be kept in the digital domain inside the console, the EQ and compression elements of the desk must meet with the approval of the engineer, which is highly unlikely for every situation. Therefore, the means to insert outboard equalizers or compressors into the signal path is critical. Although it's possible that one of the cheaper digital boards like a Yamaha 02R or Ramsa DA-7 can fit the bill in some respects, their lack of sufficient monitoring facilities (not to mention their inability to read 96kHz sample rates) means that some customization (such as the add-on Martinsound MultiMax unit—*see Figure 64*) is still required.

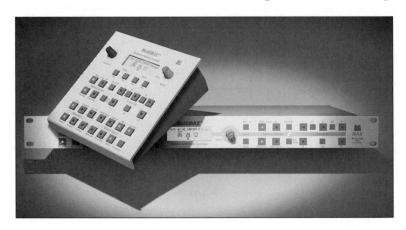

Figure 64
Martinsound Multimax
Surround Controller

CONVERTERS

While it's a given that much of the program material will be delivered in the digital domain, that still doesn't preclude the need for at least six channels (preferably eight) of high-quality A/D and D/A conversion. Many items in the mastering engineer's bag of tricks are still analog, and the ability to jump domains must be readily available. Also, there's already talk by some producers of mixing to one-inch or even two-inch eight-track analog both for the sound and for archival purposes, making these additional converters an immediate necessity.

OUTBOARD GEAR

It's not as simple as just adding extra channels; proper ergonomics must accompany any multichannel outboard unit to make its operation fast and easy for the mastering

The Mastering Engineer's Handbook

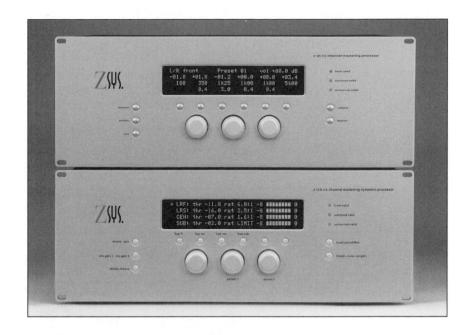

engineer. Compressors and equalizers must have the added capability of not only being ganged for multichannel operation in multiple configurations (two, three, four, five, and six channels), but must also have the ability to have each channel individually tweaked as well *(see Figure 65)*.

Ergonomics of these devices must be extremely user-friendly (a highly overused but all-too-appropriate term) since the mastering engineer by nature does many repeatable operations (such as equalization) very quickly. These operations now increase with addition of at least four channels. With the many new variables now facing engineers, great pains must be taken to avoid multiple pages and deep menus that slow the process down.

SURROUND MASTER RECORDERS

Although any multitrack format can be used as a master recorder, the de facto standard for surround program destined for DVD-Video is the Tascam DA-88 family (DA-98, PCM800, etc.), the members of which are limited by the fact that they record with only 16-bit resolution. Sometimes these machines are enhanced to 20-bit resolution with either Rane or Prism bit-splitters. Tascam has also recently introduced the 24-bit DA-78HR *(see Figure 66a)* and DA-98HR; the latter can also record four channels at a sample rate of 96kHz. Other machines being used include the

Genex GX8000 and 8500 Magneto Optical recorders and Tascam MMR-8 hard disc recorder. Some producers are even mixing to one- or two-inch eight-track analog for both sound and long term archival purposes.

For high-resolution audio program intended for DVD-Audio disc delivery, the Euphonix R-1 *(see Figure 66b)* has recently become the de-facto standard despite its being a 24-track recorder. This is because of its stability at 96Khz, ease of use, and ability to import and export the coming broadcast wave file format standard.

COURTESY EUPHONIX

The Mastering Engineer's Handbook

With DVD-Audio now a reality, the demand for at least some form of 96kHz/24-bit audio is growing rapidly. With the increased sample rate and bit depth come the obvious problems of storage and backup, which although voracious enough in stereo becomes humongous in 96/24.

Consider this: we all know that a 48/16 stereo minute needs approximately 11.5MB of storage (actually, 11.52MB, to be precise). A minute of true 96/24 stereo needs 34.56MB, and a minute of discrete 5.1 surround at 96/24 requires a whopping 104MB! This means that a 60-minute program will need 6.24GB just to get it into the DAW. With the capacity of a basic DVD 5 at 4.32GB, it's now easy to see why some form of data compression is necessary to get it to the public. As for storage, it looks like drive manufacturers will be selling a lot of 25GB (or more) drives to mastering houses!

But 96/24 operation doesn't stop just at storage. All equipment in the digital signal chain, including compressors, equalizers, A/D and D/A converters, sample rate converters, and workstations must now be able to process at least 96/24 as well. And since the DVD-Audio disc can also store a stereo program at 192kHz/24-bit, look for a growing demand for that capability to arise as well.

SURROUND ENCODERS/DECODERS (CODECS)

Now that data compression of the digital audio signal has become a fact of life, the mastering facility may need to have the three most popular data compression encoder/decoders in-house as a check on what that process will do to the final audio product. Although it's not imperative that an encoder be present at mastering, it does help to hear what the codec (the Dolby, DTS, or MLP compressor/decompressor) will do to the final product because codecs can change the sound considerably. There are also quite a few parameters (like downmixing and Late Nite levels) that the producer might like to tweak rather than leave for someone else down the production chain.

Downmixing automatically folds down the 5.1 surround program to the available number of channels. In other words, if only two speakers are available, the surround mix is folded down to stereo. Although this is less desirable than a separate mix, the Dolby Digital encoder gives a number of choices about how this is done.

Late Nite levels are essentially the same as a loudness control for surround sound. When a surround system is calibrated, it's usually done at a fairly moderate level of 85dB SPL. This level is usually way too loud for quiet listening late at night so the system naturally gets turned down, which may destroy the balance between the front and rear speakers and the subwoofer. The Late Nite parameter takes this into account and allows the mixer to somewhat compensate for the balance discrepancies.

Data Compression
Data compression is the process of using psychoacoustic principles to reduce the number of bits required to represent the signal. This is needed with surround sound so more data can be squeezed onto a finite storage space such as a CD or DVD, and also because the bit rate of six channels of 96/24 LPCM is too large to fit through the small data pipe of a DVD.

High or Low Resolution—96/24 vs. 48/20
First, understand that the first number (96) stands for the sample rate in 1000 per-second increments, or a sample rate of 96kHz. The second number (24) stands for the word length of the encoded digital data, or 24 bits.

In order to understand the significance of each parameter and how they affect quality, a brief discussion of sampling rate and word length is in order.

The analog audio waveform is measured in amplitude at discrete points in time; this is called sampling. The more samples of the waveform that are taken, the better representation of the waveform that occurs, with a greater resultant bandwidth for the signal. Audio on a CD has a sampling rate of 44,100 times a second (44.1kHz), which yields a bandwidth of about 22kHz. A sampling rate of 96kHz gives a better digital representation of the waveform and yields a usable audio bandwidth of about 48kHz. Therefore, *the higher the sampling rate, the better the representation of the signal and the greater the bandwidth.*

The more bits a word has, the better the dynamic range. Every bit means about 6dB in dynamic range. Therefore, 16 bits yields a maximum dynamic range (DR) of 96dB, 20 bits yields 120dB DR, and 24 bits (there are no true 24-bit systems yet) yields a theoretical maximum of 144dB DR.

From this you can see that the high-resolution 96/24 format is far closer to sonic realism than the current CD standard of 44.1/16. The higher the sample rate, the greater the bandwidth and, therefore, the better the sound. The longer the word length (the more bits a word has), the greater the dynamic range and, therefore, the better the sound.

What all this means is that there are now more choices regarding audio quality and resolution than ever before. For the highest fidelity, a stereo mix at 192/24 can be chosen, or 96/24 for 5.1 surround. It's also possible to choose any number of other possibilities such as 96/24 for the front channels and 48/16 for the rear or 48/20 for all channels, if that better fits the needs of the program.

Thanks to the new DVD medium, music is no longer tied to the old CD quality standard of 44.1kHz at 16 bits.

Lossy and Lossless Compression

Lossy compression (such as Dolby Digital or DTS) is built around perceptual algorithms that remove signal data that is being masked or covered up by other signal data that is louder. Think of an inner tube filled up with air. When you let the air out of the tube, it takes up less space, but the same amount of rubber remains and can fit into a smaller space. This is the idea behind lossy data compression. Because data is thrown away and never retrieved, it's what's known as "lossy."

Depending upon the source material, lossy compression can either be completely inaudible, or somewhat noticeable. It should be noted that even when it is audible, lossy compression still does a remarkable job of recovering the audio signal and still sounds quite good.

Lossless compression (such as MLP) never discards any data and recovers it completely during decoding and playback.

Dolby Digital (AC-3) or DTS Encoding

Both Dolby Digital® and DTS® (Digital Theater Systems) are lossy data compression schemes. Dolby Digital (also called AC-3, which is actually the file format of the process) takes six channels of 48kHz/24-bit information and compresses it at about an 11:1 ratio to a maximum bit rate of 640kbps, although 384 is the average data rate used.

DTS compresses at about a 3:1 ratio at an average data rate of 1.4Mbps. Because there is less data compression, and therefore less audio data thrown away, many audio professionals prefer the sound of DTS encoded product.

Meridian Lossless Packing

Meridian Lossless Packing is the compression standard used on the audio DVD in order to store six channels of high resolution 96/24 audio. MLP's main feature is that it never discards any signal information during data compression (which is why it's "lossless") and therefore doesn't affect the audio quality. MLP gives a compression ratio of about 1.85:1 (about 45 percent), and its licensing is administrated by Dolby Laboratories.

A NEW WAY OF WORKING

Where today's stereo mastering engineers are now used to dealing with the entire mix in terms of adding equalization or compression, surround mastering engineers will need more time and expertise to work their magic. For instance, when tweaking the low end (at say, 60Hz), the engineer may need only adjust the LFE channel if that's where the instrument (such as a kick drum) containing that info was assigned. However it's just as likely that all five main channels, as well as the LFE, will have to be adjusted because the frequency steering by the Bass

Manager to the subwoofer causes that frequency to appear there from multiple sources. This means that where the engineer had just one set of stereo adjustments, multiple adjustments are now needed to accomplish the same thing for a surround mix.

Mastering engineers also will now be called upon to adjust the final balance of a mix in terms of level shifts between front and rear speakers and center channel levels. Out-of-whack LFE levels due to misaligned subwoofers or monitoring without Bass Management while mixing will require severe adjustment and are bound to give engineers a level of control over the final product unprecedented by today's standards.

Other times, the mastering engineer might be called upon to create a center channel or LFE channel from the existing program. Or the mastering engineer may be supplied stems and be asked to perform a final mix himself. Stems are parts of a final mix delivered as separate elements. For instance, a mix of only the rhythm section by itself, the vocals by themselves (complete with effects), and strings or lead elements by themselves, would make up three stems that would be mixed together to form the entire mix.

Add to this the additional operations of setting downmix parameters, possibly extracting a standard stereo mix from the surround mix, setting encoding parameters such as dialog normalization and dynamic range compression settings for late night listening, and mastering and encoding in multiple release formats, and suddenly the typical five-hour album project time has at least doubled.

WHAT THE HECK IS AUTHORING?

A DVD has a greater possible level of built-in intelligence than a CD. Authoring is the process of taking advantage of this intelligence by programming not only the interactivity into the disc, but additional material such as liner notes, music videos, artist and producer bios, and promo for other product as well. Since most mastering houses are used to doing the final prep of audio material before sending it to the replicator, they assume that they will be required to do the same for DVD as well. However, this is an area fraught with potential pitfalls that must be approached with caution. Authoring for DVD is a very distant cousin to CD prep and is not a trivial matter.

Using the Internet as an analogy, an audio CD is very much like text that you want to send via e-mail. You learn the e-mail program in no time and soon you're sending mail (burning CDs) worldwide. DVD is more like designing a Web site. In order to even put up the most rudimentary site using only text, you've got to program it using HTML. If you add pictures, you've got to learn something about graphics or hire a graphic designer to produce something spiffy. If you want to add movies, you've got to learn about shooting video and video editing and compression or use an expert.

Nowadays, you can buy an inexpensive application that programs HTML for you, but what you get is a very basic site that doesn't compete too well with the big sites that use great graphic designers who have an intimate knowledge of HTML and can make those advanced Web design programs really sing.

As with most professional gear, just buying the authoring workstation does not immediately put you in the authoring game. There is a very a high cost of entry (about $150K for a workstation with all the necessary peripherals) and a steep learning curve (about six months) before you can get anything out the door in a timely fashion. This is one case where it really is rocket science at the moment, since all of the authoring tools out there have either undocumented or hidden traits that you simply can't get from a tutorial.

The bottom line is that mastering is *not* authoring, and vice-versa. Authoring is computer programming that uses the visual, not aural sense. Unless you have access to design expertise for the graphics, video expertise for video shooting and editing, and programming expertise for the authoring, you're better off leaving the authoring to a facility that specializes in it. Besides, they still need your expertise to supply the best audio possible.

ENTER DLT

The current standard media used as a DVD production master for delivery to the pressing plant is DLT (Digital Linear Tape), a tape format similar to Exabyte but with a much faster transfer rate and a greater storage capacity. Since DLT's original use was as a backup medium (with storage of up to 70GB on a tape), mastering facilities actually get a break because the same DLT unit can pull double duty as production master and backup.

But the mastering facility doesn't get off that easily. A DVD-R is also required in order to give the client a check disc. Relatively expensive at about $7,000, the unit is currently only capable of a reliable capacity of about 3.9G. Although this should be sufficient for a great number of projects, especially if they're data compressed with AC-3 or MLP, it isn't if you require the entire 4.7G capacity of a DVD-5 or larger disc.

As we move into this brave new surround mastering universe, it's become pretty obvious that there are many questions still to be answered.

Multichannel Audio Delivery Formats

Now that DVD is becoming commonplace on the shelves of the local electronics superstore, several new formats also are about to enter the lexicon of the consumer and this time they're audio specialty items. The DVD-Audio disc and Super Audio CD (SACD) are getting more and more press these days, but both the DTS music disc and the DVD-Video disc have been delivery vehicles for surround music to the consumer for some time. Here's a quick but thorough overview as to what to expect from, and how to prepare for, each format.

DVD BASICS

All but one of the formats that we'll be discussing are in some way based upon the Digital Versatile Disc (and soon the odd one may change to it as well), so some DVD basics are in order. The DVD distinguishes itself from a CD in two ways: storage capacity and file system.

Storage Capacity

While the storage capacity of a current CD is 650MB, the capacity of a DVD can actually be one of four levels, all far exceeding the CD. This is accomplished by having more and smaller pits on the substrate than that of a CD. Add to this the fact that DVD can have two layers and be double-sided, and the power of DVD becomes readily apparent *(see Figure 67)*. Because a laser with a smaller wavelength is required, a CD player cannot read a DVD. A DVD player can read a CD, however.

Figure 67
DVD types and capacities

DVD Name	Number of Sides	Number of Layers	Capacity*
DVD-5	1	1	4.7 G bytes
DVD-9	1	2	8.5 G bytes
DVD-10	2	1	9.4 G bytes
DVD-18	2	2	17 G bytes

There's some unfortunate confusion as to the actual capacity of a DVD because it's measured differently than the computer norm. For example, a DVD-5 has 4.7 billion bytes (G bytes) not 4.7 gigabytes (GB). The problem is that DVD is based on multiples of 1000 while the computer world measures bytes in multiples of 1024. Therefore, a DVD-5 actually has a capacity of 4.38 gigabytes.

File Format

Today's CD can be thought of as essentially a "bit bucket" in that there is no intelligence built into the different file formats required for audio CD, CD-ROM, CD-R, etc. DVD differs from this in that the various types use basically the same DVD-ROM–like format with a bit of intelligence built into the specification.

DVD uses a file format known as Universal Disc Format (UDF), which was designed specifically for use with optical media and avoids the problems and confusion that CD-ROMs have because of the many different file formats used. In fact, UDF permits the use of a DVD by DOS, OS/2, Macintosh, Windows, and UNIX operating systems as well as dedicated players. What's interesting is that a dedicated DVD player will access only the information that it requires; all other files will remain invisible. It also means that the file system for use with computers is already built into the format, which widens the potential market without it having to jump through programming hoops.

THE DVD-VIDEO DISC

DVD-Video (DVD-V) burst on the scene in 1998 primarily as a high quality movie delivery system, but the audio portion of the format is still quite an improvement over the Red Book CD standard. And because there's automatic provisions for multichannel audio and a built-in (but limited) 96/24 option, DVD-V may yet become a major delivery format for audio before all is said and done.

Sonics

The audio portion of a DVD-V can have up to eight bit streams (audio tracks). These can be one to eight channels of common linear PCM (LPCM), one to six channels (5.1) of Dolby Digital, or one to eight channels (5.1 or 7.1) of MPEG-2 audio *(see Figure 68)*. There are also provisions for optional DTS or SDDS encoding.

Figure 68
Audio Portion of
a DVD-Video

Audio Coding	Sample Rate (kHz)	Word Length	Number of Channels	Max Bit Rate
LPCM	48	16	8	6.144 Mbps
	48	20	6	
	48	24	4	
	96	16	4	
	96	20	3	
	96	24	6	
Dolby Digital	48	24	6	640 kbps
MPEG-2	48	16	8	912 kbps
DTS (Optional)	48	20	6	1.4 Mbps

The LPCM bit stream, which is the same uncompressed format as today's Red Book CD (which is standardized at 44.1kHz and 16-bit), can use either a 48 or 96kHz sample rate with a bit depth of 16, 20, or 24 bits. Now, on the surface this seems great and makes you wonder why another format for multichannel audio is even considered, but then you realize that the bit rate for the audio data is capped at 6.144 megabits per second (Mbps).

The bit rate (the sample rate times the number of bits times the number of channels) is equivalent to the size of the pipe that the audio data has to flow through and, in this case, the pipe isn't big enough to fit six channels of 96/24 audio. In fact, all you can squeeze through is two channels of 96/24. If you want multichannel, you're back at 48k, but at least the bit depth is raised to 20 bits for six channels *(see Figure 68)*. So now we have to use some sort of data compression scheme to fit all of the channels down the pipe at a higher audio quality.

The standard compression scheme for DVD-V is Dolby Digital (sometimes called AC-3, which is actually the name of the file format after it has been compressed), which compresses six channels (5.1) of up to 24-bit audio to fit through the DVD-V audio pipe but is limited to only a 48kHz sampling rate. In addition to this, it is a lossy compression algorithm with a maximum bit rate of 640kbps (although 384 is mostly used), which means that some data is thrown away in the encoding process (although the goal is to only throw away the data that you won't miss). MPEG-2 Audio, which can be configured as either six-channel (5.1) or eight-channel (7.1) at 48/16, is also an optional compression scheme but is hardly used (especially in the U.S.) due to the lack of decoders in the marketplace. Even though MPEG-2 does have a higher bit rate at 912kbps, the algorithm has its share of inherent coding problems, which effectively negates its lower data compression ratio.

Although an optional coding process, DTS encoding could prove to be an interesting choice since it can potentially encode up to eight channels of 96/24 with less data compression than either Dolby Digital or MPEG; however, this is according to the DTS white papers and is not yet actually implemented (see the section on the DTS music disc for more details).

DVD Video Advantages

Installed Base of Players
DVD-V audio can currently play on all DVD players in the marketplace and, with a small bit of additional authoring, all computer DVD-ROM drives as well (providing the PC has the appropriate decoding hardware/software).

Compatibility with the Greatest Number of Players
Unlike DVD-A, which requires a new generation of player, DVD-V audio is universally compatible with existing and future DVD players.

DVD Video Disadvantages

Not as Flexible as DVD-A
While there are choices for the audio in DVD-V, the format lacks the scalability and super-high quality options of DVD-A.

96/24 LPCM Available on Only Two Channels
The highest quality multichannel LPCM audio available is 48kHz at 20 bits for six channels. Using a data compression scheme such as Dolby Digital gives you six channels of 48/24.

Some Players Can't Handle 96/24 LPCM
Even if 96/24 LPCM is used, some players automatically decimate to 48kHz and truncate to 16 bits, thereby negating some of the benefits of the enhancement.

THE DTS MUSIC DISC

There's some confusion in the marketplace as to exactly what DTS (Digital Theater Systems) is. Is it a company? Is it a technology? Is it for movies? Is it for music? The answer is really "yes," to all of the above.

DTS, the company, was started in 1994 primarily with the intention to bring higher quality audio in surround sound to motion pictures than what was available at the time. This was done by way of the DTS data compression process, which is a lossy data compression that reduces the data less and with a different method than its competitor Dolby Digital. DTS claims their compression scheme sounds better as a result.

This data-compressed film audio was then burned to a CD, synced to the film, and translated back into analog 5.1 sound in the theater via a decoder. Since putting audio on a disc was already being done by DTS for film sound, the next logical step was to make a CD strictly for commercial distribution of surround sound music. Hence, the DTS music disc was born.

The DTS music disc is actually the only multichannel delivery system of the four discussed that isn't based in some way on the DVD spec. In fact, the DTS compressed bit stream is encoded onto what amounts to a CD-ROM. This can then be played back on any CD player, laser disc player, or DVD player that has a digital output and passes the digital bit stream to a DTS decoder that separates the channels back out to 5.1.

In order to promote their technology, DTS has started its own record company, DTS Entertainment, which licenses previously released and new recordings and remixes them in surround sound.

Sonics

The DTS music disc provides up to 74 minutes of 5.1 audio at a sample rate of 44.1kHz at 20 bits, at the relatively high bit rate of 1.4Mbps. As stated before, the big attraction to DTS is that the compression algorithm used is a gentle 3:1 ratio, which many claim makes it sounds better as a result.

The DTS coding technology is potentially much more flexible than what is currently being used on either the music disc or in film sound however. According to a paper given at the 100th AES convention, DTS encoding is capable of one- to eight-channel multiplexing, sample rates of 8 to 192kHz, 16- to 24-bit word lengths, a variable bit rate lossless coding mode, various downmix algorithms, and a host of other features not implemented on the current DTS music disc. If these features were ever to be used on a larger and more flexible platform such as DVD, the combination could well prove to be formidable indeed.

DTS Music Disc Advantages

Sonic Superiority
Thanks to its low compression ratio and high bit rate, many audio professionals (though not all) feel that the DTS encoding system is the best sounding of the current lossy compression systems.

A Large Catalog
A wide library (150 discs in all musical genres already released) of DTS music discs can be found just about anywhere that DTS equipped receivers or decoders are sold.

DTS Music Disc Disadvantages

Requires a Decoder to Operate
Without a DTS decoder, the only output you get from your player or receiver is white noise. However, many receivers, even the most inexpensive, now come with a DTS decoder built in.

Distribution Limited Due to Noncompatible Discs
Because of possible consumer confusion with Red Book CDs (the customer puts it in his CD player only to get a white noise output), many of the biggest music retailers have refused to carry the DTS music disc at this point.

No Value-Added Information
Because the DTS music disc uses the limited storage capacity of a CD, there's no room (or provision) for additional text, graphic, or video material.

THE DVD-AUDIO DISC

Introduced in late 2000 after several years of preparation, the DVD-Audio disc provides significantly higher audio quality than its video cousin. Just having the ability to do so doesn't necessarily mean that the highest fidelity audio will automatically happen though, because for better or worse, the final decision as to the sonic quality is largely in the hands of the content producer.

Sonics

DVD-A differs from the audio portion of DVD-V in that the data pipe is a much larger 9.6Mbps compared to DVD-V's 6.144Mbps. Even with the wider audio pipe, six channels of 96/24 LPCM audio still exceeds the allotted bandwidth (multiply 96k by 24 bits times 6 channels to get the resultant 13.824Mbps bandwidth). Therefore, there has to be some type of data compression to not only fit the required amount of data through the pipe, but increase the playing time as well.

For this requirement, Meridian Lossless Packing (MLP) was selected as the standard data compression for DVD-A. MLP, which provides about a 1.85:1 compression ratio, is seemingly lossless, meaning that no data is thrown away during the compression process. Dolby Digital is listed as a lossy compression option. Also possible is the use of other coding technologies such as DSD and DTS.

Of special note is the fact that DVD-A is what is known as extensible. This means that it's relatively open-ended and can utilize any new audio coding technology that becomes popular in the future.

Scalability

One of the more interesting but possibly confusing traits about DVD-A is what's known as scalability, which simply means "lots of options." Audiowise, those options are truly extensive. The program producer is able to choose the number of channels (one to six), the bit depth (16, 20, 24), and the sample rate (44.1, 48, 88.2, 96, 176.4, or 192kHz) *(see Figure 69)*.

What's more, the producer can also mix and match different sample rates with different bit depths on different channel families. For example, the front three channels (family 1) can be set to 96/24 while the rear (family 2) and subchannels are set to 48/16. This is important for more efficient bit budgeting if additional space for videos or stereo mixes is required.

Figure 69
DVD-A audio scalability

Audio Coding	Sample Rate (kHz)	Word Length	Number of Channels
LPCM	192	16, 20, 24	2
	176.4	16, 20, 24	2
	96	16, 20, 24	1 to 6
	88.2	16, 20, 24	1 to 6
	48	16, 20, 24	1 to 6
	44.1	16, 20, 24	1 to 6
MLP	96	16, 20, 24	1 to 6
Dolby Digital	48	16, 20, 24	1 to 6
DTS	48/96	16, 20, 24	1 to 6

Playback Time

Even with DVD-A's increased storage capacity, there's still not enough room to contain 74 minutes of discrete multi-channel linear PCM (LPCM) program at the high sample rates and bit depths, so the option exists to compress the audio data several ways.

As stated before, for the high sample rates and bit depths (88.2, 96, 176.4, or 192kHz/24-bit) Meridian Lossless Packing, or MLP, is provided. This method is attractive in that it almost doubles the playing time with supposedly no loss in data or audio quality *(see Figure 70)*. For the lower sample rates and bit depth (48k/24-bit), Dolby Digital (AC-3) is also provided as an option.

SMART Content

One of the more interesting aspects of DVD-A is a new feature known as SMART (System Managed Audio Resource Technique) content. SMART content is an auto downmix provision that lets a consumer with only a stereo system have the multichannel mix automatically down-mixed to that format. In other words, the six-channel 5.1 mix automatically becomes a stereo mix if there are only two channels in the playback system. While it might seem like a scary thing to have that great multichannel mix auto-matically fold down to stereo, SMART content actually gives the producer a choice in how this downmix will take place by allowing the producer to select one of 16

Figure 70
Approximate playtime
for a DVD-5

Audio Coding	Sample Rate (kHz)	Word Length	Number of Channels	Approx. Play Time
LPCM	192	24	2	65 min.
	192	20	2	78
	96	24	2	129
	96	20	6	52
	48	24	6	86
	44.1	16	2	422
MLP	192	24	2	117
	192	20	2	141
	96	24	6	78
	96	20	6	94
	48	24	6	157
	44.1	16	2	767
Dolby Digital	48	24	6	1550
DTS	48	24	6	425

downmix coefficients that get stored along with the audio data. SMART content also potentially eliminates the need to include a separate stereo mix on the disc, thereby freeing up space for either higher quality audio or additional data information.

Copy Protection and Watermarking

Of primary concern to all the committees and groups working on DVD-A was the inclusion of strong antipiracy measures and copyright identification. In fact, the encryption and watermarking issues have actually taken longer than any other technical aspect to resolve and held up the release of the format.

A point of concern regarding the inclusion of watermarking (which identifies the manufacturer, artist, and copyright holder by embedding a digital code in the noise floor) has been about the possible degradation of the audio quality as a result. After extensive listening tests among many of the "golden ears" of the industry, the chosen watermarking scheme is now said to be virtually undetectable even under microscopic studio conditions and may not prove to be a deterrent to audio quality in any way. However, its implementation and application has yet to be determined as of the writing of this book.

Watermarking should prove to be a boon to content owners in general since it will work on any digital transmission, including Web downloads. This should result in a lot less pirating and a lot more royalties. One thing is for sure: most record companies feel that watermarking is the key to their future survival in this increasingly digital world.

Value-Added Content

One of the attractive features of DVD-A is the ability to add additional content such as liner notes, music videos, and even Web URLs that enable the consumer to access related material on the Internet when played from a computer's DVD-ROM drive. Consumers have always complained about the lack of information found on CDs, but if you mix DVD-A's Internet abilities with additional artist commentary, discographies promoting back catalog titles, bios, links to Web sites (and therefore after-market sales), and even a place to finally put those videos that MTV never played, the value-added material brings the format to life.

Each track (song) has the ability to display up to 20 still images that can run like a slide show in an automatic or manual mode. This can either be a great way to display artist or song information, or a lame attempt to add some info that no one wants to see, depending on how it's implemented. Videos can also be added in the video portion of DVD-A (there is always a video zone), provided there's sufficient room.

DVD-Audio Disc Advantages

Extensibility
Open technology has provisions for new innovations beyond LPCM in the future.

Scalability
The program producer chooses the number of channels, bit depth, sample rate, and encoding method.

DVD-Audio Disc Advantages (cont.)

Value-Added Material
Liner notes, album cover artwork, music videos, artist commentary, and Internet links can all be included.

Copy Protection
Strong encryption methods makes DVD-A harder to pirate than any previous digital medium. Watermarking provides easy copyright identification.

DVD-Audio Disc Disadvantages

Will the Consumer Accept Another Format?
Will 96/24 make enough of a difference to the average consumer to purchase yet another piece of entertainment hardware?

Lack of Moving Pictures During Songs
Many in the production community believe this to be a liability, even though up to 20 still pictures per song may be used. However, material such as liner notes, artist-producer bios, and even engineer bios and commentary actually make this a nice adjunct. After all, one of the main complaints about CDs was the lack of information relative to what was previously found on LPs.

Some DVD-A Discs Won't Play in Some Current DVD Players
Since DVD-A was specified well after DVD-V hit the marketplace, DVD-A discs will not play on the first generation of players already in the marketplace. This can be gotten around by authoring the video zone of the disc with identical, albeit lower quality (48/24 Dolby Digital–encoded) material, but it's up to the content owner to provide this added authoring. Also, universal or "combi" players will play all DVD formats (as well as SACD) when released.

Thanks to the promise of improved sonic performance as well as backward and forward compatibility, the Super Audio CD (SACD) is certainly an intriguing prospect in the multichannel delivery wars. With the massive corporate muscles of Sony and Phillips behind this format, SACD is quite a formidable challenger in the multichannel sweepstakes. SACD's vision has changed somewhat from what was first announced, as the product that was initially released was scaled back in terms of features.

In theory, the SACD can be a dual-layer disc (basically, a DVD-9) with one layer dedicated to normal Red Book CD–type audio and the second to a high density layer for a six-channel surround mix, a two-channel stereo mix, and potentially extra data such as text and graphics. What makes this interesting to the record companies is the ability to be both backward and forward compatible, meaning that consumers can play an SACD on their current CD player *and* play a current CD on a SACD player. Because of the requirements for new watermarking circuitry, SACD discs are not playable in existing DVD-ROM drives, however.

Sonics

SACD touts an improvement in sonic quality due to a new twist in a current recording process known as Direct Stream Digital (DSD). DSD uses essentially the same delta sigma oversampling method used in most modern high-quality analog-to-digital conversion systems where a single bit measures whether a waveform is rising or falling rather than measuring an analog waveform at discrete points in time. In current systems, this one bit is then decimated into LPCM, causing a varying amount (depending upon the system) of unwanted audio side effects (such as quantization error and ringing from the necessary brick wall filter). DSD simplifies the recording chain by recording the one bit directly, thereby reducing the unwanted side effects.

Indeed on paper, SACD with DSD looks impressive. A sampling rate of 2.8224MHz (which is 64 times 44.1k, in case you're wondering) yields a frequency response from DC to 100kHz with a dynamic range of 120dB. Most of the quantization error is moved out of the audio bandwidth, and the brick wall filter, which haunts current LPCM systems, is removed. To enable a full 74 minutes of multichannel 100/24 recording, Phillips has also developed a lossless coding method called Direct Stream Transfer that gives a 50 percent data reduction. Yet some critics speculate that DSD is a closed system with little room for improvement in that both the frequency response and dynamic range cannot be improved much beyond the current spec. Others note the fact that no data interfaces, DSP chips, and little supporting software exist, while their LPCM counterparts abound.

Other Data

As in DVD-A, text and graphics but no video can accompany the audio data. This will take the form of today's Blue Book Enhanced CD, which doesn't look to be quite as elegant an implementation as the UDF file format utilized by DVD. This area of SACD doesn't seem to have been given much thought since the disc is intended for the audiophile market, but it is likely that new features and execution will be implemented as the format matures.

Super Audio CD Advantages

Sonic Performance
Wide bandwidth goes from DC to 100kHz with a 120dB dynamic range, and there are no adverse filter artifacts, thanks to elimination of the brick wall filter. There have been widespread positive reviews regarding audio quality.

Plays on Current CD Players
With both backward and forward compatibility, consumers won't feel forced to buy expensive new hardware or give up their current libraries.

Super Audio CD Disadvantages

Yet Another Format

As with DVD-A, will the average consumer be willing to buy another piece of expensive hardware? Will consumers be confused with yet another format choice?

Is The Sonic Performance Really Better?

While DSD seems every bit the equal to the current state of LPCM, advances in converter technology could eventually move LPCM beyond the seemingly closed format of SACD.

For more information on Surround Sound production, delivery methods, and calibration, visit the Surround Sound FAQ at **www.surroundassociates.com/ssfaq.html**.

PART THREE: THE INTERVIEWS

Chapter 13:   The Interviews

The Interviews

ABOUT THE INTERVIEWS

The interview portion of this book is the part I most enjoyed writing. It's a wonderful thing to finally meet (at least, over the phone) the people that I've been listening to for many years. Not only were the contributors very willing to share their working methods and techniques (something that mastering engineers as a whole are not known to do), but they were very gracious in taking time from their busy schedules to do so. For this I am very grateful and extend to them my heartfelt appreciation.

Since this book is about mastering as an entire profession, I've included a cross-section of the industry. Not only are the legends and greats represented, but also some engineers that deal in specialty areas of mastering (the near greats?). Regardless of their perceived industry stature, they all toil in the everyday trenches of mastering, and much can be learned from their perspective. The interviews are presented in alphabetical order.

Greg Calbi started his career as a mastering engineer at the Record Plant New York in 1973 before moving over to Sterling Sound in 1976. After a brief stint at Masterdisk from 1994 to 1998, Greg returned to Sterling as an owner, where he remains today. Greg's credits are numerous, ranging from Bob Dylan, John Lennon, U2, David Bowie, Paul Simon, Paul McCartney, Blues Traveler, and Sarah McLachlan, among many others.

Do you have a philosophy on mastering?

GC: I do. It really depends on the relationship with the person who brings me the tape. My philosophy in general is to try to figure out how to improve what the person brings me and then try to figure out what his intent was. In other words, I don't just plug in my own idea without first really communicating with the client. It's a little tricky. It really is different for every project. You really have to get a good communication flow going, which sometimes is actually one of the most difficult parts of the jobs.

One time somebody said something to me that I thought was the best compliment that I ever got in mastering. He said, "The reason I like your work is because it sounds like what I did, only better." And that's kind of what I've always tried to do. I try not to change the mix, I just try to enhance it. I just go with the spirit of what was given to me, unless I really feel that it's totally missing the mark. And occasionally it does, because we're now in an era where you have a lot of people in the beginning of the learning curve because of the availability of the technology. People are getting into recording who have the resources because the cost of entry has gone down, but actually the qualifications for doing it has kind of diminished. The bar got lowered a little bit.

In terms of mixing?

GC: In terms of being a recording engineer. I hate to sound like I'm criticizing the guys that have been getting into it because I would do the same thing if I was young and musical. I'd buy the stuff and try to record at home and do a lot of what they try to do. But the fact is that they really haven't had the experience, so you get to the mastering stage now with a much greater need to augment what you've got rather than the way it used to be back in the days when studios had staff engineers with an internship program. There was just a higher level of expertise that it took to get to the level where you could make a major record. You don't necessarily have that now, so we need to try to help them where we can.

Is there a difference between mastering from coast to coast or city to city?

GC: There's really more of a difference from person to person. I've listened many years to all the different sounds that different guys have, and they really all do something different and I respect every one of them for it. I could be blown away by something that any of ten guys do, it's so recognizable.

We recently hosted a great symposium that NARAS ran for their members. They had about 90 people come up, and the four of us, George Marino, Tom Coyne, Ted Jensen, and I, had the same mix to work on. We had ten people in the room at a time and we had a make-believe producer who was asking producer-type questions so people could see how a session went. We all EQed the same song and, after it was over, we all went out to the main room and listened to it with everybody there. All four sounded like four different mixes, and they all had their own thing about it. None of them sounded bad, but it was amazing how different they all were.

You really don't know what your own sound is. Maybe other people know and can identify with your sound more than you can and every once in a while someone comes in because they heard something on a record that you mastered and knows exactly what you tried to do with it. Even if it's only one person that picked up on it, it's just a great feeling.

Can you hear the final product in your head as you're running something down?

GC: Yeah, I can hear where I want it to go. I use kind of an A/B method most of the time so I'm always referring to other mixes on the album. What I try to do is get a listen to everything on the album before I start to work on it.

That's something which I've started doing over the last two or three years and now I almost do it religiously. I really want to know what the producer and the engineer are capable of doing at their best before I start to force it in a direction.

In other words, if the first song on the A side is like a nightmare, all of a sudden you're plugging things in and trying things and going back and forth and you're just going crazy. You get into a certain negative mindset at that point where you think that this whole album is going to be tough. Then all of a sudden about an hour or two later you find that all the stuff after that is starting to sound really good and you realize that you might not have done your best work because you were forcing a mix into an area. Whereas if I go to the stuff that I really like hearing in the beginning, it gives me more of a realistic expectation of what I'm going to be able to get from this stuff later on. It's just a good way to give your ears something to compare to.

I even used to do it back before we had digital, where I'd cut a little piece onto the acetate behind me and go back and forth to listen. Every once in a while there would be a real eye opener because it's a combination of ear fatigue and the way the mixes work where you think something is really working, but then all of a sudden your ears pick right up and you realize that you really didn't take it far enough. Or it could be the other way around, where you get a little ear fatigue and you start overhyping some things and then you listen to what you know is good from earlier in the day and all of a sudden that thing sounds nice and smooth and the thing you're working on is starting to sound a little brittle. I use that method a lot to try to keep my ears fresh and keep my aural memory locked in. It really helps me make the records cohesive from song to song, too.

Do you listen to the whole record before you start?
GC: I'll listen to snatches of everything. I'll listen to maybe a minute or two of a few songs. You know the question I always ask? I'll say, "What's your favorite mix on the album?

What's the one that everybody seems to really like?" because that'll give me an indication of what their expectation is. If they point me to something that I think is horrible and they think is great, then I know I have a combination of engineering and psychology because I need to bring them to where I know it might have to be. The funny thing is that as the years have gone on, they will throw it into my hands almost totally and I have to drag them back into it. I find I work better when the client gets involved because when they take some responsibility for the project in the room, they'll also take that same responsibility when they're listening out of the room. A lot of mastering guys kick the people out and are really secretive about what they're doing, but I'm completely the opposite. The black magic thing is really totally overrated. It's kind of a fallback for a certain amount of not taking responsibility.

What do you think makes the difference between a really great mastering engineer and someone who's just competent?

GC: Just a great musical set of ears. That's so important. I mean, there are some guys who just have a tremendous talent for creating something that's musically and aurally satisfying. But then the communication skill is another thing that makes somebody great, as well as a real good understanding of how to push the equipment and a willingness to try different things. It's kind of a combination of creativity and tenaciousness.

I think you have to really have a lot of pride in what you do. The aspect of pride is very, very important. There's no way that you can do this without being personally attached to the work. I always try to figure out whether this is an art or not. It's not really an art per se, but it has shared elements of what an artist does. You take possession of the thing.

How do you feel about the "level wars"?

GC: It's gotten so insane. I'm a huge music fan and I listen to CDs constantly at home. I have to say that the CDs that always please me the most sonically are not the real hot ones when I bring them in here and look at them on the meters. I tell people, "If you want yours to be hot, I know how to do it, and I'll make it as hot as we can possibly make it and still be musical. But I just want to tell you that you may find that it's not as pleasing to you if you get it too hot."

The genre that I'm dealing with a lot though is not necessarily the genre where people really want to crank. I did something this week for Jay Beckenstein from Spyro Gyra. He's been around for 20 some-odd years, although I've never worked for him before so I wanted to blow him away. I really wanted him to put this thing on and go, "Oh man, this guy's great." So I laid it on there pretty hot for him and he calls me back and says, "I just want to tell you that this doesn't have to be the hottest record ever made. With this kind of music, it's really not that important." And I just thought "Thank God. This guy is not in that mode."

What do you think is the hardest thing for you to do?
GC: Hard rock and metal have always been the hardest thing for me to make sound good because the density of the music requires a lot of aggressiveness. But what happens is, if the aggressiveness goes just that one step too far, it diminishes the music. You reach a point where all of a sudden it starts to reverse itself, where big becomes small and exciting becomes overbearing and it works against the rhythms of the music. So you have to push it to the point, but if it's just one step past the point, it loses impact. It's a very weird phenomenon.

I've heard other people say exactly the same thing.
GC: You go right off a cliff. There was one record that I did last year with a band called Reveille, which is a bunch of 16- and 17-year olds. It was really good and I did everything I could to make it as loud as I could. What happened was this thing was put on a compilation with like maybe 13 or 14 other metal things and man, the other ones were so much louder. Some of them were terrible, but some of them were fantastic. It's the continuous puzzle of this trade, especially with that heavy kind of music.

I do a bunch of stuff that is more jazz and world music with kind of acoustic rhythm that's so powerful when it's nice and smooth because it's not so dependent on the level. But the metal and the hard rock is very, very dependent on it. If you catch it right, you've really created something really great.

How do you go about getting your level?
GC: I wouldn't mind talking about it to a certain extent, but I'm still working on that all the time. What I do in general is try to use three or four different devices to a point where each one is just a little past the point of overload. I overdrive two, sometimes three and even four pieces of gear, one of them being an A/D converter and the other ones being digital level controls. I find that if I spread the load out amongst a couple of different units and add them together, then I'm able to get it as loud as I can. I don't like to put soft limit or finalizing on things. What I find is there's a point where you're trading in rhythmic clarity and subtlety for loudness. I don't want to do that, although there are some types of music which do really lend themselves to it, particularly if a lot of the rhythm instruments have been sampled already and the overtones have already been knocked off it. Again, it's pretty much content-based.

But I'll go back to what I said before where a lot of times, the things that seem the most powerful and the most pleasing in the home listening situation aren't necessarily the loudest ones. The loudest ones seem to be the ones that are the most blurry sounding. Anybody who's working on trying to max their levels out has to see what happens to the strong dynamic elements when they start to get squashed.

I had a TC 5000 for awhile. I used to use it as a multiband compressor, and I tried all kinds of different ways of getting that thing to max levels out. But if you take your original source tape and just forget about overloads and do an A/B at some peak level, I guarantee that you'll find that you've lost a whole bunch of depth, and that's a depth which people cannot recreate in their listening situation.

What's your signal chain like?
GC: On the analog side, what I try to do is combine light and dark, solid-state and tube. So I have a bunch of tube

equipment. I have the EAR compressors and the EAR EQs—the MEQ and the regular one, like the old Pultec. And I have an Avalon compressor and Avalon equalizer, which is a little bit more specific. Then I have something that we all have here at Sterling, which is a sum and difference box that was designed by Chris Muth that enables you to EQ and compress the center channel differently than the side channels. It's the most fantastic box; it almost eliminates the need for vocal up mixes because you can just EQ the center. You can also take sibilance away from the center without affecting the brightness of the guitars on the side, so you can really get pretty creative. I also have a Manley tube limiter compressor, one of those Vari-Mu's and one of Doug Sax's level amplifiers, which I'll use sometimes in-between my console.

Occasionally if something sounds really good I'll just bypass my console and patch it directly into my A/D converter and use the analog machine as a level control. A lot of times with the DATs I'll go into a Doug Sax line amp that I have to make them a little more analog if I don't need to be EQed a lot.

I have an ATR analog deck with tube electronics and one with solid-state electronics. I also have a Studer 820. Most of the time at the beginning of an analog session, I'll play it off each of those three machines and see which one sounds the best. I usually work with two different A/D converters. I have a dB Technologies converter, and I have one that the guys at JVC were fooling around with for a while, which is excellent. I try to have two different converters at all times, one that maybe has a deeper bottom and better imaging and another one that's maybe a little more exciting in the midrange.

That's what I have on the analog side. The EAR compressors I also use as a level control. If you call me in a month from now, I'll probably have all different stuff. I don't buy a lot of gear, but I'm constantly changing what I'm doing and the order in which the gear gets plugged in all the time. We use the Z-Sys for digital EQ. I have a Weiss compressor for digital compression, and Z-Sys has been

GREG CALBI

fooling around with a compressor, which I also have.

I haven't had too much luck with digital compressors. With this Weiss thing I'm always trying to come up with something that works for everything, and every time I think I have a good preset and then try it on something else, it doesn't seem to work. I had that TC 5000 for a while and we had a Finalizer in here, which I'm actually supposed to start fooling around with more. I have probably the same stuff that a lot of the guys have. I think the sum and difference box gives us a little bit of a more chance at being a more creative.

As far as the person who might be trying to learn how to do his own mastering, or understand mastering in general, the main thing is that all you need is one experience of hearing somebody else master something. Your one experience at having it sound so incredibly different makes you then realize just how intricate mastering can be and just how much you could add or subtract from a final mix.

I would also say to anybody who is trying to learn about mastering, realize that there's a hidden element that the more flexibility you have and the more time and patience you have, you can really come up with something that's going to be better. There's no shortcut to it. You just have to keep A/Bing back and forth and back and forth. It's pretty amazing how far off you can be sometimes even when you think you're doing everything right. But then the satisfaction of knowing that you really got something great is just an amazing feeling.

How important is mono to you? Do you listen in mono at all?
GC: I don't except to check for azimuth. I don't really work that way. I've had some clients who want to do it in mono but it's not something that I do. I would imagine that there are guys who have fooled with it and really find that they do really great work that way because there's also guys that EQ a lot differently from channel to channel to get dimension and everything. I always feel by doing that you're taking balances in the mix and fooling around with them and I'm very, very hesitant to do that unless an engineer comes and

says to me, "You know, the guitar player made me push the guitar too far up on the right. Could you do something?" I really don't want to give somebody something back and have them say, "What the heck did you do?" I just want them to listen to it and go, "Wow, it sounds better."

What are you using for a workstation?

GC: We all have Sonics here and actually they just changed the software now. They have a new version, and we all have to learn it over the next couple of months because we're building our new studio, which is going to be open in about four to six weeks. The new studio has the latest version of Sonics.

What are you using for monitors?

GC: For six years it's been ProAc Response 4. It's a big floor standing model almost like the size of a Dunlavey, but not as deep. I'm really happy with them. To me, they're well balanced and musical. They're powered with an Audio Research Stereo 300. I'm always fooling around with a whole bunch of crazy cables and with AC cords. There's a guy in L.A. doing some great AC cords for about $1,200 a shot.

Do you find it makes a difference?

GC: I do blind tests with clients all the time where I plug this cable into a converter or onto a machine and they hear it right away. I'd like to buy like six more of them, but they're very expensive.

There's a guy over at Sony Mastering apparently who found that if he works between midnight and 8 a.m., there's so much less going on in the building that he thinks the power is better. You start getting crazy with stuff like this. It's only two tracks, so you take any little advantage that you can come up with.

Do you do your own production, or do you have someone there to do it for you?

GC: The production here is done in my room. I have an assistant, Steve Fallone, who's a full-blown mastering engineer, but he works as my assistant and as a production guy in the studio. We get it to the point where the final EQ is approved, then we capture it as a 16-bit file in the Sonics. Once it's in there, then all the production engineers take it and make any 16-bit media that needs to come out, be it a DAT or a PMCD or CD or 1630.

What are you mostly sending to the plants these days? 1630s or PMCDs?
GC: Pretty much 50/50.

Do you do any DDP?
GC: We've been discouraging them, but they are ordered a lot. One of the big reasons is that every time I've ever done a comparison, they never sound as good. I never really understood why, but I think it has to do with the high-speed transfer to the glass master.

Do you do much processing in the Sonics at all?
GC: The only time I ever do anything is if there's like a thump on the tape and you want to do a quick rollout at 80 cycles or something. Or if there's an extra hard snare hit that just sounds too loud and you just want to take a little 4k off of it. Outside of that, I never use anything in the Sonics. It just doesn't compare to anything else that I have.

Do you cut lacquers?
GC: We actually have two lacquer rooms going pretty much all the time. We have a tremendous amount of cutting business because we do a lot of dance and rap music. I personally haven't cut a lacquer in six years, but I had 20 years of it before that.

Do you think cutting lacquers helped you in the way you work now?
GC: There's nothing like cutting lacquers because of the attention that you have to pay to dynamics. It's so unforgiving. In terms of helping me, I think that you learn to concentrate on the dynamics because it's so critical to whether you're actually going to have a successful cut or not. You probably train yourself to see the VU meters and the music in one continuum. I think that it probably helped to focus me on how to concentrate on listening to music. Somebody today could say to me, "Did you like the way the

song took off in the second bridge?" and I'd say, "I wasn't even listening to the structure of the song at this point. I'm listening to the whole." There's a whole other thing that's going on. There is a way that you listen to music when you have to cut a lacquer. You have to watch those meters and you have to make sure there's no hits that are going to make that record skip, so you're conscious of the rhythmic element.

See, that's the thing. There are guys that know how to make things sound really loud and big, but overcompression will keep the rhythm from working right. That's the thing that drives me nuts about the Finalizer and all this other stuff. Once you take away the beat, then you just don't have the same intensity any more. Maybe from cutting lacquer all those years, I started listening to drums a lot.

What makes your job easier? Is there something that your client can do to make things go faster, easier, better?
GC: It's really common sense stuff. One, stay off the phone; let's get locked in and not have to constantly get our ears back up to speed. Two, know where everything is. Don't make me spend four hours rewinding tape because that's not really productive work. I always tell people that, as stupid as it may sound, probably the most important thing that they could do is just go into the session being organized so that they know where the mixes are. Three, be honest with the mastering engineer. Don't try to pretend that everybody likes something and then later in the day start to reveal all the doubts that people had about certain aspects of the project. You'll just waste a tremendous amount of time that way. These are really basic human things.

What's the hardest thing you have to do in mastering? Is there a particular type of project that's harder than others?
GC: I don't have any idea exactly why it happens, but the hardest ones are the ones that don't sound a hundred percent, but yet you can't figure out what it is that could make it better. That's why I'm glad I have a lot of different things that I can plug in and just do signal path kind of stuff rather than EQ.

Another thing that's hard is when the low end is thin and light, because it's really hard to create low end when there is none. If you have a real muddy project, you can always clear stuff away and find something in there, but it's really tough when the bottom end isn't there. Most of the problem projects have to do with the bass being recorded poorly. If you made a book of excuses, the chapter on bass would be eight times bigger than the chapter on everything else. He brought the wrong axe, we couldn't get another bass player, it was an acoustic bass, the room, the miking, the direct, the buzz, the hum. It goes on and on. But the fact of the matter is that you never have a great-sounding CD if you don't have a great bass sound. It can't be great unless the bass is great. It could be good, but bass is what takes it to the level where it's really something special. It's just a constant thing that you try to get to improve. It's the thing that engineers are the most frustrated about.

David Cheppa began cutting vinyl in 1974 and since that time has cut almost 32,000 sides. He is the founder of Better Quality Sound, which is currently one of the few remaining mastering houses dedicated strictly to mastering vinyl. Thanks to his intense interest and design engineering background, David has brought a medium once given up for dead to new, unsurpassed heights of quality.

Not too long ago, everyone thought that vinyl was dead, yet you're really, really busy.

DC: I don't think anybody else does as much vinyl cutting as we do. We do about 500 masters a month here, but only because that's the niche that it worked out to be. When things were waning back in the '80s, I was still acting like nothing had changed insofar as I was still looking for ways to develop and improve the medium.

You never think about vinyl being "improved."

DC: We've actually developed it quite a lot. In the old days, way, way back in the '50s, the first cutting systems weren't very powerful. They only had maybe 10 or 12 watts of power. Then in the '60s, Neumann developed a system that brought it up to about 75 watts per channel, which was considered pretty cool. Then in the '70s, the high-powered cutting systems came into being, which was about 500 watts. That was pretty much it for a while. I mean, it made no sense beyond that because the cutter heads really weren't designed to handle that kind of power anyway. Even the last cutting system that came off the line in about 1990 at Neumann in Berlin hadn't really had changed other than it had newer panels and prettier electronics. It wasn't really a big difference.

One of the things that I did was look for a way to keep the signal path as simple and clean and free of anything that would affect the signal. I figure that a mastering engineer spent a lot of time and money to get it to where he wanted, so I didn't want to alter the program when I finally got it. All I wanted to do was give them as faithful a reproduction as possible. What I went for was to keep the warmth of the vinyl, but have the power of the CD. But because we had CDs by then, nobody even cared about vinyl anymore. I mean, everyone in the cutting end was old school in their thinking in a lot of ways and didn't care much about improving the medium other than just trying to do what was always done. So using my background as a design engineer, I improved the cutting system, mainly the amplifiers. I pushed the power levels way beyond anything that we ever had.

In doing that, I sacrificed a number of cutter heads, and these cutter heads are about 20 grand apiece, if you can find one. In fact, Neumann doesn't really make them any more, but if you want them to build you one from scratch, they'll charge you $35,000 for it. If you can find one, you can pick it up somewhere between 10 and 15 thousand dollars right now, and maybe a burned out one for about 5 or 6 thousand dollars. It costs about $10,000 to repair it, just the way it is. Last year alone, I burned out four cutter heads to get everybody's product out the way I wanted. Nobody knows what we go through to get a really good faithful recording on the disc because when you master for CD, you don't usually master with vinyl ears. You master with an ear to whatever it is that you want and as a result you don't consider anything else.

When you get stuff in that hasn't been mastered with vinyl ears, what are the problems that occur?

DC: This is what I notice and it's really the secret. The balance of the sound is the most important thing. You get a good mix where the elements are balanced well and it cuts well as a result.

Frequency balanced?

DC: Yeah, in the sense of equalization, every aspect of it is balanced so that you don't have these anomalies poking out that you don't really want. It seems obvious that this is what you would strive for, but that's not what mastering guys generally do. They'll tweak things in all different directions.

I used to voice rooms to flatten out monitors so that they sounded good, and the way you get rid of all the problems is to feather any EQ that you used. The same with limiting and compressing. The best mastering I see is where people have feathered their work. It's almost like you're just fine-tuning. It's so subtle that you almost don't notice it. If it's a good mix, you can make a great master because the best masters have the best balance. It seems obvious, but it just bears out, especially in cutting.

Do you have to do a lot of mastering in the sense of having to do a lot of EQ and compression, or do you just do a lot of straight transfers?

DC: My goal is to take someone's work and keep it faithful and not touch it, but there are very few engineers that I don't have to do anything with their program. But my first approach is a subtle one. I'll do things where nobody even notices it because I don't want them to hear that I did anything.

The problem is taking something that's now in the digital domain and putting it in the physical realm. You're basically making that little stylus accelerate sometimes as much as 5000 times the force of gravity at times, especially when you have a program with a lot of percussive brilliance or sibilant sounds created by S's. The demands are so great.

And by the way, that's where all the power is required in cutting. In the physical world with sound systems, all the energy is in the low end. But in cutting, it's the exact opposite. All of the energy is in the upper spectrum, so everything from about 5,000 cycles up begins to require a great amount of energy. This is why our cutting systems are so powerful. One lathe has 3,600 watts of power and our least powerful one is about 2,200 watts. It's devastating if something goes wrong at that power. If I get a master that's raw and hasn't been handled at all and there is something that just tweaks out of nowhere, it can take the cutter head out. So that's always a big concern.

If I'm not familiar with the material or the mastering engineer, then the first thing I'll do is dump it into our system here and look at what the sound spectrum is like to find out what kind of energy distribution exits. I can overview the entire project just at a glance and determine if there's anything that looks like it's going to be a problem.

Unfortunately, it does take time, and it's not something I usually charge for.

We do everybody's work here, MCA, Sony, Warner Brothers, but I treat every project as though I'm doing Babyface's album. Even when it's somebody's garage band, I'll give it the same care and interest because to me, every project is important. But that project may be a mess. If it's beyond anything I think I should be messing with, I'll call them and say, "Listen, this hasn't been premastered for vinyl." "What do you mean by that?" "Well, there's percussive brilliance that's out of control." This is the problem in almost every case because sibilant distortion can occur on vinyl that doesn't occur anywhere else. It's because the velocities are so high and so quick that the person's playback stylus will literally chatter in the groove. That chattering sound seems to be a distortion, when in truth, the record might not have any distortion, but nobody can track it. I can actually cut records that nobody can track, which is useless.

The other problem with having the high-power levels that we have today is that I have to figure out what kind of client this is going to and what kind of turntable and cartridge he'll be using. My lab turntable uses a high-compliance cartridge but that isn't what they're using in a club. If they're going to use a DJ setup, let's make it so they can play it. So that's another consideration.

Where does most of the vinyl go?
DC: Today there's so many markets. The DJ market, or the dance/rap/hip-hop market, is probably the greatest number. I think 80 percent of it goes there. The other percentage is really only a few percent, like classical music. We're having a resurgence of swing music and big band that's incredible, and a lot of music that we're remastering was done in the '60s and '70s. Everything that Polygram ever did and everything that Motown ever did, they're being remastered, and we're recutting them.

We're actually getting a better record now than they had back then because you're hearing things that they couldn't hear on the original masters. Also, the cutting systems weren't that evolved back then either. Everything's been improved so much.

What else has improved?

DC: One of the things that people used to do is compress and limit and EQ to try to make it go to vinyl. My goal is to take whatever the person had and make it go to vinyl without going through anything. That's a real feat at times because again, with a master that was prepared digitally, people don't think there are any limits. They do whatever they do to make it good for CD. I try to keep a straight path from whatever master machine I'm working from, whether it's an analog or a digital source.

That's a big task for me because some things are not physically possible. I'll get masters that I can't cut, and the reason is they're so rich in harmonics in the upper spectrum, which you can't even hear.

Because it's so distorted or squashed?

DC: What's happened is it's almost limitless in the way you can control the sound now, where the equipment in the earlier days wouldn't handle the frequency or transient response or the power levels. Most of the gear today is much more responsive. When people EQ, they don't realize that they may be adding harmonics that they're not hearing. Where something like a flute's highest fundamental frequency may be just under 5,000 cycles, its harmonics go out to 15–18,000 cycles and beyond.

My biggest challenge is that they're EQing this top end so that it sounds crisp and nice, but they don't realize that things like bells and cymbals are adding harmonics that they're not hearing, and may make it impossible to cut. I'll try to tame that portion of the sound spectrum that they can't hear in the first place because it won't go to vinyl otherwise.

A lot of guys who are cutting today can't figure out why they're having trouble so they just back off on the level or they smash it or just EQ it all out. The only problem with that is you then affect the brilliance and the air and the transparency. So sometimes I'll go in and I'll just tailor those harmonics.

What is the master format that you usually get in?

DC: I get everything but most of the stuff comes on optical, like a CD-R or a PMCD. The reason I prefer that is, and I don't care what anyone says, it's the most stable format we have right now. DAT was never intended to be a professional format. I was appalled that we had to work with it for so many years, but there was nothing else to bridge the gap. And of course, nobody has 1630s in their homes. And even on those, the error rates are now pretty high since all the machines are older. Plus maintaining them is very costly. The best new DAT machine has the same error rate as a 1630 today, so there's no tape format that I know of that's free of digital errors.

I have 12 DAT machines in this room and the reason I have so many is because we get DATs from all over the world that are recorded on every kind of machine you can imagine to make sure that they track. Despite all those machines, sometimes I'll get a DAT that I still can't play. I would always prefer it if someone can give me an optical format because I know, no matter where it was burnt, unless their burners are bad or they have a defective CD, it will always work.

Do you load it into a Sonics?

DC: We're using several systems here. Some of my cutting is done off a hard drive so I can assemble something quickly if you send it to me out of order. That happens a lot. I may actually do some EQing in there if I notice something. I'll maybe taper the high end a little bit, or if there's sibilant problems, I'll do some de-essing. Again, I don't like doing any of this stuff because it affects the program as far as I'm concerned, but I'll try to be so subtle and feather it.

A lot of times I will cut a little test on the outer diameter of the record. Not the area that we're sending for processing, but an area that I can play with. I will do that until I make sure that whatever is done is faithful to the original master, because there's so many variables in cutting that the response can change drastically by the stylus temperature, the stylus being dull, even the temperature in the room if the room is very cold and the lacquer is cold. I might turn up the temperature on the styli. The higher the temperature of the styli, by the way, the more resolution you can get. If you increase the temperature a little bit, it will cut more easily and maintain the response. But I only run styli for a few sides or a couple of hours total and then I discard them, because I try to maintain a certain standard. As soon as they get dull, then the response goes way down and that's not good.

With a lot of rap and hip-hop, do you have problems with the low end?

DC: The answer is yes and no. It's almost always no good if they haven't really mastered it because the kick may be boosted so severely that there's no way that you can get any apparent volume.

That's the other thing that I try to do; get the most apparent volume I can get on the medium. I had a Sublime record that I was cutting last year and the sides were 28 minutes, which is just too long (the longest side I ever cut was somewhere around 35 minutes and that was a spoken word record). But what I did was alter the EQ just a little bit to give them a sense of volume where there really wasn't one. Again, I think I did it in a way where nobody knew but the result was okay. It was kind of a compromise, but there are so many compromises you have to make sometimes, you just don't want them to be noticeable.

So what's your signal path then?

DC: The signal path is direct. I mean once I go out of the converters, I'm going right into the cutting system. Sometimes I'll cut off the converters; sometimes I'll cut right off the analog source, but I try to avoid anything that's going to alter that signal path at all. That's where I have the danger of destruction on the cut because of the power levels, because if there's a high frequency that's not controlled, the cutter head can't dissipate the heat fast enough and it's going to blow.

Normally you'd go through a limiter/compressor, maybe some kind of EQ, all kinds of amplifiers and transformers. I've eliminated everything. In fact, I even went through and pulled all the transformers out of all the equipment because I didn't want the changes that occur from the transformers. Most guys that cut around the country still have older systems, and because they've accepted the way things have been for so long, nobody thinks about it. But the signal path is so blocked with things that actually kind of blur the original source a little bit, and they don't even know it.

Another thing that I do and no one else does is run my helium pressure (used to cool the cutter head) seven or eight times of what is normally used because of the power that I now have. Because if I don't cool that cutter head down, I know I'm going to lose it. I found that I was able to cut higher levels with more high frequency that way. The factory settings work but they never intended their cutting systems to be pushed as hard as we push them.

It really must take a lot of experience to cut a good record.

DC: If you just want to cut a mediocre record, you don't need to know a lot of anything. If you want to cut a better record, it's good to know something. If you want to cut an incredible record, you need to have an understanding of the physical world and the physical laws that govern it. You have to know what the limits really are, physically and electronically. So I think it's a balance of art, science, and technology.

How many sides do you cut a day?

DC: Some days I'll do maybe 25 or 30 masters. That's pushing it and about the most that I can do. Now if they're short I can do more. I have some that are 25-minute sides, so they take a half hour to cut, but sometimes the preparations are pretty hard. Like when I was doing those Sublime masters, because I wanted to get it loud I spent hours preparing for something that was only going to take a half-hour to cut on each side. But on the short side, on dance records like the seven-inch singles, I may be able to do four an hour, or sometimes even more.

That's assuming that you don't have to do any fixes.
DC: Yeah, like I said, we can do premastering here, but I usually reserve that for fixing problems. I figure I'm going to stick with what we do best. We cut here and we'll do premastering when we need to, but I don't want to compete with the people that supply us with masters. My goal is to give them something beyond anything they expected on vinyl. In other words, whatever it takes to get this guy's record to sound incredible, that's what I want to do.

Dave Collins has been a mainstay at Hollywood's A&M Mastering (recently purchased by Jim Henson Productions) since 1988. In that time, he has brought his unique approach to a host of clients such as Sting, Madonna, Bruce Springsteen, and Soundgarden.

What is your philosophy on mastering?

DC: The first philosophy is like the Hippocratic oath and "Do No Harm." The client is investing a tremendous amount of trust in the mastering engineer when he gives you the tape and expects it to sound better than it did when he brought it to you. I personally think experience is as valuable as equipment in a large sense because after you've done it for 10 or 20 years, you've heard almost everything that can possibly go wrong, and go right, on a mix. So you can, in one respect, quickly address people's problems.

Today we are in kind of a funny situation because the definition of mastering has become a little diluted in my opinion. A Finalizer does not a mastering engineer make. Just because it says "mastering" on the box and there is a preset called "rock and roll" in it, that's not what it's all about. When a guy writes a book, he doesn't edit the book himself. He sends it off to an editor and the editor reads it with a fresh set of eyes, just like a mastering engineer hears it with a fresh set of ears.

Every so often I'll have a client whose budget is gone by the time he's ready to master. And so he says, "Well, I'll go in the studio and I'll hook up a Massenburg EQ to my two-track and I'll do a little equalization, and I'll put a compressor of some type on the output of it." But he'll ultimately call back and say, "Well, I don't know what I'm doing here. I'm just making it sound worse."

And that's kind of analogous to some guy trying to edit his own writing. It is the impartial ear that you get from your mastering engineer that is valuable. All this equipment and new technology that we've got is a great thing, but you're really asking for someone who has never heard the record before to hear it for the first time fresh.

When I listen to a record I've never heard before, I don't know that the guitar player was fighting with the singer through the whole session, or everyone hated each other by the time the record was done, or whatever political bullshit entered into the equation. I just listen to the sound that comes out of the speakers and take it from there.

What distinguishes a great mastering engineer from someone who is just merely good or competent?

DC: It's probably two things. The best mastering engineers have a sensibility to the widest range of music. And I think some mastering engineers get kind of pigeonholed into a certain style of music, that, "Oh, you've got to take your rap record to studio X and you have got to take your guitar/pop record to studio Y," and I don't really subscribe to that. I think the best mastering engineers understand a wide range of music. Believe me, I buy tons of CDs and listen to everything so I can stay current with what is going on because I have got to get what the fans are hearing and understand that. So having aesthetics for a wide range of music is probably a fundamental skill.

Secondly I would say that having a technical background, especially these days, certainly doesn't hurt because both recording and mastering now are far more complicated than ever before. The palate of signal processing that you have today is enormous, both in analog and digital, and it is growing all the time. Unfortunately, only 1 percent of all the gear that is out there is really optimized for mastering. Mastering is a really small market, and only a couple of companies really build stuff for mastering. TC will tell you that some of these boxes are made just for mastering, but they really aren't.

Yeah, you don't see many pieces.

DC: I actually use one of their boxes, called the dB Max, which is designed to be a radio station processor and is not even designed for mastering. If you spend a little time fooling around with it, it actually works great.

What does it do?

DC: It's a great de-esser and it's a really good limiter. The

Waves L2 is a better peak limiter, but we still use this TC box (which has a million different functions) just for de-essing. People kind of look at it sideways when they come in because it sort of looks like a Finalizer, but it's a good box. I'm really anxious to hear the new TC 6000 as well.

It does some other things that are handy too. It will make compatible mono, if you have a mix that doesn't sum to mono properly. It has a 90-degree phase shift that you can introduce to the signal that will stop elements of the mix from canceling out in mono. I have done that when we've sent stuff overseas for music videos, where stereo TV audio is not as popular as it is in the U.S. So making a good compatible mono program is sometimes useful.

How important is mono to you, and do you listen that way often?
DC: I always check in mono, and I think mono is very important. One thing that is overlooked sometimes is the fact that the signal on your FM radio becomes increasingly mono as the signal strength decreases, so it is important to check mono.

One thing that happens after you've listened for a long time, I can tell by how phasey it sounds to me in stereo if it's going to sum to mono. And once I get a certain amount of that eyes-sort-of-crossing feeling, I can pretty much tell that it is not going to sum to mono. But yes, we always check for compatibility. I've certainly had mixers come in with stuff and I'd say, "Man, that is some wide-ass stereo you got going there. How does it sound in mono?" And the guy goes, "I don't know. How does it sound in mono?" And of course you put it in mono and now one of the guitars has disappeared. So, it's an issue, but probably less important as time goes on. But I think it's still significant.

Can you hear the final product in your head when you first run through a song? Do you know where you are going with it before you go there?
DC: No, not always. And in fact, I frequently go down a dead end EQ-or processing-wise. There are some styles of

music that I will intrinsically get faster because the sonic presentation is pretty standardized in a lot of ways. So, there are times when I can hear 90 percent of what it is ultimately going to sound like immediately when I put it up, and there are other times when you go around in a big circle.

I guess when we were talking about the philosophy of mastering, what I should have added was, one of the hardest things, and it took me forever to get this, is knowing when to not do anything and leave the tape alone. As I have gained more experience, I am more likely to not EQ the tape, or just do tiny, tiny amounts of equalization. I think some people feel like they really have to get in there and do something. They really have to put their stamp on the tape somehow.

I don't really care about that. I only care that the client is happy and he comes back. I don't really feel that I need to put any particular personality on it. And hey, if the tape sounds good, let it sound good. To backtrack on the whole philosophical aspect, I am a fanatic about being able to reproduce the master tape properly. I've built an entirely custom analog tape playback system to get every bit of information and music off the client's tape to begin with, and what I have found is as I optimized that system, I have to EQ less. The music will require less EQ as you improve your chain.

Sometimes people are fighting their own electronics. They have a piece of gear in the signal path that sounds dark, for instance. Now suddenly you must compensate with equalization at some other place. As I got my system dialed in I found that I EQ less than I did ten years ago.

What is your signal chain?
DC: I used to work in electronics before I got into audio so I had some background in analog engineering. It started by finding things that sounded good, like say an ATR-100 which everybody likes, and doing some modifications and optimizations of the circuitry. Some of these are due to the fact that when the ATR was built, some of these components and technologies just didn't exist in the mid-1970s, and today they do. So we can bring some of it up to date.

The tape playback system that I use now is a half-tube, half-transistor system that sounds great. I have had a lot of people come in and really be surprised at what was on their tape that they didn't hear in the studio because you're reproducing it in a much more resolute, much more accurate way. More often than not they're hearing things that they like that they didn't hear in the studio.

But my philosophy is, optimize every inch of the chain and really get it as clean and as pure as you can, because you can always screw it up some other way. You can always distort it or do whatever you want to do. But if you don't start with something that is clean and transparent, that always hampers you. You have to begin there.

What is the ratio of analog-to-digital masters that you get?

DC: That number is hard to pin down because it changes. Say, 70 percent half-inch, 20 percent high-resolution digital sources, and 10 percent DAT. We're seeing much more bit-split DA-88s right now, and I just did some stuff off Genex 24-bit MO format. Those things really sound great.

When a client mixes to half-inch and DAT and he brings in both and we do a very careful level-matched A/B between the two sources, whenever the DAT wins, it is because they couldn't set up their half-inch machine right, in my opinion. A properly aligned half-inch machine should always be a given, but in the year 2000, it's kind of a lost art. I get stuff where the azimuth is on the moon, and they obviously haven't put an MRL tape up on the machine for 20 years.

Not that many people really know how to deal with analog nowadays, which makes your DA-88 with the Apogee 8000 look really good. Because man, you plug that sucker in and you set 1kHz to zero and you don't have to deal with anything. There is no bias; there is no azimuth; there is nothing to worry about. You get some level on there and go. And that system can sound good. We worked on that Santana record [*Supernatural*] and they mixed to half-inch and bit-split DA-88 and the bit-split DA-88 beat the half-inch soundly. It was better in every way. So I think when you get to these 20- or 24-bit formats, then it really can compete with the best analog. I personally think the jury is still out on 96k, but I guarantee that some 24-bit storage mediums can really sound good and can compete with the best analog. It's not a popular opinion, but I think it's true.

Are you getting anything in that is recorded at a higher sample rate?

DC: Yes, I just did some Tori Amos stuff that came in on a 96k Genex. It sounded terrific. But when we do blind tests on 48k versus 96k, no one can consistently hear the difference. Everyone loves the sound of 96k when you're sitting there and you know what position the switch is in, but, at least in our tests which used analog tape as the source, no one could consistently tell whether it was 88.2 or 44.1.

I'm not convinced either.

DC: Well, it's technologically a funny question because I guarantee, if you like 96k better, it is not because you are hearing to 48k. Our hearing has not evolved another octave of range just because 96k is being marketed. What it does do, and it is kind of an arcane technical point, is relax the anti-alias and anti-imaging filter requirements by half so you need half as much filtering at 96k for the same bandwidth. But to me these tests are a little hard unless you had a band set up live on the floor and took the signal right off a mic preamp or something like that. I'm sure that would be a more accurate test of 96k. I mean, when we use half-inch, I can see that there is some slight ultrasonic information present on the tape. But so far as we've been able to tell, I don't really hear any significant difference.

The average person is not going to hear it.

DC: That is something that we definitely have cried in our beer about because my mom can tell the difference between stereo and 5.1, but I can get a room full of professional audio engineers and we can barely hear the difference between 44 and 88k. So you have to be careful from a marketing point of view where this stuff goes because the audiophile market is like one-tenth of 1 percent of the total audio sold, and it's a strange world to be in. I'd rather present compelling multichannel stuff at 44k.

I really wanted to like 96k because from a technical point of view, there are some interesting things that can be done with it, and it just gives you twice as much room to work from a processing point of view. But when we tried to do blind tests (I've done it twice now, once with the Prism gear and recently with the dB Technologies gear), the results were statistically about the same as flipping a coin.

What converters are you using?

DC: We're using dB Technology A/Ds, and for 96k I'm using the dB Technology D/A. For 44.1 I'm using one I built myself based on Ultra Analog components. We just went through a big shootout of all these converters and tried the HDCD, DCS, Prism, dB, and Mytech. It's funny, the Prism and the dB Technologies sound almost identical. I mean, we were just pulling our remaining hair out to hear the difference. But ultimately when you compare it to the half-inch tape, the dB was ever so slightly closer to the master tape. If I didn't have the master source to compare to, I would not have been able to tell you one was better than the other. If somebody just gave me a CD that had two tracks on it, and I didn't have the master to refer back to, I could not have told you. They are both good products.

What is the hardest thing that you have to do? Is there one type of operation or music that is particularly difficult for you?

DC: Well, the hardest thing to do is a compilation album. These "Very Special Christmas" albums are a good example where you have 13 songs with 13 producers and 13 engineers and in some cases ten different mix formats. Those are the hardest, just from a strictly sonic point of view, to try to get any consistency to it.

Second to that is working on projects that have a "too many cooks and not enough chefs" condition where you've got a lot of people kind of breathing down your neck and a lot of people with different, usually contradictory opinions. Some of those projects, and usually they are your major name artists, can be a little problematic because you have so much input and everyone is trying to pull you in a different direction at once, so that can be a little nerve wracking. But it's all in a day's work.

What do you enjoy the most?

DC: The day after the session when the client calls and tells you everything sounds great and, "I can't believe how good my CD sounds. I had no idea my mixes sounded that good." Seriously, they do come. That's the best, when I have someone who really got what I was doing and really got what my room is able to produce. It's not every session of course, but those are a good call to get.

What are you using for monitors?

DC: Presently I'm using Genesis 500s for the mains and Quested 108s for the minis. The mains are soon to be changed to B&W 802.

They seem to be popular these days.

DC: It's a good speaker. I never liked the old B&W 801s. This new one is really amazing. I don't find much to criticize in it other than it is bloody expensive.

The 801s seem to be the classical standard, both for recording and for mastering.

DC: They were. I've heard them many places, and I never really understood why. It's like saying my car only turns right. What good is a speaker that only works on classical music? That means it's not accurate. You mean it won't play a kick drum?

I can tell you those 802s are great. I'm putting together a new surround mastering room with five of them. The only possible disadvantage is that it's a very wide dispersion speaker, and in a five-channel room, it may require some additional treatment of the side walls. But it sure sounds good.

Tell me more about your signal chain.

DC: The analog signal path is a Studer 820 used just as a transport. We use a Flux-Magnetics playback head that's connected to the outboard tape playback electronics that we talked about before that is a half tube, half solid-state. That feeds an all custom analog console. Basically, the tape machine feeds some passive attenuation, and from there I've got a custom EQ that we use.

I've got a Prism analog EQ, a Manley Vari-Mu compressor, and a heavily modified SSL console compressor.

That thing is great. I was just telling somebody at lunch today that if you take a Manley Vari-Mu and an SSL compressor and have those in your console, that covers an enormous range of dynamic possibilities. You've got the kind of in-your-face nervous sound that an SSL can give you, which is something that people respond to very well, and then you've got the Manley, which is much more polite. The Manley has some sort of magic features to it; just running stuff through it sounds good. It is probably phase shift and distortion, but it sounds good. And we've got a Waves L2 limiter (serial number 0) and a dB Technology A/D converter. I also use that TC dB Max that we discussed.

Basically, what I do is A/D convert the output of the console and then from there we'll do maybe a tiny bit of EQ. I've got one of those Weiss digital EQs, which is a wonderful box, but to me, if you've got good analog EQ, it's really hard to beat it digitally. But sometimes for a few touch-ups here and there I think it's very valuable.

As far as limiting, a digital limiter is just far superior to any analog limiter. You just can't get analog to do the things you can do in digital. And with today's kind of stupid dB level war that you have to fight, you're just skirting the hairy edge of distortion every step of the way. I mean, to get a CD to the level of the loudest CDs today, it really requires kind of tiptoeing around distortion.

I never would've thought that we would be cutting CDs at this level. It's to the point where a large amount of our day is optimizing the gain structure in the console and checking what kind of limiter you're going to use and how you're going to use it just to get the CD as loud as you possibly can. I don't get it. I have to play the game because if you want to stay in business, you've got to compete on absolute level, but it's really a horrible trend. I wish all mastering engineers would speak out about this because it sucks.

I buy records that I really want to listen to, and they are so fatiguing. It's impossible to get that amount of density and volume on a CD and not make you want to turn it off after three songs. I don't know how to put it in print in a diplomatic way, but when you get mastering engineers together and you get a couple of beers in them, they'll all agree that CDs are too loud. We hate it and wish we didn't have to do it, then it's right back to work on Monday and squeeze the shit out of it all over again.

Part of the problem is everything gets squeezed to death even before you get it.
DC: I have a client that says before he sends the client home with a CD-R, he has to run it through some kind of compressor, limiter, Finalizer, you name it, just for their take-home copy, or the artist doesn't respond to it.

My joke about this is the whole problem started when they came out with multidisc CD changers. Because before, by the time you took the one CD out and put the new CD in, you forgot what the volume was on the last one. If you had to adjust the volume control, no problem. But now when you've got the six-disc changer, one CD comes on and it's ten dB quieter than the last one, and this next one comes on and it blows your head off. It's a problem. I don't know what the answer is. The frightening part to me is when we're right at the threshold of a 24-bit home format, we're still probably going to squeeze it into the top of its dynamic range. I hope we don't because I would love to hear some of these new DVD audio releases actually using the available dynamic range. Nobody uses any of the available 16-bit dynamic range as it is.

In mixing, if you don't squash it, the client isn't happy.
DC: It's true. And believe me, it's the same way in mastering.

When I get it to where I'm almost uncomfortable with the amount of processing I'm doing, the client responds to it and loves it.

What kind of workstation do you use?

DC: Sonic Solutions U.S.P. We've got one of the new Sonic HD systems too, but it isn't quite ready for primetime yet.

Do you cut lacquers?

DC: We still have one lathe set up. Every year we get together and say, "Well, this will be the year when we pack the lathe up and sell it or put it in storage." And every year there's just a little bit more work than the last, and it's frankly enough to keep us in business with lacquers.

Lacquers are funny. You have three types of clients. You've got the guy who can't afford to make CDs and can press a white label 45 for 30 cents. You've got the total high-end boutique client who wants to put out 50,000 copies of his new record on vinyl because it's cool. And then you've got a DJ who just wants to take a 12-inch lacquer to play in a club. They bring in a CD and you basically give them a flat constant pitch transfer to a lacquer so they can scratch on it in a club.

Do you cut yourself?

DC: I have, but not really. Andrew Garver does all the cutting here. I have to say, cutting is really fun in a sense because it's a skill. Cutting a loud record is very difficult and it requires an enormous balancing act of physics and sonics. Any idiot can make a loud CD, but not any idiot can make a loud record. And in a way, I miss it a little bit. But I guess I really don't because all the physical limitations of a record are gone on the CD and nobody ever worries about the laser jumping out of the groove.

Do you ever have to use effects? Anybody ever ask you to add reverb?

DC: Oh, sure. We've done a lot of soundtrack mastering at A&M, and it's very common to add a touch of reverb at the final stage. Generally, you won't want to add reverb to a whole pop mix because it gets too washy. But five times a year, I bring up an Eventide DSP4000 because I want to flange the whole mix like you hear on that Lenny Kravitz track, ["Are You Gonna Go My Way"], where the whole thing goes through a flange and you cut it back into the regular track. And sometimes we'll go to the telephone-limited bandwidth kind of sound for a measure or two and back again, or something like that.

But generally speaking, I hope that by the time the record gets to mastering it doesn't need effects. But I've done things like overdubbed vocals in the mastering before. I've overdubbed guitar solos in the mastering room too. Live, right to the master. I remember the last time we were doing vocals, the guy was like, "So, what kind of cue mix are you gonna send me?" I said, "I'm gonna turn the level down low on these speakers and you can listen to it and you're gonna sing. How's that?" It does happen, but fortunately not often.

When you have to add effects, what box do you use?

DC: Well, for reverb, I like the old Lexicon 300. I think if you get into the parameters on that thing and spend some time with it, it's really a good box. I've heard some good results on that little Sony 77 whatever it's called, but it seems like there are a million menus and each one was ten deep. For general purpose, I think that Eventide Orville has just got some great programs in it. Whenever I need to flange something or add some weird slapback to a section or something, I always reach for that because it's got a digital I/O.

Do you ever have to do something where somebody cuts the heads or tails off and you have to fix it?

DC: Oh yes, sometimes you'll have to add a little reverb at the end just to give you something to fade over. It's not that common, fortunately. I generally try to caution people, if you're going to bring your tape assembled on a 14-inch reel, don't leader it too tight because it's a lot easier to take it off than it is to put it back.

What do you deliver mostly to the replicator these days? DDPs or 1630s or PMCDs?

DC: All three. I would say the majority of our releases still go out on 1630. What they get transferred to at the CD plant, I don't know. I'm actually warming up to DDP. I've heard some CDs that came back that we did off DDP that sound fine. They're not significantly different from the master.

I still try to talk people out of PMCD just because I've heard so many horrible sounding CDs that originated off PMCD. I'm sure it can work and from a technical stand-point any of the delivery mediums should sound the same, but the reality is somewhat different.

It seems in my experience that the 1630 is the one that comes out sounding the most like the original tape. I guess I should backtrack. The one that sounds the best of all is the Sony PCM-9000 but nobody else uses them. That really was the one that won all of our tests. Second to that was 1630; next to that was DDP. The DLT is really the best of all these formats, but I don't know of any CD replicators that accept it. Those are the contenders.

Do you do much processing within Sonics at all?

DC: I use zero processing in the Sonics. The only processing I do will be level adjustments, if you want to bump up the chorus up two-tenths of a dB or something like that. I've never used the EQ or compressor in the Sonic, which is weird, considering they've got the smartest guy who has ever worked in digital audio. This guy is just head and shoulders above everybody else. But they've never had a great EQ or compressor, so I don't know.

What do you think the mastering house of the future is going to look like?

DC: I think it'll look fundamentally the same as it's always looked because the basic requirement for accurate moni-toring in an accurate acoustical space will never change. It will always have recognizable elements of it.

The mastering house of the future will have at least five loudspeakers. The mastering house of the future will have much more digital processing, and there will be a much wider palette of digital processing to choose from. I'm sure you're going to walk in and it's going to look like the bridge of the Enterprise, but the basic requirements of good acoustics and good monitoring will always be there. That's one thing that will always stay the same.

One of the most widely respected names in the recording industry, Bernie Grundman has mastered literally hundreds of platinum and gold albums, including some of the most successful landmark recordings of all time. Michael Jackson's *Thriller*, Steely Dan's *Aja*, and Carole King's *Tapestry* have all benefited from Bernie's touch. A mainstay at A&M records for 15 years before starting his own facility (Bernie Grundman Mastering) in 1984, Bernie is certainly one of the most celebrated mastering engineers of our time.

Do you have a philosophy on mastering?

BG: Well, I think that mastering is a way of maximizing music to make it more effective for the listener, as well as maybe maximizing it in a competitive way for the industry. It's the final creative step and the last chance to do any modifications that might take the song to the next level.

There's a couple of factors that come into play when we're trying to determine how to master a recording. Most people need a mastering engineer to bring a certain amount of objectivity to their mix, plus a certain amount of experience. If you (the mastering engineer) have been in the business awhile, you've listened to a lot of material, and you've probably heard what really great recordings of any type of music sound like. So in your mind you immediately compare it to the best ones you've ever heard. You know, the ones that really got you excited and created the kind of effect that producers are looking for. If it doesn't meet that ideal, you try to manipulate the sound in such a way as to make it as exciting and effective a musical experience as you've ever had with that kind of music.

Now, you can only go so far. Mastering has certain limitations. You can't completely change the mix, but you can certainly affect it a lot. Sometimes you can affect it dramatically so much that it really becomes much more engaging musically for the listener. And if somebody brings in something that's better than what you've heard, you have to be open enough and sensitive enough to let that music affect you. So you have to really be willing to admit sometimes that, "Hey, this is actually better than anything I have ever heard before." All it means is that you have a new ideal.

So, I think one of my biggest philosophies is that the music really has to tell you where to go. What that monitor is telling you is the truth, as long as you have a good monitor. You manipulate the song in one direction and you go, "No. Now the music is aggravating me. I'm not getting as good an experience." Instead of the things that are supposed to contribute to the effectiveness of the music, you're hearing all the elements of the mix getting obscured and muddy when you're manipulating the sound. You have to be aware of that and be aware of the elements that are important to make that thing effective. It's one of those back-and-forth kind of things.

In the end, you really have to be sensitive to whether you're really making it better, rather than just some intellectual pursuit where it's as bright or as loud as somebody else's. That's not really a great criterion for a musical experience. The real question is whether it's really communicating better musically, emotionally. And I think that's something that all mastering engineers struggle to open themselves up to, whether or not this manipulation is really going in the direction that's beneficial for the product.

What about the interaction with the client?
BG: Yes, you have to interface with the producer or the artist too, because they might have a vision that may be slightly different than where you intuitively want to take it. They might want to emphasize some aspect of the music that you may not have noticed. So a lot of it is definitely trial and error on your part, but it's also give and take between the producer and the artist because you can't sit there and arrogantly think that you know where this recording ought to go and that they don't.

Not that you shouldn't suggest things, because more often than not, the producer will say, "Yeah, I like where you're going with it. You're making it better than it ever was." Hopefully, you get that kind of response. And then sometimes they'll have comments like, "Yeah, I like that part but it's hurting this other part of the music. When you're pushing it here, it's hurting it over there." Or, "This is an element that I don't want to lose." It's all a learning process. I always say that we're all trying to get to the same place, but we're just trying to figure out how to get there. We want to get the best musical experience and be competitive.

So we've got all of these aspects that we're kind of struggling to maximize, and sometimes it takes two or three passes before it's right. They take it home, listen to it, and say, "No, let's try to get a little more of this out." Or, "Can we do this or that?" You try to do the best you can, but mastering is usually a little bit of a compromise in a lot of cases.

Can you hear the final product in your head when you first run something down?

BG: Well, you do get ideas. If you've been in it a while and you've heard a lot of things, then you know where to go. Like if you put on a rap record, you know that it's very rhythm oriented, and it has to be really snappy and punchy on the bottom end. You know that some of the elements are really important and that this kind of music seems to feel better if it has them.

Or they may have had a monitoring system that had a lot of bottom end and the tape comes out bottom light as a result, but they thought they had it right. That's why probably the single most important piece of equipment that a mastering engineer can have is his monitor, and he has to understand that monitor and really know when it's where it should be. If you know the monitor and you've lived with it for a long time, then you're probably going to be able to make good recordings. The only problem with that is, if the monitor is something that is a little bit esoteric and only you understand it, it's very insecure for the producer or the artist because they don't think it's there, and you have to reassure them all the time. That happened to me when I first worked at A&M and I had a monitor system where I knew what it should sound like, but it was really kind of wrong for everyone else. They had to trust me and they did, but I could see them get really insecure and concerned. So in my studio I've gone to great lengths to make it a very neutral system that everyone can relate to.

What are you using?

BG: We put it together ourselves. We build our own boxes and crossovers and we use all Tannoy components. We have it all mixed in with different elements that we feel are going to give us the best sound. It's not that we're going for the biggest or the most powerful sound; we're going for neutral because we really want to hear how one tune compares to the other in an album. We want to hear what we're doing when we add just a half dB at 5k or 10k. A lot of speakers nowadays have a lot of coloration and they're kind of fun to listen to, but boy, it's hard to hear those subtle little differences. We just use a two-way speaker system with just one woofer and one tweeter so it really puts us in-between near-fields and big soffited monitors.

Do you use only that one set or do you use near-fields as well?

BG: We have some NS10s and some little Radio Shack cubes. These are things that a lot of people around town like to hear what it's going to sound like on. Usually, if you can get it sounding good on our main system, it's just that much better on the other ones.

What is the ratio of tape to DATs that you get in?

BG: We get about 50/50. Most of the major jobs are done on analog at half-inch 30 ips. I'm just looking around my room and I've got three projects right there that are mostly analog. Sometimes they'll have a mix or two on a DAT, but I've got three albums sitting there that are almost 100 percent analog.

Do you have anything coming in that's 24-bit DAT or bit-split?

BG: A few. We've had some of those 24-bit Tascams come in, and we also had some DA-88s that are bit-split. But the most common formats are DATs and half-inch 30 ips. That's still around.

What are you delivering to the replicator?

BG: PMCDs and 1630s. I'm not sure but I think we might do 60 percent 1630s and 40 percent CD-Rs. We're doing a lot more CDs lately because the factories don't want to mess with 1630s because they're just a headache.

When you're processing, are you doing that prior to going into the workstation? Are you doing that in the analog or digital domain?

BG: We do a lot of our processing analog. A lot of times we'll put it right on the computer already EQed and processed. Sometimes we don't. It depends on the project. Some of the stuff I'll put on the computer and then I'll run it through the board.

Is your console custom-built?

BG: Yeah, we build our own equipment. It's built mostly as an integrated system to avoid a lot of extra electronics and isolation devices and so forth. When you buy most pieces of audio equipment, each one has its own isolation transformers or electronically balanced outputs, or however they arrive at a balanced output. But when we buy outboard equipment, we completely rebuild it and put all of our own line amps in and take out the transformers or the active transformers. You'd be amazed at how much better they sound as a result.

We have all separate power to each one of our rooms and a very elaborate grounding setup, and we've proven to ourselves that it helps, time and time again. We have all custom wire in the console. We build our own power supplies as well as everything else—the equalizers, everything.

It must take a long time.

BG: Yes, it takes about three to four months to build a console. Sometimes six months. We just built one for our studio in Japan that's a 5.1 six-channel board. We had to design it specially so that we could go from two-channel or six-channel with just a push of a button.

Are you going to do surround sound?

BG: Japan is already running 5.1 just for DVD-Video. We

have a room that's designated for it here and we're building a second six-channel board that will go in there.

What are you going to use for subwoofers?
BG: We're using two Vandersteins, one on either corner of the room up front on either side. The five main channels are all full-range speakers.

Do you still cut lacquer?
BG: Oh yes, we sure do. In fact, I'm going to be cutting lacquers all afternoon. We have one room where we cut all of our lacquers now. We used to have lathes in every room in our old studio, but we figured there would be less vinyl work in the future, so now we have just one room that has two lathes in it.

One of the lathes is for the audiophile guys, and it's got all tubes. The other one is solid-state and has more power for the hip-hop and rap and club stuff. The three key engineers here all use that same room to cut, and almost every day there is somebody cutting something. We were very, very surprised at how much is still going on in vinyl. I don't even know where you buy them (records) anymore, but I know they must be around somewhere.

There's one store down on Melrose (in Hollywood) that only has records.
BG: Well, that might be where they are. But if the labels really merchandised them, they could probably sell even more because a lot of kids really like those things.

Most of the stuff we're doing is either really high-end audiophile stuff on the tube system done from the original masters from the late '50s and early '60s, or we're doing almost like promo records where they've got a 12-inch single with three or four cuts on there. We're doing more and more current albums too, and they don't even want to take tunes off to make them fit. On long CDs, we're doing them on four sides and they're putting it on a gatefold jacket. It's amazing, if an artist has any notoriety at all, they'll do it on vinyl as well as CD.

How do you think that having experience cutting vinyl has helped you in the CD age?

BG: Well, the problem with vinyl is that it has more limitations than CDs, so it takes a lot more knowledge to cut a good vinyl disc than it does to do a CD. With CDs, except for artifacts and various changes that occur in the digital domain, what you get on the monitors is very close to what you get on the disc and you don't have all the various distortions that vinyl can come up with. Vinyl has inner groove distortion and it has tracing distortion because of too much energy in the high frequencies. But this doesn't happen on CDs. With CDs, of course, the quality is the same from the beginning to the end of a CD, which isn't the case on vinyl. High frequencies might get a little brittle, but they don't distort on a CD, whereas they will on vinyl. So there is this whole grab bag of problems with vinyl that you have to consider. So part of being a good vinyl-cutting guy is knowing how to compromise the least.

All of us here have been in the business a while and are very experienced with vinyl, so we can probably get about as much as you can out of it. But they're harder and harder to cut with the way these digital tapes sound. They have all of this energy now because people don't have to worry about being conservative on the bottom or the top end of a CD. Whereas, if you listen to old vinyl discs, you notice that they don't have anywhere near the bass or high end that CDs have nowadays because there was a cutting limitation. You just couldn't play a record back then that had too much energy in the high end. That's why things have gotten so bright and aggressive on CDs I think, because now you can get away with it.

Talk about the level wars for a minute.

BG: That's one of the unfortunate things about the industry, and it was even that way with vinyl. Everybody was always trying to get the loudest disc, and then if you got into a new generation of playback cartridges that could track cleaner, they would push it again until even those were on the edge of distortion. So it didn't matter if you had better and better cartridges because that just meant that you could go that much louder and get right up to the same amount of distortion you were at before. Hopefully, it was louder than your competitor's record because that's a very basic, almost naive, kind of competitive area that people can identify.

Usually anything that sounds louder gets at least some attention. It might not hold up on the long haul, but the main thing that a lot of promotion guys want is to at least attract attention so that it gets a chance. What happens is everybody is right at that ceiling level as high as you can go, so now guys without a lot of experience try to make things loud and the stuff starts to sound god-awful. It's all smashed and smeared and distorted and pumping. You can hear some pretty bad CDs out there.

Would you have any words of advice for somebody that has one of those "mastering processors" to stay out of trouble?
BG: Well, I just don't think that you should do anything that draws attention to itself. Like if you're going to use a compressor or limiter on the bus, if you use it to the point where you really hear a change in the sound, you're going a little too far. You always have the consolation of knowing that the mastering engineer can take it to another level anyway, and he's experienced in how to do that.

Some of the automatic settings in these devices really aren't as good as they make them out to be. And when you use them, you have to realize that you're going to degrade the sound, because compressors and limiters will do that. It's just another process that you're going through no matter if it is in the digital domain or analog.

This is another thing that is very true that I've studied for quite a while. Analog and digital are very, very much alike when it comes to signal processing. If you put an equalizer in the circuit, even if it's all in the digital domain, you will hear a difference. If you put a compressor in the circuit, not even compressing, you will hear a difference and it will sound worse.

Do you do all of your processing in the analog domain then?

BG: No, we do some processing in digital. We do compression and limiting sometimes in the digital domain because some of that stuff is pretty good if you use it right. But, our equalization is all analog because I have yet to find a digital equalizer that is as good.

What are you using for a compressor?

BG: It's something that we have actually put together. It's kind of an oddball thing, but it works for us.

So you build digital gear as well.

BG: Yes. We can hybrid stuff if we want. We could do part of the processing and even do the equalization in the digital domain if we felt we had a good equalizer. Our boards are built to accommodate anything you want because at some point we convert it to digital and after that we can hang more stuff on it.

So the consoles are digital?

BG: No, the main console isn't, but we have outboard equipment that we can put in the digital chain if we want. We have a whole desk area for digital stuff right next to the analog console so we could add in digital compression, limiting, or equalization if we wanted to.

What are you using for a workstation?

BG: Right now we're using (Studer) Dyaxis. When we did all of our testing about three years ago, it was the best sounding one that we heard, and it still is. But when we go into these higher sampling rates and higher bit rates, we won't be able to use those. Since we are still in a 44.1/16 world, they're fine for now and do a great job.

How important is mono to you? Do you listen in mono often?

BG: No, I very rarely listen in mono. Sometimes I do it just to test the phase, but I never listen in mono any more.

What is the hardest thing that you have to do?

BG: One of the things that is really hard is when the

recording isn't uniform. What I mean by uniform is that all of the elements don't have a similar character in the frequency spectrum. In others words, if a whole bunch of elements are dull and then just a couple of elements are bright, then it's not uniform. And that's the hardest thing to EQ because sometimes you'll have just one element, like a hi-hat, that's nice and bright and crisp and clean, and everything else is muffled. That is a terrible situation because it's very hard to do anything with the rest of the recording without affecting the hi-hat. You find yourself dipping and boosting and trying to simulate air and openness and clarity and all the things that high end can give you and so you have to start modifying the bottom a lot. You do the best you can in that situation, but it's usually a pretty big compromise.

If the client just had a bright monitor system and everything in the mix was just a little bit dull, that is easy. It's almost like a tone control because you bring the high end up and everything comes up. But when you have inconsistencies in the mix like that, it's tough.

Then there's something that's been overly processed digitally where it gets so hard and brittle that you can't do much with it because once you've lost the quality, you can't get it back. If I am starting out with something that is really slammed and distorted and grainy and smeary, I can maybe make it a little better, but the fact that a lot of that quality is already gone is going to handicap that recording. It is never going to be as present as the way something that is really clean can be.

That is part of what gives you presence, when it's clean. The cleaner it is, the more it almost sounds like it is in front of the speakers because it's got good transients. Where if it has very poor transients, it just stays in the speakers. It sounds like it's just coming out of those little holes. It doesn't ever fill up the space between the speakers.

Do you have to add effects much these days?
BG: No, sometimes if it's lacking spatially really badly,

we can put the B.A.S.E. [spatial processor] unit in. We have a couple of those around and every now and then they come in handy because they can give a little more of an expansion to the ambience. But other than that, we don't. We almost never add echo either, unless it's like a classical recording where there are one or two instruments. There you can do it, but usually it messes things up if you try to put it on something that is really complex. It just confuses it.

What makes a great mastering engineer as opposed to someone who is just competent?

BG: I think it would be what I was talking about at the beginning. I think it would be trying to get a certain kind of intimacy with the music. It doesn't even have to be music that you like. Music is a human expression, and you have to be willing to open yourself up to wherever it is that the artist is trying to go with their music or whatever he's trying to communicate. There is no reason why you can't get on that same wavelength, because you're also a human being and we're all basically alike. But that is sometimes hard to do because you're not always on, so you can't always do it. It's like any artist. They are not always on, and they're not always open to where their internal, basic humanity comes out. And that's the thing that will communicate to everyone because that's the thing we have in common.

So the real test is if you can really not be a snob, or not have all kinds of preconceived ideas, and just open yourself up to it and see how the song is affecting you emotionally and try to enhance that. I think that a lot of it is this willingness to enter into another person's world and get to know it and actually help that person express what he is trying to express, only better. I think that is a big factor when it comes to mastering.

You're going beyond the technical, in other words. You're going to the spiritual.

BG: Oh, yes. Because that's what music is. My wife is an artist, she's a painter, and she has the same experience. When she goes in her studio, it's almost like it's not her painting when she's really on. And anyone that's played a musical instrument knows that there are these moments when it almost feels like you're not doing it. You're in touch with something really greater than you. It's going through you. It's a very elusive thing and hard to know how to get there. This is part of being concerned about how things are affecting others rather than just being all wrapped up in yourself.

How long do you think it takes to get to that point?

BG: I think it varies. It depends on the emotional issues that people have, their personal defenses and their sense of self-esteem. Some people have such low self-esteem that it's really hard for them to even admit that there's a better way to do something. If a client suggests something, they're very defensive because they feel that they have to have the answers. A lot of engineers are that way, but mastering is more than just knowing how to manipulate the sound to get it to where somebody wants it to go.

We have a double board here where we can compare EQs, and one artist used to sit over there and do an EQ himself. I would do one on my side and then we would compare them to see who wins. Now a lot of engineers would be deathly afraid to do that because that would mean that, "God, what if he wins? That means I'm no good." That's low self-esteem. You think that if one thing is off or there's something that somebody had thought of that you didn't think of, that means you're no good. But maybe it's just how you're feeling that day. There are a lot of other things that you've done that are great. People have to know that about themselves. That one little thing that might not be right doesn't mean your whole world is gone.

Co-owner of Orlando-based Digital Domain, Bob Katz specializes in mastering audiophile recordings of acoustic music, from folk music to classical. The former technical director of the widely acclaimed Chesky Records, Bob's recordings have received Disc of the Month in *Stereophile* and other magazines numerous times, and his recording of *Portraits of Cuba* by Paquito D'Rivera, won the 1997 Grammy for Best Latin-Jazz Recording. Bob's mastering clients include major labels EMI, WEA-Latina, BMG, and Sony Classical, as well as numerous independent labels.

What's your approach to mastering?

BK: I started very differently from many recording engineers that I know. Number one, I was an audiophile, and number two, I did a lot of recording direct to two-track. That's my orientation. I am a very naturalistic person. I work well with rock and roll and heavy metal, but the sound and tonal balance of a naturally recorded vocal or naturally recorded instrument is always where my head turns back to. I find that my clients, while they don't necessarily recognize naturalistic reproduction as much as I do, love it when I finally EQ a project and make it sound what I think to be more natural. Now, there are exceptions. A rock and roll group that wants to have a really big heavy bass, well, I'll go for that. But, at the same time, I'm more inclined toward projects that sound good when the EQ is natural.

Do you think there's a difference from the way people master from geographic area to geographic area? Do people master differently from New York to Nashville to L.A., for instance?

BK: Well, there used to be a West Coast sound.

Do you think there is now?

BK: I think that I can identify the product of Doug Sax and Bernie Grundman a lot. But if you compare a lot of Ludwig against Doug Sax or Bernie Grundman, I think you'll find more similarities than differences even though they're on different coasts.

I think that as the years have gone on, without mentioning names, some mastering engineers have succumbed more to the "crush it" campaign while others are still holding their ground, and when that happens, you hear a big distinction between engineers. But I see that same phenomenon on the West Coast as on the East Coast as well as elsewhere. I think it's more of an individual mastering engineer in the fact that some of them happen to be located in the same location, rather than a city by city thing.

What do you think makes a great mastering engineer? What differentiates somebody that's great as opposed to somebody that's merely competent?
BK: Great attention to detail and extreme persnicketyness, stick to it-iveness, and discipline. The desire to just keep working at it until it's as good as the sound that you have in your mind, and to keep trying different things if you're not satisfied. I will bend over backward to get something right, even if I have to do it off the clock. Not to say that I don't charge for my time, but if I make a mistake or I feel that I could've done it better, the client will always get my best results.

As good as you have in your mind. Does that mean that before you start a project, you have an idea where you're going with it?
BK: I think that another thing that distinguishes a good mastering engineer from an okay mastering engineer is that the more experienced you are, the more you have an idea of how far you can take something when you hear it and pretty much where you'd like to go with it, as opposed to experimenting with ten different pieces of gear until it seems to sound good to you. That distinguishes a great mastering engineer from an okay mastering engineer in the sense that you'll work more efficiently that way. That's not to say that there aren't surprises. We're always surprised to find that, "Gee, this sounds better than I thought it would," or, "Gee, that box that I didn't think would work proved to be pretty good." And sometimes we will often experiment and say, "Let's see what that box does." So it's a combination of not being so closed minded that you won't try new things, but having enough experi-

ence to know that this set of tools that you have at your command will probably be good tools to do the job before even trying it. Also, a real good sense of pitch and where the frequencies of music are allows you to zero in on frequency-based problems much faster than if you have a tin ear.

It's hard to be in this business if you have a tin ear...

BK: True, but I know a lot of medium level people who get away without that degree of precision. There is another area, and that is the ability to be a chameleon and get along incredibly well with all different kinds of people from all walks of life. If someone brings in a type of music toward which I'm not necessarily inclined, I'll psyche myself up and do pretty well with it, but I think that there are other people out there who perhaps do that even better than I do. So, being a chameleon and being adaptable and versatile is what distinguishes a great mastering engineer from an okay one.

What's the hardest thing that you have to do?

BK: Make a silk purse out of a sow's ear. It's a lot easier to take something that comes in at an A-minus and turn it into an A-plus than to take something that comes in as a B-minus and turn that into an A. That is the hardest thing I have to do.

The next hardest thing is to teach my clients that less is more. When they're preparing their work to send to me, and also when I'm working on it, we'll often go in a big circle. I may know in my head that putting three different compressors in a row isn't going to make it better, but when they suggest it, I'll never refuse their suggestions. When it's all done though, they usually realize that passing it through less is more. The exception being that Phil Spector kind of approach where you think that more is more, but in that case the purity of the sound is less important than the bigness and the fuzziness and all the other things that it does. That's not necessarily my kind of sound anyway. I'd rather make something sound really good and clean than good and dirty if I can.

What kind of project do you enjoy the most?

BK: Music that is acoustic-based. That doesn't mean that they don't have electric instruments, but there are musicians playing together and the music's been performed all at the same time with few overdubs. I love those kinds of projects because I can really make them shine. Fortunately, people seek me out for that stuff so I tend to attract that. It keeps me off the charts though, darn it.

What makes your job easier?

BK: This is almost becoming a ubiquitous answer, but I have to say that if I get the highest resolution, highest sample rate, earliest generation, uncut, unedited by anyone (or if they do cut it, leave the heads and tails alone) version, then things are easier. Unfortunately, I get more and more chopped up material these days.

Today I just finished a CD for Telarc that's an interesting record. It's a children's record, and Meryl Streep does the voiceover in a number of places. Now, they left her dry so if I needed to add reverb to put in-between sections, I could do pretty much anything I wanted. But there were three cuts where they mixed the voiceover with the music, and when I finally put the CD in, three of the four worked fine in context with the songs they came in front of and after. But on the fourth one, the original mix engineer chose to mix the music fairly low against the voice and after she finished talking, brought the music up to a certain level. When it was put in context in the mastering against the song before and the song after, the music was too low but the voice sounded at the right level when placed at the proper level to fit to the cut before.

I was stuck with a problem of the music being too low. So in my first revision I sent to them, I cheated the music up gradually after Meryl stops speaking, but not enough, because the cheat doesn't sound as good as if I had gotten separate elements and had been able to cheat the music up underneath without raising the voice.

So, what I am leading to is that you run into certain situations that are special or different. The problem is that many mix engineers don't know what is special or different. It's good to consult with the mastering engineer ahead of time, and in this case I would have said, "Send me the elements. Don't mix it, because when you finally put an album together in context is when you'll discover that you may need the separate elements." I think that the future of mastering increasingly will involve some mixing.

So you'd be getting stems essentially.

BK: More often, and as we move to surround, we're going to be getting stems. I think that even two-track mastering will start moving into stems if we can ever standardize on a multitrack format.

If you get program material in that's already been edited (and of course a lot of times what they do is they chop the fades), does that mean that you have to use outboard effects sometimes in order to help that along? And if so, how often do you have to do that?

BK: More often than I'd like to. But sometimes the fixes are so good that the guys never realize how much they screwed it up when they brought it to me. I've always been a great editor and that always helps. If you're good at editing, you can supply artificial decays at the end of songs with a little reverb and a careful Sonic Solutions crossfade that's indistinguishable from real life.

At the head of things, it's not as easy. The biggest problem with the head-fades is that people just cut it off. The breath at the beginning of a vocal is sometimes very important. I think part of it is that, number one, they don't have the experience with actual editing over the years and don't recognize it as being an important part of the engineer's art. And number two, if you have a system such as Sonic or SADiE, you have great flexibility with crossfades. You realize that you can do things that other people can't, which is to carefully massage a breath at the beginning of a piece so that it sounds natural. But if you cut something, and not just the breath but something which I guess we would call the air around the instruments prior to the downbeat, it doesn't sound natural.

And how to fix that? Well, I'm not sure I can give a general answer. It's a lot easier to talk about how to fix fadeouts and end fades than it is to fix beginnings. The bottom line is, send us the loose material. If a client has a real good idea on the fadeout that they want to do, fine. Then send us both versions; the faded and the nonfaded. That way, if it proves to be a problem in context, we can still use the unfaded version.

What piece of gear are you using to help the fadeouts?

BK: Being a naturalistic engineer over the years, the first digital reverb that I really felt sounded natural was the EMT 250 and its variations. Anyway, they got smaller and smaller and finally made a 32-bit unit that is only two U high that had the same sounds in it [EMT 252]. That was the first digital reverb that I felt sounded very natural, but I couldn't afford it at the time. So I was always searching for a poor man's EMT and renting them whenever I needed one.

A reverb chamber is used surprisingly a lot in mastering to help unify the sound between things. I might use it on 5 percent of all my jobs. So, I still needed a pretty good unit. Then I discovered the Sony V77, which is already obsolete (in Sony's typical way). After you spend a couple of hours fine-tuning it, it can sound just like an EMT.

I've heard that from other people as well.

BK: It is really good. Now we're not talking about things that immediately attract people to a Lexicon, like smoothness and lack of flutter echo. Those are basic things that anybody can put into a reverb. What distinguishes the EMT and the V77 from the rest of the pack is the ability to simulate a space and depth. I've gotten it down so quickly that I can supply tails with a combination of Sonic and a few keystrokes in the verb and it's all patched in in a matter of a minute or less for any tail.

What's the ratio of tape to DAT that you get in?

BK: It's bad and getting worse. It's up to about 70 percent DAT verses 30 percent half-inch now. But here's the good thing. Many of the customers that used to send me DATs are now using cheap digital mixing consoles and bring the signal into the computer at 24 bits and cut me a CD-ROM. So as a result it's become more like 40 percent DAT, 30 percent 24-bit files, and the other 30 percent half-inch analog.

Perfect segue for this part. What is your signal path like? Do you have an analog and a digital signal path?

BK: Yes, but I'm a purist, and I try to avoid doing an additional conversion whenever possible. The logical place to do analog EQ is when an analog source comes in. My analog path starts with a custom-built set of Ampex MR70 electronics, which in my opinion is the best playback electronics that Ampex ever invented. They were designed to be mastering EQs and there were only a thousand built. It has four bands of EQ itself; a high shelf, a high peak and dip, low shelf and a low peak, and dip for the playback at 15 or 30 ips. I have that connected to a Studer C37 classic 1964 vintage transport with the extended low-frequency heads that John French put in made by Flux Magnetics. It's just real transparent and not tubey-sounding at all, just open and clean. And nothing ever goes through a patch bay. It's all custom patched.

Usually, I try to avoid any analog compression at that stage, and I try to make the tape sound as great as possible with either its own EQ or through the Millennia Media (NSEQ-2) so it's just real transparent. That goes directly, with a pair of short Mogami cables, into my A/D converter. So that's my analog chain. I don't have any other analog processing. I built a compressor once, but after playing around with the Waves Renaissance compressor and a few other digital compressors, I'm convinced that I'm just as happy staying in the digital domain once I'm already there. So at that point I convert with the best analog EQ possible, and the rest of the processing is done digitally after it's in Sonic.

Is most of your processing done prior to the workstation?

BK: I think that there are two different types of engineers. I'd like to think the old-fashioned and the new-fashioned, but that's my slant on it. There are the engineers who like to process during load-in, and there are the engineers who like to process on load-out. Many engineers will set up an entire chain, either analog or digital or a hybrid of both, and process on load-in, and then if it doesn't work in context, they'll go back and reprocess and then load it in again.

I find that to be a very inefficient way of working so I'm really puzzled why they put themselves through this. The most I will do with the analog tape, as I said, is go through this great EQ on load-in only because I don't want to go through another conversion again. After that, I favor having as many processors automated as possible. It just shocks me that there aren't that many mastering engineers who work that way.

I think that as the years go on, more and more mastering engineers will be working my way. I think they'll have to. When you start getting into surround, I think it's just going to become the norm. It's very much like the way you work with an automated mixing console

What format do you deliver mostly to the replicator?
BK: Five percent 1630 over here. Most of what I send out are DDPs.

How about PMCDs?
BK: Oh, they suck, but I do it whenever it's requested. First of all, PMCD is, for all intents and purposes, just hype. The term stands for premastered CD. Way back in the Dark Ages when 1630 was the only format, Sonic Solutions was looking for a solution whereby a compact disc could be made to look like a 1630 and therefore be used as a master. They took the same PQ information that you put on the cue track of the 1630 tape and used a portion of the CD-R at the outer rim at the end of the track (as we know, CDs are recorded from inside to outside), to put the PQ burst. This was then defined as the PMCD. The rest of the system only existed at this point at a couple of plants, some of them owned by Sony, and what they do is make the system look like a 1630. They put the PMCD into a CD-ROM reader, they read the PQ burst off the end track of

the PMCD, and then they run the laser beam recorder as if a 1630 were running. From that point on, it's just playing back the regular CD-ROM as if it were a 1630 and having read the PQ code as if it had been read off the head of the 3/4-inch tape.

This system does not exist any more at 99.9 percent of all the plants in the world. The reason is that Doug Carson Associates, the inventors of the DDP protocol, found a way of taking an ordinary CD-ROM reader, reading the table of contents at the head of every CD, and using that to generate the PQ codes rather than reading a PQ burst on the end of the PMCD. So, in reality, when Sonic Solutions users make a PMCD, the portion which distinguishes it from an ordinary CD, that little tiny burst at the outside rim, isn't being used. And that is the only thing that distinguishes a PMCD from an ordinary Orange Book CD-R. So, in reality, we've been saying PMCD to impress the public, but it's really just hype at this point.

How important is mono to you?

BK: I forget to listen in mono more often than I intend to. I have good enough ears to detect when something is out of phase; it just sounds weird in the middle. In fact, I'm usually the first person walking into a stereo demo saying, "Hey, your speakers are out of phase." So I usually don't have that much of a problem with mono, but I'm always using a phase correlation meter and an oscilloscope to make sure things are cool. If I see something that looks funny, then I'll switch to mono. But, half the time I just look at the scope and listen and won't switch these days.

Do you ever normalize?

BK: "Normalize" is very dangerous term. I think it should be destroyed as a word because it's so ambiguous. If you mean, do I ever use the Sonic Solutions normalize functions so that all the tracks get set to the highest peak level, the answer is no. Or do I ever use TC Electronics Finalizer normalize function to find the highest peak and bring it up to 0 dB? No, I never do that. Do I use my ears and adjust the levels from track to track so that they fit from one to the other, then use compressors and limiters and expanders and equalizers and other devices to make sure that the highest peak on the album hits 0 dB FS? Yes, I do. I don't call that normalizing, though.

Tell me why you don't do it.
BK: I'll give you two reasons. I advise my clients not to do it and I've written about it extensively on my Web site, "Seven Reasons Why You Shouldn't Normalize." The first one has to do with just good old-fashioned signal deterioration. Every DSP operation costs something in terms of sound quality. It gets grainier, colder, narrower, and harsher. Adding a generation of normalization is just taking it down one generation.

The second reason is that normalization doesn't accomplish anything. The ear responds to average level and not peak levels and there is no machine that can read peak levels and judge when something is equally loud.

Tell me how you came about choosing your monitors. And then, how you would suggest someone else go about it?
BK: Let's start with the first question, which is a lot easier to answer. A great monitor in a bad room does absolutely nothing for you, so if you don't start with a terrific room and a plan for how it will integrate with the monitors, you can forget about it. No matter what you do, they will still suck and you will still have problems, so let's just say that I first started out by designing a great room.

The first test that anyone should do for a system is called the LEDR test. It stands for Listening Environment Diagnostic Recording and was invented by Doug Jones of Northeastern University. Basically he determined the frequency response of the ear from different angles and heights. Then he simulated the frequency response of a cabasa if it's over your head, to your left, behind you, beside you, in the middle, and also beyond the speakers. In other words, from at least a foot to the left of the left speaker, over to at least a foot to the right speaker, all done with comb filtering that simulates the response of what the ears would hear.

The LEDR test is a substitute for about 30 to 40,000 dollars worth of test equipment. If the sound for the up image doesn't go straight up from your loudspeaker, six feet in the air as you sit there in your position, then you've got a problem with your crossover or with reflections above the loudspeaker. If the sound doesn't travel from left to right evenly and smoothly with the left to right test, then you've got problems with objects between your loudspeakers. And the same with the beyond signal, which is supposed to go from about one foot to the left of the left speaker, gradually over to one foot to the right of the right speaker, which detects reflections from the side wall.

So the first thing you should ever do as an engineer is to familiarize yourself with the LEDR test, which is available on Chesky Test CD, JD-37, and also on the ProSonus Test CD which is about 50 dollars more. Just test your speakers and room with the LEDR test. And believe me, if you ever want to know how bad it can sound, just take a pair of cheap bookshelf loudspeakers and play the LEDR test through it and see what happens. It also shows how bad the lateral image is if you take a pair of monitors and put them on their sides with the tweeter and the woofer to the left and right of each other as opposed to vertically.

So my room passes the LEDR test impeccably, so then it comes to the choice of loudspeakers. The speakers I chose are made in Switzerland by a man named Daniel Dehay. They're called Reference 3As (**www.reference3a.com**) and they are your classic two-way high-quality audiophile loudspeakers. I'm sure that there are about half a dozen high-quality audiophile equivalents from other manufacturers that can do just as well, but the whole thing is that these do not have a crossover per se; the woofer is directly connected to a pair of terminals in back of the speaker, and the tweeter goes through a simple RC crossover. They're wired to my Hafler amplifier. The woofer is an eight-inch speaker, and it's ported in the back, and the speaker has a really tight clean response down to about 50Hz.

The Mastering Engineer's Handbook

With an eight-inch?

BK: Yeah, the guy did a really nice job. It's really an excellent speaker, the Reference 3A. They can only be bought in Canada right now. I don't think there is a U.S. distributor. But like I say, you can find some things that are reasonably equivalent. Right now, if somebody would ask me for a recommendation, I'd say PMC or the Dynaudio and so on. Anyway, these speakers play loudly and cleanly without a problem since they have a 93dB sensitivity. To top of it off then, I have a pair of Genesis Servo subwoofers and they have their own crossover amplifier. There is no separate high-pass or Bass Management type of device on these speakers. I let the main speakers roll off with their own natural rolloff, and then I carefully adjust the subs to meet seamlessly with them. I could go on, but I think that covers it.

You're running stereo subwoofers.

BK: Right. That's absolutely essential.

What are you using for a console?

BK: Aha! Mostly, you mean, for EQing and leveling and stuff?

Are you using a console at all?

BK: No. I've never been impressed with the whole console concept. Most of the time I take the signal through the Sonic Solutions desk at 24 bits with the Sonic set for unity gain so that it doesn't do any calculations. I don't like the EQs in Sonic. I'll use them for certain patches if I have to, but even the high-pass filter in Sonic has its own characteristic sound on the high end.

The first thing that it feeds, nine times out of ten, is the Z-Systems equalizer. Then I patch various forms of external outboard digital gear using the Z-Systems digital patch bay and eventually bring it right back into Sonic and cut the CD master from the Sonics M1-M2 outputs.

How do you adjust the control room level?

BK: I have an audiophile Counterpoint D/A converter with Ultra Analog Module and it sounds as good as the Mark Levinson or one of those similar quality D to As. I went into the Counterpoint and installed a stepped attenuator with metal film resistors at an interstage point. That is my volume control. It's calibrated in 1dB steps, and the output of the DAC feeds my power amp directly. It is the cleanest, purest signal path that you've ever heard. So I have no preamp or no console, and I'm using absolute minimalist circuitry.

Well, I think the whole console concept is really a throwback to the lacquer days anyway.
BK: Yeah, where you need a preview and all that stuff. Well, as we get into surround, we're going to need some console features. Mastering engineers are getting away from the console concept, although people like Bernie [Grundman] and Dave Collins will build a purist high-quality console because they want to do analog processing. I'll simulate that by patching gear one into the other into the other with short cable.

There are definitely two schools of thought on this.
BK: Yeah, they are real purists. But it just reminded me of something. I've been in many mastering studios and almost every mastering engineer that I know of sits in front of some kind of a table, which sits at some height, with maybe a monitor in front of him. And then six or eight or nine feet in front of him are his stereo loudspeakers. As far as I'm concerned, there is some compromise there. Now anything that breaks into the listening triangle between my ears and my monitors is verboten in my studio.

My solution is that I have a listening couch where I and/or my clients sit, which is exactly like a high quality audiophile living room listening environment. We have the perfect 60 degree triangle there, with nothing in between except the floor and the side walls which are far away from interference from the monitors. It's a reflection-free zone. Then behind the couch is the back of the display of my Sonic Solutions workstation. When I want to edit or do some preliminary setup or segues, I go back there and do my primary work. It keeps my heart working. I get up, walk to the couch, sit down, listen, and go back. I don't EQ from back there though, which prevents me from making those awful immediate judgments that are so often problems. Too many highs, well, listen for a few minutes. "Oh, wait a minute. That was just the big climax with the cymbal crash."

I have a Mac PowerBook sitting on the arm of the couch connected by Ethernet to the rest of the system. I can remote control the Z-Systems equalizer from the arm of the couch, start and stop Sonic, or switch the Sonic desk between its record and playback desks which allows me to monitor two different digital paths. So I can effectively insert or remove any set of equipment from my chain at the critical listening point without having any interfering tables or consoles in the way. Just a pair of function keys on the PowerBook over there sitting on my right. Can you picture it? You're sitting there on the couch, your right arm is off to your right, and you just push a little button on a little portable computer sitting on the arm of the couch. And that's it.

After having worked on hundreds of platinum and gold records and mastered projects that have been nominated for scores of Grammys, Bob Ludwig certainly stands among the giants in the mastering business. After leaving New York City to open his own Gateway Mastering in Portland, Maine, in 1993, Bob has proved that you can still be in the center of the media without being in a media center.

What do you think is the difference between someone who's merely competent and someone who's really great as a mastering engineer?

BL: I always say that the secret of being a great mastering engineer is being able to hear a raw tape and then in your mind hear what it could sound like, and then know what knobs to move to make it sound that way.

You know where you're going right from the beginning then, right?

BL: Pretty much. It's a little bit like the Bob Clearmountain school, where after 45 minutes of mixing he's practically there and then spends most of the rest of the day just fine-tuning that last 10 percent. I think I can get 90 percent of the way there sometimes in a couple of minutes and just keep hanging with it and keep fine-tuning it from there. It comes very, very fast to me when I hear something. I immediately can tell what I think it should sound like. And the frustration is, sometimes you get what I call a "pristine piece of crap." I call it that because it's like a bad mix, and anything you do to it will make it worse in some other way. But 99.9 percent of the time I hear something and I can figure out what it needs, and fortunately I know what all my gear does well enough to make it happen.

Like today, I was doing something while training one of the guys that works with me. I put this song up and said, "I know this piece of gear would be perfect for this thing." He said, "Man, I haven't seen you use that in like nine months or a year." I said, "I know it's gonna be great." I fired it up, plugged it in and boom, it was right there.

How many of your sessions are attended?

BL: When I started my own business after working at Masterdisk and Sterling Sound before that, our business plan called for a 20 percent reduction in overall business, but the opposite actually happened. We thought that half the people that had attended sessions in New York would attend up here. It turns out more people attend sessions here than in New York, which was a total surprise.

Why do you think that is?

BL: I'm not sure. To tell you the truth, I think a lot of people have heard about the effort we've gone through to make our room as acoustically perfect as possible. And they know that we've got speakers that retail for $100,000 a pair, so a lot of people just want to come and see what it's about.

It's a real pleasure. So many times people come into the room and they go, "Oh, my God!" or something like that. It's a trip to get that kind of reaction from people. When I was at Sterling and at Masterdisk, everybody thought I owned those companies but I never did, and to me it was always frustrating that I was always dependent on my employers dictating my conditions. That was one of the reasons I left. I felt that if I stayed in New York, I'd never be able to have a room that was acoustically as perfect as we knew how to make it. I don't know about the new place, but Sterling and Masterdisk always were in high rises, so you're always limited to very low ceiling rooms. But in order to get as near perfect a situation as possible, you actually need a fairly large shell that's at least 30 feet long and accommodates a 17- or 18-foot high ceiling.

Do you think that there's a difference between the way people master from coast to coast?

BL: I don't think there's so much a difference between coast to coast as there is just between some of the major personalities in mastering. Some engineers might master almost everything into the analog domain because they love working with analog gear. I certainly do that sometimes, but I would say that I've tried to accumulate what I think is the very best new gear as well as funky old gear that has a certain sound. If a tape comes in sounding really, really good, I have gear that will stay out of the way and do exactly what I need without inflicting any damage on the thing at all.

Occasionally we'll get a tape in that's so good that I'm just happy to change the level on it if needed. The level controls I have are made by Massenburg and some engineers over at Sony are as audiophile as you can get. If you're not using the level control, you can take it out of the circuitry so it's as much a straight wire as possible so at least I'm convinced I'm inflicting as little damage as possible on a great sounding tape if all it needs is simply a level change.

Is that in the digital or analog domain?

BL: Analog. Talking about different engineers, there are some engineers that just like to slam the hell out of everything. It seems like their only criteria is how loud they can make it, not how musical they can make it. And for me, I'm under pressure from A&R people and clients to have things loud, but I try to keep the music at all costs. I'll think nothing of doing a Foo Fighters record one day where it's totally appropriate to have it smashed, then the next day do something that's perhaps even 4dB quieter than that because it suddenly needs the dynamics for it to breathe.

The dynamics wars...where did that come from?

BL: I think it came from the invention of digital domain compressors. When digital first came out, people knew that every time the light when into the overs or into the red that you were clipping, and that hasn't changed.

We're all afraid of the over levels, so people started inventing these digital domain compressors where you could just start cranking the level up. Because it was in the digital domain, you could look ahead in the circuit and have a theoretical zero attack time or even have a negative attack time if you wanted to. It was able to do things that you couldn't do with any piece of analog gear, including an Aphex Compellor or [Empirical Labs] Distresser. It will give you that kind of an apparent level increase without audibly destroying the music, up to a point. And of course, once they achieved that, then people started pushing it as far as it would go. I would say the average level of a CD has peaks on a VU meter that are at least 3.5dB hotter than they used to be, if not as much as 6dB hotter than they used to be.

I always tell people, "Thank God these things weren't invented when the Beatles were around because for sure they would've put it on their music and would've destroyed its longevity." I'm totally convinced that overcompression destroys the longevity of a piece. Now when someone's insisting on hot levels where it's not really appropriate, I find I can barely make it through the mastering session.

Another thing that has contributed to it is the fact that in Nashville, the top 200 country stations get serviced with records from the record company, but apparently there's some kind of an agreement that the major record companies have for stations 201 on up to get serviced with a special CD every week that has the different label's new singles on it.

It's called CDX. Glenn Meadows does that.
BL: And of course, when they started doing that, the A&R people would go, "Well, how come my record isn't as loud as this guy's record?" And so that further led to level wars even in Nashville, so that everyone's record would be the hottest record on the compilation. And of course when the program director of the radio station is going through a stack of CDs, a mediocre song that's twice as loud as a great song might at first seem more impressive, just because it grabs you by the neck. It has a certain impressiveness about it so you listen to it before realizing there's no song there, but at least on first listen it might get the program director's attention.

I suppose that's well and good when it's a single for radio, but when you give that treatment to an entire album's worth of material, it's just exhausting. It's a very unnatural situation. Never in the history of mankind has man listened to such compressed music as we listen to now.

In mixing too, if you don't put bus compressors on, or if you don't compress something, clients inevitably say, "Why are you not doing that? That's what I want." You can't get into trouble if you squash something, but you can if you don't.

BL: I know some very famous mixers that complain to me about A&R people who will not accept their mixes unless they already sound as though they had been mastered, already devoid of any dynamic range.

Do you think we've reached the limit of that?

BL: Yeah, I honestly do, because we're not that far away from music dynamics approaching steady-state tone! If you look at many of today's CDs on a digital level meter, the peak levels barely go lower than the maximum. It would be a steady stream of digital overlevels if the digital domain compressors didn't artificially prevent the red Over light from coming on. It's difficult to believe that it could be compressed much more than it is now. That's why I'm so excited about 5.1 because there's no radio competition, at least for this year anyway.

How do you see the mastering room of the future? How do you see surround affecting mastering in general?

BL: I think it's going to make for very long weeks. Already we're starting to do more and more projects where they are both stereo and 5.1, and each one of them is a long day. Fortunately most of the 5.1 stuff that I've been doing has been mixed by really good engineers so the projects have been coming out sounding really great.

The 96/24 multichannel tools are starting to come, and hopefully we're going to get these tools by the time we start to get some of the bad mixes that really need some help. And believe me, those are coming. I've seen more and more engineers doing their first 5.1 mix and I don't know how it was for you, but usually your first 5.1 mix isn't as good as your last one.

I have done projects where the engineers have treated the LFE as a true LFE—no effects in the music, thus nothing fed to the LFE. Then we get requests from A&R people asking us to create something to put in the subwoofer just for marketing purposes!

I was speaking with a very famous mixer when I was out in Las Vegas for CES. He was telling me how he's listened to all these 5.1 mixes that people were making, and his opinion was that they weren't putting nearly enough stuff into the subwoofer. He was putting the bass instrument into the subwoofer alone, none on the main speakers as usual, to the point where if you turned the LFE off, there was no bass in his mix at all! And I said, "Do you realize that when Dolby Digital folds down to two channels that there's no subwoofer in that fold down?" He says, "No."

Do you find mastering surround is more difficult?

BL: It's more difficult right now because of the lack of tools and having to make up for tools that don't exist quite yet. Like if someone came in said, "Boy, this mix is too dry, I need five channels of reverb added," I'd really have to scramble to do that with the present tools until the M6000 or somebody else's comes out. Part of it is a lot easier in that I think you need less compression for it to sound great. I think it's easier to mix because you're not trying to jam everything into two channels, and because of that freedom, it seems like we need less equalization too. That part of it's been good. I don't know how many projects I've done, but it's really quite a lot now between DTS and all the DVD stuff. At first I tried it on an O2R, then I did it on a Neve modified Logic 3 before I finally settled into the Daniel Weiss, the TC Electronics stuff, and some Waves things that I'm using.

You mentioned people asking you to add reverb and effects. Does that happen often?

BL: Oh yeah, it happens often enough. A lot of people assemble mixes on ProTools, and they don't listen to it carefully enough when they're compiling their mix, and they actually cut off the tails of their own mixes. You can't believe how often that happens. So a lot of times we'll use a little 480L to just fade out their chopped off endings and extend naturally. I do a fair amount of classical music mastering and very often a little bit of reverb is needed on those projects. Sometimes if there's an edit that for some reason just won't work, you can smear it with a bit of echo at the right point and get past it. Sometimes mixes come in that are just dry as a bone and a small amount of judicious reverb can really help that out. We definitely need it often enough that we've got a 480L in our place and it gets used probably once every week.

What is the ratio of analog-to-digital source masters that you get in?

BL: I would say it's pretty much about 65 or 70 percent analog, which is fine with me. Pretty much the rule that I found is that if someone's mixing on a 16-bit DAT, especially one with internal converters, the analog tape will almost always sound better if it's made on a decent analog machine. But at 88.2/96kHz, it's often a toss up. Sometimes the digital sounds better; sometimes the analog sounds better. A lot of it depends on who the mixer is. Some of the premier mixers like Bob Clearmountain get exactly what they want on digital tape. He sends me stuff at 88.2/24-bit and I'm sure it's a very, very close match to what comes out of his console.

For most engineers, analog tape serves as wonderful kind of acoustic glue that sounds better than the output of the console. Analog is very forgiving, and our ears really seem to love it. We place a lot of attention on analog at our place. We've got six different ways of playing back analog tape. We've got a stock Studer A820. We've got a Studer that's got Cello class A audiophile electronics. We've got a stock ATR, a tube ATR, and an unbalanced ATR. We also have one of the Tim de Paravicini one-inch two-track machines with his fantastic tube electronics. When you record with his custom EQ curve at 15 ips, it's basically flat from eight cycles up to 28kHz. It's unbelievable. You put an MRL test tape on his machine and it comes back zero VU all the way.

Do you get a lot of stuff in that is bit-split or ROM files that are 24-bit?

BL: Yes, both. We primarily get bit-split tapes. It used to be the Prism and the Paqrat boxes but nowadays it's almost all Apogee PSX-100 or the AD-8000. Lately we've been getting more and more CD-ROMs that have ProTools 24-bit mixes. And of course we've been getting 24-bit Sonic Solutions mixes for years. ProTools is still far away from catching up with Sonic Solutions' ability to handle 192kHz/24-bit files.

Is that what you're using for a workstation, Sonics?

BL: Yes. When I was at Masterdisk, I think we were the first studio on the East Coast to buy Sonic Solutions (I think it was release 0.9 or something like that) and so I've been with them ever since.

Tell me about your monitors.

BL: I used to have Duntech Sovereign 2001 monitors. I think around '86 when I was at Masterdisk, I decided to find the best monitors I could so that when I was working on digital I would have something that could really reproduce subsonic defects. So I went down to New York to some of the audiophile shops to see what kind of audiophile speakers I might be able to find for mastering that would be professional enough that I wouldn't have to change the tweeter every other day.

I found these Duntech Sovereign 2001 speakers. Tom Jung, the engineer that owns the DMP label, had a pair at his house in the basement. His basement had very low ceilings. The Duntech speakers are in a mirror image arrangement; the tweeter is in the middle and then there are the midrange speakers and then there are the woofers on the top of the speaker and the bottom. So in the basement of his house, that upper woofer was coupling with his ceiling as well as the bottom one coupling with the floor and he had bass for days. So he sold me his pair of Duntechs, and that's what I used at Masterdisk from then on.

I also bought one of the first Cello Performance amplifiers from Mark Levinson when he was there at the time, and subsequently he told me that somebody in Japan had actually bridged a pair of these things and it was really worthwhile. Of course his amps are mega expensive, so he loaned me another pair so I could try to bridge them together. Doug Levine, who ran Masterdisk and was in charge of all the money, could actually hear the difference between the bridging and the nonbridging enough that he thought it was worth spending the extra money on it.

Then when I started Gateway, I got another pair of Duntech Sovereigns and a new pair of Cello Performance Mark II amplifiers this time. These are the amps that will put out like 6,000 watt peaks. One never listens that loudly, but when you listen, it sounds as though there's an unlimited source of power attached to the speakers. You're never straining the amp, ever. So I used those Duntechs for quite a while.

Then when I began doing 5.1 surround music, Peter McGrath, a classical engineer friend of mine, had fallen in love with these Eggelston Works Andras speakers that are made in Memphis. Bill Eggelston has been designing speakers for many years and Peter told me that he thought those were the best speakers that he had heard at the time. Peter used to own an audiophile hi-fi shop and he's heard everything under the sun. As he's a very good classical engineer; I give what he says a lot of credence. So I had made it a point to seek them out. I really fell in love with these Andras and for the 5.1 music, I use five of them. They retail for around $14,000 a pair, and I have 2-1/2 pairs of them. They were *Stereophile* magazine's Speaker of the Year. With five of them in the room, they move plenty of air with no problem whatsoever, but I felt that there needed to be a bigger speaker to work right in stereo.

I told Bill Eggelston if he ever decided to build a bigger version of the Andras to let me know and maybe I'd consider changing my Duntechs if I thought they sounded better. He decided to build what he thought was the ultimate speaker, which is called the Eggelston Works Ivy speaker (he names all of his speakers after former wives or girlfriends). These speakers are a little bit taller than Duntechs and they weigh close to 800 pounds a piece. They've got granite on the sides of them. There's three woofers on the bottom, a couple of mids, the tweeter, and then a couple of more mids on the top. Actually, each cabinet had 23 speakers in it.

You know how M&K uses the isobaric principle in their subwoofer? The Eggleston Works Andras use that same isobaric principle in their woofers. Well, Bill extended that principle to all of the speakers, so behind each speaker is two others. I guess if the isobaric principle is carried out to purity, you'd have an infinite number of speakers. But he has two behind each of them and they're amazing. Every client that comes in, once they tune in to what they're listening to, starts commenting on how they're hearing things in their mixes that they had never heard before, even sometimes after working weeks on them. It's great for mastering because they're just so accurate that there's never much doubt as to what's really on the tape.

One reason I've always tried to get the very best speaker I can is I've found that when something sounds really right on an accurate speaker, it tends to sound right on a wide variety of speakers. I've never been a big fan of trying to get things to sound only right on an NS-10Ms.

Do you listen only with that one set of monitors or do you listen to near-fields?

BL: Primarily just the big ones because they tell you everything, but I do have a set of NS-10Ms and some Proacs and stuff like that. Lower resolution near-fields have their place. In the case of the NS-10Ms, the reason we have them there is just so the client can hear what he thought he had on tape! The NS-10M kind of dials in a little bit more reverb than you think you have and more punch than is really there. When I'm teaching people, I make sure that they listen on NS-10s and Proacs and speakers like that a lot so they can learn in their head how to translate from one to the other.

Do you still cut lacquers?

BL: We do. We still have a lathe. We just did an audiophile release for Classic Records, the Springsteen *Born to Run* vinyl record, which got very good reviews.

But we're thinking of closing the cutting lathe down. The reason is that I think with the mergers at the major record labels, a lot of the A&R people now just don't relate to vinyl anymore and they're starting to treat the vinyl lacquer cutting process as if it was like CD manufacturing. They ask, "Why do I need a reference disc?" Or, "Why do I need a test pressing?" They think, "Isn't it just a transfer?"

They're so illiterate when it comes to vinyl records that we found that if the plants ever mess something up, the record company would never know it. It's just too frustrating for me now. I don't want my name going out on a product that is not going to be subjected to normal quality control. And as you know, when you cut a lacquer, you never hear it back. So if something went wrong, there's fewer quality control people out there that care to find the problem any more.

Do you think that having experience cutting lacquers helps you now in the digital domain?

BL: It does. I'm certainly more concerned about compatibility issues than a lot of the mixers are, especially as more people are getting into either Q-Sound or other kinds of synthetic ways of generating outside-of-the-speaker sound. Some people just get into this and don't realize that their piano solo is gone in mono. It just happened to me recently. A very famous artist came in and the piano solo has this wild spatial effect on it, and the piano is just not there when you listen in mono, so I had to point it out to them. And much to my surprise, they said, "We don't really care." Well, people do still listen in mono, but some artists just don't seem to be bothered by the lack of compatibility. Nevertheless, I'm probably more hypersensitive to sibilance problems than I would otherwise be if I hadn't cut a lot of discs.

Does that mean you listen in mono a lot still?

BL: I certainly check in mono. We have correlation meters on our consoles. Even though my room is huge, Q-Sound works perfectly in it on the large speakers because the first reflections are so well controlled. So any time there are Q-Sound like effects, one can hear it in a jiffy. In my room, if you're sitting in the sweet spot and flip the phase on one of the speakers, the entire bass goes away. It's almost as if you were doing it electronically. So you can hear any phase problems instantly and then of course you just monitor in mono. Plus, I have the ability to monitor L minus R as well to hear the difference channel if I need to.

What are you delivering to the replicator these days?

BL: Still mostly 1630s. When the 1630 was invented, I remember all the guys on the West Coast screaming about how awful it was. And now that plants are doing 4X cutting and glass mastering off of CD-Rs, that 1630 is like the Holy Grail of professional audio. The fact is that the error rate is very low on it and you can computer verify it with a DTA 2000 to make sure that everything is precisely just as you want. And if you send it to a replicator that still has a 1630 and insist on doing it single-speed, you might get a CD back that sounds something like what you sent to the plant.

That's a huge problem—replicators that want CD-Rs or DDP Exabyte so that they can glass master at 4X. They treat it like CD-ROM material and it just doesn't work well to do it that way.

Tell me about your signal path.

BL: In the analog domain, it goes from the tape machine into George Massenburg/Sony electronics that are as minimal and audiophile as one can get. The output of that goes into either a dCS, Pacific Microsonics, or sometimes Apogee analog-to-digital converter. When I need other outboard gear, we've got Neumann EQs, and NTP and Manley compressors. Between the Manley, NTP, and digital domain compressors, that normally fills the bill for me, but I do have some Aphex Compellors. In the digital domain I have all the Weiss 96/24 stuff. The bw102, which has the 96kHz de-esser in it as well, is complete with a mixer, compressor, and equalization.

We use a lot of the Waves products because they are 48-bit internally and sound good. If you have to do work in ProTools, using the Waves components will sometimes get you an OK sound because they have their own DAE [Digital Audio Engine] that isn't subject to the crunch of ProTools as much.

I know that once I used ProTools as just a level control and found that just raising the level 6dB sounded not so good on ProTools but sounded okay with the Weiss controls. It's amazing. I think that ProTools is okay to record to and store music on and play it back, but for optimal quality I think one should mix on something else.

Do you have a Waves L2?

BL: Yeah, we have three of the production units and one of the beta versions right now. We also have SPL units and before that we had the Junger units.

What's the hardest thing that you have to do? Is there a certain type of music or project that's particularly difficult?

BL: I think the most difficult thing is when the artist is going through the period where they just can't let go of the project. You get into the psychological thing where in the same sentence they say, "I want you to make the voice more predominant, but make sure it doesn't stick out." Just contradictory things like that. They'll say, "This mix is too bright," and then you'll dull it up like half a dB and they say, "Oh, it doesn't have any air any more." It's that kind of thing.

Letting go is so hard for some artists. One of my favorite artists is Bruce Springsteen. I think he realizes mastering means he has to finally let go of the record and crystallize it. I think, unlike new artists, he has the ability to put out the record exactly as he wants to, and I've seen him live with records for a long time as a result. And in his case, he's correct in not putting it out until he is completely happy.

Do you have a specific approach to mastering?

BL: To me music is a very sacred thing. I believe that music has the power to heal people. And of course a lot of the music that I work on, even some of the heavy metal stuff, is healing some 13-year-old kid's angst and making him feel better, no matter what his parents might think about it. So I treat music very, very seriously.

I love all kinds of music. I master everything from pop and some jazz to classical and even avant garde. I used to be principal trumpet player in the Utica, New York Symphony Orchestra, so I always put myself in the artist's shoes and ask myself, "What if this were my record? What would I do with it?" So I try to get some input from the artist. If they're not there, at least I try to get them on the phone and just talk about what things they like. I just take it all very seriously.

Glenn Meadows is a two-time Grammy winner and a multi-TEC award nominee who has owned the Nashville-based Masterfonics since the '70s (most recently purchased by Emerald Entertainment). He has worked on scores of gold and platinum records for a diverse array of artists including Shania Twain, LeAnn Rimes, Randy Travis, Delbert McClinton, Widespread Panic, and Bananarama, as well as for producers and engineers such as Tony Brown, Jimmy Bowen, and Mutt Lange.

What's your philosophy on mastering?

GM: I think that mastering is, and always has been, the real bridge between the pro audio industry and the hi-fi industry. We're the ones that have to take this stuff that sounds hopefully good or great on a big professional monitor system and make sure it also translates well to the home systems. We're the last link to get it right or the last chance to really screw it up and make it bad. And I think we're all guilty at times of doing both.

That being said, do you listen on typical home hi-fi systems?

GM: No, my mastering room is an in-wall Kinoshita monitoring system. It's about an 80 or 90 thousand dollar speaker system when you include the amplification. What we found is that when you have it sounding really great on that, it sounds good on everything else you play it on. Yeah, it's a different characteristic than a home system without the dome tweeters and that thin, ethereal top end that comes out of there, but if the components in the big system are in good shape and they've been maintained properly, you're going to get that same perspective. It also doesn't rip my head back and forth trying to go to different monitoring systems.

What I think is really difficult is that if you put up two or three different monitors to get a cross section, then you don't really know when anything is right because they all sound so different. I used to run little B&W 100s and I'd also have the requisite NS-10s in the room, and during that time when I was switching back and forth, I found my mastering suffered radically because I didn't have an anchor any more. I didn't have a point where I knew what was right because the character of the speakers was so different from each other. Once you listened to one for a couple of minutes, you lost your reference point on the others.

The reason people come to a mastering engineer is to gain that mastering engineer's anchor into what they hear and how they hear it and the ability to get that stuff sounding right to the outside world. So if you start putting all this stuff up on small speakers, and try this and try that, you've basically created a big confused image for the mastering engineer.

Well that being said, does that mean you only listen on one pair of speakers?
GM: Yeah.

So you never go to a smaller pair?
GM: I do at home. I do in the car. I do outside of the mastering room. I'll pop it on in another room in the building. All of our rooms are cross-connected fiber optically so we can literally walk into another room and dial the first room up and listen on those speakers. It's really very handy having that. But in the room itself when I'm working? No, it's the one set of monitors.

If I get a producer that says, "Well, I've gotta listen on… fill in the blank," then we get a pair, and it's like, "Okay, here's the button that turns them on. Here's how you start. Here's how you put the EQ in and out if you want to listen that way. Call me when you're finished listening." And I leave the room, and let them listen because it literally rips me away from my anchor. If I start listening on different sounding monitors, then I'm completely lost. But on the monitors that I've worked on for 13 years in the same room, I know how they sound. I know what they need to sound like and the repeat clients go, "Yep, that sounds right. Yep, that sounds good." What you find is typically within a song or two of working with somebody who has been in here, they settle into it and say, "Okay, yeah. I really can hear all that detail. I understand exactly what you are doing." We put other things up for them to listen to that they're familiar with to get a crosscheck on what I'm used to hearing.

Do you think that there's a difference between the way people master from town to town? Is there a difference because of where you're geographically located?
GM: I don't think that's as much true any more as it used to be. I could probably put a vinyl record on and tell you where it was mastered and who did it. To some extent the early CD transfers were very similar to that as well.

Right now though, it's all blended in to be a big jumble of sound, and you almost can't pinpoint anybody's characteristic fingerprint any more. Everybody has basically the same kind of tools and is doing the same kind of thing to satisfy the customers. And unfortunately, satisfying the customers is, in my opinion, not where the music needs to be right now, but that is a whole other story.

Let's go there. What brought that about do you think?
GM: The level wars? We had level wars in vinyl right near the end of it, where everybody was trying to get the vinyl hotter and hotter and hotter. And at least in vinyl you had this situation where when the record skipped, the record label would say, "Well, it's too loud and you're gonna have returns." What put the fear of God into the producer was returns. By God, we don't want any returns. So they would tend to back away, and we could kind of stay within the limits of the medium where you got a 23-minute side here and you couldn't cut it any hotter because it just won't fit at that level. Those were the realities that you had to live with.

We originally thought we had that type of limitation on digital, but what ended up happening is there's so many tools out now for doing the dynamic range squash that you can literally get tracks now where you put them in a workstation and it looks like a 2 by 4. It comes on at the quietest passage on the beginning of the intro and it's full level. You get into what I call "dynamics inversion." Spots in the record that should get louder actually get softer because they're hitting the compressor/limiter too hard.

I don't think that the record companies and the producers at this point have enough insight or understanding about what radio has learned a long time ago, which is the tuneout factor for distortion. Radio has spent a lot of time researching how far can you push it before people are annoyed and won't listen any more. As a result radio is tending to back down a lot with their compression, but it still gets compressed when they mix it, we compress it when we master it, and they compress it when they broadcast it. If you look at some of the radio stations on a VU meter on a calibrated system, they have maybe 3dB of dynamic range. We are putting out CDs that maybe have 6dB of dynamic range.

I'm mastering one right now, actually making 1630s on it, that's a French Canadian album, and it's a joy to listen to because it's got dynamics. It's an independent release and the artist sells probably 50–100,000 on her own in Canada. It's great; it has dynamics. It lives. I challenge any mastering engineer to go back and listen to music that they did four or five years ago when they were putting greatest hits packages together and listen to the mastered versions compared to what they're getting now. Then ask themselves, "Have we really gone forward or have we gone backward?" This happens to me all the time.

Whose fault is it?
GM: I think it's a wrap-around effect from broadcast. To be very honest with you, there is the impression that if the song doesn't jump off the CD from the program director's initial listen, then he's going to hit the "next track" button. So, we get into this round robin deal where we've got to make the cuts louder and louder so that they jump off the CDs faster.

We do an every other week compilation called CDX, which is a collection of all of the country stuff coming out in the next four- or five-week period and is a service to all the nonreporting *Billboard* R&R type stations. The labels actually buy slots on this so it relieves them of having to send release CDs on singles to thousands of radio stations. All they then have to concentrate on are the 150 or 200 reporting stations because this service handles the 2,500 others. So they buy a slot on this for every one of their releases. We compile it for them, and we have ever since it started. The sequence of the songs on the CD is alphabetically based by song title, so Aaron Tippin doesn't always go first, or Arista Records doesn't always get their stuff first. Every single release is a jumble so there's no preferential positioning on the disc. We've spaced those five, six, eight seconds apart, trying to make them less like an album so it's just like a collection of songs.

All the producers and the record labels get copies of this and the first thing they do is compare their cut to somebody else's, and if theirs isn't as loud, they go back to their mastering engineers and say, "What's wrong with this?" Or they call us and say, "You screwed mine up. You didn't make mine as loud." Wait a minute, all we're doing is compiling. If you do a digital compare, what's on the CD is exactly what was given to us by whoever mastered it. We don't play with it, we don't change levels, we don't have preferences. We are a fulfillment center and that's all we're doing, so don't blame us. So they go back to their mastering engineer and say, "The next time a track is going on CDX, make sure it's good and hot." So we get specialized releases for CDX that have been run through additional processing and have even less dynamic range. Then you have the situation where the record label listens to this advance copy and pulls out their mastered album and says, "The one on the CDX is louder than the one on the full album. Why is that?"

Catch-22.

GM: It's a complete Catch-22. I just had a one-inch two-track rolled in while we're talking because I'm remastering a ref on a shoot-out again. They came to me first and everybody loved it. One of the people involved in the project said, "Well, I really think we ought to go over here [to a competitor] to master." So they pulled the tapes, went over to this other place, took my ref and said, "Here's what he's done. Can you beat it?" So of course, he got more level and they said, "Wow, look at that." So the producer and the head of the label said, "You know, we really like what you did, but we don't feel it's fair that you went first. Do you want to take another shot at it and hear what the other guys did?" So here we go. The tapes are coming back today. I'm going to get a copy of what they did to see if I think I can do it any better or any differently. But the irony is that the producer was here when we did it the first time. This is what he said he wanted. Now why are we doing this again? The problem is if you stay in a situation where you're always going first and end up not doing the mastering, then you have people go, "Well, why should I even go over there?" It's a horrible situation and I don't personally know how to break the cycle, other than getting people to listen.

As the quality of the music is going down, so are the record sales. I don't think anybody has tried to make a correlation between the fact that if it's fatiguing to listen to, the people at home are going, "I can't even listen to the whole record. It comes on, it's in my face; it never gets quiet; there are no dynamics. I could only listen to five songs. Take it off and throw it away. It's irritating."

Do you think the problem lies in mastering or is it in mixing?
GM: God, that's a hard question.

I must admit that if I don't use the buss compressor when working on an SSL, I have clients that will get upset. And no matter how bad it sounds, you never get in trouble if you use it. But you get in trouble if you don't.
GM: Right. And unfortunately there is no easy provision on the SSL to give a version without it. And of course you alter your mix because it's in there, so it wouldn't do any good really to have one without it because it's not going to have the right balances. It really is a Catch-22. I've tried to get a lot of people to back away from it. We just did a project a year ago on Diamond Rio and Mike Clute, the producer, is not one who likes to be involved in these level wars. He thinks it's damaging to the music. So he mixed it on one of the late prototypes of the Soundtracks digital console. It sounded magnificent. It had dynamic range. We stepped on it ever so slightly in mastering just to get a little bit of average level up.

My typical approach to do that is to use like a 1.15:1 compression ratio and stick it down at –20 or –25 so you get into the compressor real early and don't notice it going from linear to compressed and basically just pack it a little bit tighter over that range. I'll get maybe 3dB of compression, but I've brought the average level up 3 or 4dB, and it just makes it bigger and fatter. That's what we did to it, and the record label goes like, "Wow, how did you do that? It doesn't sound limited and compressed!" And he and I just looked at each other and smiled. It sounded great on the radio, and that's the whole point. People think that they have to be heavily compressed to sound loud on the radio and they don't.

When you use your compression technique, are you using the typical radio attack and release settings? Long attack, long release?

GM: No, it varies. It depends on what the tempo of the music is doing. I'll adjust it track by track.

Breathing to the music.

GM: Yes. Most everything I do is tailored to what the music dictates that it needs. There's no preset standard that I'm aware of that I use, although I have had a producer come in and had me master a record, and then he went back and matched it with a Finalizer and stored the setting; "Ah, there's the Masterfonics setting." He told me he did the same thing for Gateway. He had a couple of things mastered up there and then found a common setting and now he's got it as his Gateway preset. He does his own mastering now. "Ah, make it sound like Gateway. There it is." I told Bob [Ludwig] that, because he and I have been friends for probably 20 years, and he just died laughing. He said, "If you can find out what that setting is, send it to me. I'd love to have it, because I don't know what I do."

What makes a great mastering engineer?

GM: The ability to use discretion. The ability to listen to a piece of product and say, "You know, this really doesn't need much of anything." At this point in my career (I've been doing this for almost 30 years now), if I put a client's tape up and I don't have a pretty good clue by the time I'm at the end of the first run of the first song as to what that song needs, they ought to go back and remix. I find that the real value of a mainstream mastering facility versus trying to do it yourself or doing it in a small backwoods-type place or a basement place, is that the experience of the engineer comes into play and it can save you money and time. We have had situations where clients say, "Oh, we can't pay your $210 an hour. We know how long it takes to master." And I said, "Well, tell me about what you did the last time." "Oh, we went to this guy and it was $25 an hour." "How long did you spend?" He said, "We spent four days." "Three or four hours a day?" "No, he worked ten, twelve hours a day. It cost us a fortune." I'm just shaking my head in disbelief and saying there is no reason that an album of what you're putting out should take more than seven or eight hours at the most. I said, "To be real honest with you, if I had to spend more than four or five hours on the record to get 98 percent of what can be gotten out of it, I'm wasting your time."

I don't mean to be arrogant, but it has to do with the experience of the engineer working in his environment. He's in the same room every day for years. I can walk into this room in the morning and know if my monitors are right or wrong just by listening to a track from yesterday. To me, that's the value of a mastering engineer. What they bring to the table is the cross section of their experience and their ability to say, "No, you really don't want to do that."

Speaking of which, what makes a great facility? Is it possible to have a great mastering engineer in a facility not up to par with his abilities?"
GM: Yes, it can be done because he knows the facility and he knows its limitations, how to work around them and how to get the most out of the facility. You can put a mediocre engineer in a great facility, and if he doesn't know what he's doing and doesn't know how to get the most out of what tools he has at his disposal, you are never going to get there.

Tell me about a great facility. What makes it great?
GM: It is not something that necessarily has the latest and greatest bells and whistles. It's a facility that's able to capture

what you started on tape and see it through to where the client is happy with what he walks out the door with, and be able to do that on a consistent basis as well. It doesn't necessarily have to be exactly right the first time because that's why you give a client a reference. You let them go listen in the environment they're familiar with because you're forcing them into your environment to start with. That's why they've come to you, because they value your opinion and your ears and what that brings to the table. By the same token, we all can't expect to get them a 100 percent right every single time.

What's your typical day like?

GM: For me, usually in by 8, 8:15. I get caught up on last minute projects where clients might need some copies by mid-morning or there's an emergency single that gets pulled from an album—that type of stuff. If it's a day with clients, then we pretty much try to hold to one project a day unless it's singles, then maybe we do two or three a day. If it's an album, we'll start at 10:00, break at 12:30 or 1:00 for lunch, then come back and finish up. In the afternoon, we're running references for the client. If we're done early, then we're able to get onto our production work for albums that are approved or references that need level tweaks or changes done to them. We're kind of unique in Nashville in that we're very close to Memphis, so our FedEx pickup is 9:15 at night and it allows us to run a long day. If we finish with clients at 4:00, we can then start cranking out 1630s or CD-Rs or whatever it may be that has to go out the door. Where on the two coasts, the last pickup is at 5 p.m., so if you miss that, it's like another day before it gets done. Here, we've got another four-hour shift that we can run.

Do you do your own production work?

GM: I do my own production work. That's just part of what I bring to the table with the clients. I've got almost 50 gig of hard drive space available, so a lot of projects can stay online for a long time until they are approved. I'll listen to them while they are being transferred if we're doing 1630s. If we're doing CD-R masters, we run them at real time with audio present so that we can hear what goes down, because I'm the one that did the work so I'm the one who is going to notice if something is wrong. If I pass this onto somebody and there's a process that's not working right or an automation move that sounds weird, they're not going to know. After all, it's my name that goes on the project as "mastered by." I did the same thing on vinyl for quite a few years when I did all of my own lacquer cutting.

Do you still do any vinyl?
GM: No, we just sold our last lathe.

Do you farm it out?
GM: Yeah, there are a couple of places here in town we can have it done. Most of them are kind enough to actually let us come in and run the lathe ourselves.

What's the ratio of CD-Rs to 1630s that you send out?
GM: On major label projects, it's probably mostly all 1630 and DDP. It's mostly the smaller guys that are doing CD-R. We run into those situations where they say, "Oh, just give me a ref disc," and they'll take the ref and approve it and send it straight on to the plant. It leaves you kind of like scratching your head going, "Okay, but how do you know if the disc is good?" because we don't run the CD-Rs references through the verifier. Verified masters are run through the Stagetech verifier and the print-out sheet is put in a Ziplock bag, and the jewel box is taped closed with a note to the plant saying that if it's opened and there's a problem, we don't warranty it. We tell the client, "If you take it out and play it, it's yours. If there's a problem on it, we've verified it. We've listened to it by ear." While we verify we also have a guy listening on headphones for any extraneous clicks or pops or anything strange, so it's been listened to twice. That's why we charge $350 for it.

You should catch something by that time.
GM: Absolutely. And he also checks that the start cues are working, and then we look at the printout of the error report and make sure there's no extraneous E22s and things like that on the disc that should reject it. If we catch that, we just burn it again. But we don't want the client to listen to it because they've already approved a reference disc and they're paying us to make sure that their master is what they've approved.

That's the value we bring to the table rather than cutting the CD master and saying, "Okay, here it is. You go listen to it and decide if it's okay." That, to me, is passing the buck.

We're getting paid a large number of dollars to do these. They look at us like, "$350? The disc only costs two bucks." And I say, "Yeah, but you're not paying for the disc. You're paying for the time it takes us to create it to give you exactly what you are supposed to have." So that's kind of the way it works and we don't have any problem with clients trying to listen to them as a result. It gets to the plant and the plant says, "Yes, it came in sealed," so it seems to be working.

How about the ratio of DDP to 1630?

GM: It's probably about 20 percent. MCA wants all DDPs. Capitol wants 1630s in their vaults but they'll run DDP to the plant. BMG Nashville/RCA Records will go one way or the other depending on the project; sometimes they do 1630, sometimes they do DDPs. They will ship to JVC and use that cutting method on all their product, and the difference sonically is audible. The JVC disc just sounds great all the time. It's never, "Well, it doesn't sound like my master." It's like, "Yep, that's what we sent."

Is there a particular situation that's more difficult than others?

GM: Probably I put myself in the situation where I continue to work with custom people—guys who are just putting out 500 CDs. I've always felt that they deserve as much of an opportunity to have their product handled by a pro as anybody else does. But you get some stuff and you just kind of have to roll your eyes like, "Wow, this is really bad." You have to be diplomatic about it because that's the best a client can do sometimes. I think that's the hardest thing—being diplomatic in situations when you know that in reality they are only going to sell these to their friends and family.

Do you do a lot of these?

GM: I do enough of them. I used to not be available to do that type stuff and I personally felt bad because part of how I started out in this business was doing custom disc mastering.

These people want to pay the rate, so they deserve to have what can be done to help their product. In many cases it's a whole lot easier to make dramatic improvements on bad sounding stuff than it is to take something that sounds great and make it dramatically better. That's even harder—to try and make a dramatic improvement in a great sounding tape, and know when to leave it alone.

What do you enjoy the most in mastering?

GM: I enjoy anything that is well recorded and the music is good. Be it this French Canadian project I'm listening to while we do this, be it a jazz thing, or a classical project. If the music is good, I really enjoy it. We do most all of the mastering on the Cirque de Soleil soundtrack albums for their shows and that is just a joy to work on because the music is great. There is no pretense that we're trying to make this radio friendly or anything else. This is a piece of music that has got to sound great at home and that is the enjoyable part, when it doesn't have to be commercial.

Is there something that a producer can do beforehand that makes your job easier, or something that just makes it a lot harder? Maybe that's two questions.

GM: I really hate, and have a much more difficult time, working with material that has been pre-premastered. I actually think what we have done is we have created a new Scotch tape in the industry that's called Finalized. That word from the Finalizer has almost become a generic term. Just to encompass that whole large scope of things that people stick at the end of their mixing chain before they go to their storage medium.

I'm not crazy about any of those mastering-in-a-box type deals, because most of what they do is undoable. Most people using them are listening in less than ideal environments, and they can't hear a lot of the stuff that's going on. Plus, your ears become so used to it that it becomes like an addiction where more is better. If it is louder, it is better. If it has got more bass and more top, it is better. Just whatever more is, that is better. As a result you have a tape that is sitting right at zero or clipping on the DAT and they want you to master it. You're going like,

"Well, there's barely much left to do. You have kinda killed it already."

Do you normalize? Do you ever use normalize function?

GM: No. I don't use a computer to decide how much to bring something up. Typically, I will process on the way into the workstation. I am not a load-it-in-and-then-master kind of guy. I prefer to take the original source material and go through whatever processing gear I decide I need or would like to use on the project, and come into the workstation and deal with it that way.

I have a reference point where I park the monitors when I start working on the cut, and I kind of get a feel for what it is doing and then look at the head room coming in to see where I am at. Invariably I end up within 1/4 or 1/2 dB at the top, maybe because there is a little bit of a peak limiter sitting there as a protection. But once in the workstation, I will use the processing only as subtle final tweaks. I don't use the internals of the workstation as my mastering tools per se. The workstation is an editing area. It is a scratch pad to do all the work in and compile it and put it together. The outboard gear is what I use for mastering, and that is just the way I have grown into it.

Is that signal chain digital, analog, or a combination?

GM: It can be a combination, but my path is typically 99 percent digital because 99 percent of what I am getting is digital.

So in other words, you're getting mostly DATs.

GM: DATs, or we are getting 24-bit sources in at various time. For example, with this one-inch two-track that I am working with, if I decide I need an analog EQ I will come through a Millenium Dual [the mastering version with the detents on it], then run into my Prism AD2 converter, and then come into the rest of the mastering chain 24-bit digital. Then we will store it 24-bit digital and do anything else that we have to do at 24 bits internally. Then on the way back out the door, I can now loop out and back in and pick up my Z-Sys equalizer, using the power of POW-r word length reduction if I need to. The SADiE has the Apogee UV22 built in, if I decide to use that. So I have got the ability to handle it whichever way is most appropriate for the music. But the processing gear at the moment on the digital side is the Z-Systems six-channel EQ and Weiss EQ and compressor/limiters.

Do you ever get a request to add effects or have to add some tail to something that has been cut off?

GM: Every now and then we do, yes. We just did a thing for Lorrie Morgan and one of the cuts on the album is a live piano/vocal track done live at a show. The mix that they ended up doing was a bit too dry, so we just added some verb and mastering to it and they are all happy.

Generally, what do you use?

GM: I use a Lexicon 300L if we need it and route through the mixer in SADiE. In this particular case, the stupid little plug-in that SADiE had gave just the character it needed, so it literally was added inside the workstation and is part of the project which in itself is strange, but it works.

Do you use subwoofers?

GM: No. The monitors in the room I am in and the room measure flat to 28Hz. One of the rooms here in the building, the audio for video post room, is currently set up with an M&K system and I find the use of the subs in that room to be very disturbing. I have a very difficult time getting an accurate handle on what is really happening on the low end.

One of the problems is that people misalign the sub.

GM: Very well could be. To do 5.1 we set up a Genelec speaker system in here and ended up using an M&K subwoofer. That was okay, but I sure wouldn't want to try to make any value judgments on it without listening to it for a couple of weeks.

Do you have any plans for surround sound mastering?

GM: Yes, we do. We haven't finalized them yet since we are seeing what is actually going on at the moment. That is probably one of the biggest question marks of all; is John Q Public going to buy into this, or is it going to be like the original quad was? Is the public going to say, "Why do I need this?"

After cutting his first number one record (Stevie Wonder's "Uptight") at age 18, Bob Olhsson worked on an amazing 80 Top Ten records while working for Motown in Detroit. Now located in San Francisco and mastering predominantly for the new age label Hearts of Space, Bob's unique view of the technology world and his insightful account of the history of the industry makes for a truly fascinating read.

What exactly are you doing now?

BO: I'm kind of spread out. I do all of the mastering for Hearts of Space Records, which is a new age label that does primarily composer-produced recordings. I do some pretty long, involved mastering projects for them. We do a lot of work to try to make the most with a minimum budget for recording and mixing.

The relationship that I have with Stephen Hill, the guy that started the label, came up when I first moved to California in 1972, and we've just been working together on various and sundry things since. I think we actually took what amounted to the first project studio recording into the mastering lab back around 1972 or '73. So I'm kind of on the bleeding edge of the project studio thing to the point where now I am kind of kicking my heels in the sand and going, "Hey, wait a minute! This has its place, but the old ways have a very important place too."

Do you have your own facility?

BO: Yes. I do work at the label's facility, and then I have my own setup at home. I also do freelance recording and mastering along with a bit of film sound editing and consulting work for a wide variety of people.

How do you think mastering has changed from the vinyl days to the way it is now?

BO: Well, I was thinking about that. In the vinyl days we were very concerned with mechanics, meaning the playability of a record and whether it could be manufactured. A mastering error in those areas would mean thousands of returned pressings. It was a big financial factor. Tapes, for the most part, came from larger studios with more experienced people, so you didn't really have that much to do in a lot of cases. You might use a little EQ, a little level correction, filter some low frequency and de-ess some highs so you wouldn't run into skipping problems, but other than that you pretty much tried to go with the sound on the master tape. It was a lot more nuts and bolts. You'd always think, "How do I get it off from the tape onto the disc and still have something resembling the same thing come back?" So it started out very much as that kind of consideration.

Then as the recording industry moved to the use of independent studios, we began to get a new generation of independent mastering studios. They got more involved with working on the audio itself, partly because the studios either had less experience, or had less feedback than, say, you would get in a record company studio. In a record company studio you hear about it in a big hurry if something doesn't sound good, whereas in an independent studio you may or may not hear about it because by the time the salespeople are involved, the studio is completely out of the loop. So Sterling Sound and the Mastering Lab and so forth were kind of the first generation of mastering studios that were not part of record companies.

At the same time, the record company studios became more involved in what we called "creative mastering." This was where Bernie Grundman at A&M, for example, made a very large impact from a record company studio. On the East Coast, I guess Sterling was probably the first. There was a studio, Bell Sound, which was both a recording studio and a mastering facility and they were a very big deal. Motown used to send their stuff to Bell.

In 1948, the majors decided they were going to stop doing anything other than middle-of-the-road pop music, and so a whole bunch of people left the majors and started the independent record companies; Atlantic, VJ, Chess, and so forth. Later on, Motown was actually part of the second generation of that evolution. This was a whole parallel thing that was created by the advent of tape recording. The idea that you didn't have to record to disc and go through all that stuff that required this specialized expertise was a revelation. You could now go into a studio that had done broadcast advertising or you could go into a radio station. Atlantic used to use radio stations all over the country. They would find an artist they wanted to record and sign them to a contract on the spot. Then they'd find a local radio station, make a tape, and send it back to New York. A lot of their early records were done that way. They eventually built their own studio, and the rest is history. A friend of mine, Joe Atkinson, was their mastering engineer from 1959 until he came to Motown around 1969.

When you were at Motown, were you in Detroit or L.A.?
BO: I was in Detroit, the real one.

You did the mastering?
BO: Well, it was a complicated thing. Basically Berry Gordy is a man who tried to never make the same mistake twice, so he had his own system that was integrated into RCA's manufacturing. If at all possible, he wanted the mixes to be able to be mastered flat. So in many cases, if it didn't work well flat, it got sent back to mixing rather than attempting to fix it in mastering. He also had a policy that he wouldn't evaluate anything other than off a disc since he wouldn't have a tape recorder in his office. He wanted to hear how it stacked up against other records on the market, and he wanted that perspective on everything he listened to. So we basically did an acetate of every mix that was done. We would occasionally suggest a change, but for the most part they wouldn't approve anything at all radical. Anything beyond a couple of dB at 4,000 was sent back for another mix.

So what I was doing was basically cutting these acetates. We would cut a 33-1/3 of all the mixes and then they would pick which ones they wanted to go to the next step. If there was some marketing reason why it had to happen fast, we would do the mastering. But if there was time, we would send the acetate and the master tape to RCA and tell them to match it. They were willing to absolutely guarantee pressings and turn around any mistakes in 24 hours. We went that route because Berry's first business was a record store and he knew all about defective pressings.

The Mastering Engineer's Handbook

What was the reason for them doing the mastering? Did he think that there would be fewer rejects if it happened there?

BO: He had a guarantee. Basically, the way it was set up is we would hardly even know about a problem because they would deal with it all internally at RCA. So they were actually matching an acetate that we had sent, and we would check their acetate to make sure that it matched what we had done before letting it go. That was the process.

That's far different from what you would think.

BO: Yes, it was pretty unique. Basically the secret of the success of Motown was being able to coordinate appearances of the artists with records in the stores at the right time.

You saw firsthand something that may not ever happen again. That was probably a wonderful experience to live through.

BO: Oh yes. I'm convinced Berry Gordy is absolutely the smartest person I've ever heard of in the record business. All my experience since then has been looking at how people are doing things and scratching my head and wondering why on earth they are taking the long way around. I've watched various labels go through their changes, and my perspective is sort of an odd cynicism because I haven't seen much new. I would love to see somebody put together a book about how he actually ran the company. They have done all these books that have been basically written for the fans of the artists, but they haven't really gotten into how the company worked and what they did.

The neat thing about doing mastering there was that we saw everything. We had to relate to virtually every part of the company, and we were among the only people that ever saw the whole thing. It was really brilliant. Of course, I am also not sure that he realizes how brilliant it was. He was just a very bright and very, very, very logical man. He was always thinking, "How can I make this simpler? How can I make this better?" And it meant that we did everything in a somewhat different way than the rest of the industry, but often it was a much smarter way.

Like, for example, the Motown artists never paid for any studio time. They never paid for promotion. They didn't pay a manager's fee out of the record royalties. They didn't pay for a lot of stuff, and they got a lower royalty rate as a result. But you have all these people running around believing they really got ripped off because they don't realize that the higher rates that the other companies paid would then get whittled down to next to nothing. So, it's an apples and oranges thing.

I was doing mastering there until about 1968, and then I got moved into the studio because I had a background in music. So from that point on I was doing vocals, strings, horns, rhythm dates, the whole bit. I was one of the two people that held every engineering job there. The other one is Larry Miles.

The musicians were all jazz players. Berry is a big jazz fan. His record store was a jazz record store and it completely failed, but he learned his lesson. Just because he loved something didn't mean that it was commercial, so after that he began doing the most universally commercial stuff he could. His goal for the company was for it to be another RCA or Columbia.

And he almost got there.
BO: I think what finally brought it down was the whole MTV thing, spending hundreds of thousands of dollars on videos and that kind of thing. Of course, Motown was much more oriented around the music than the video.

I think the one effect of the Internet may be to completely turn that back around again. I think in a lot of ways it is like '48 all over again, the numbers aren't going to work for these big new conglomerates, and a new complete independent scene will develop.

The actual sales that are happening on the Net now are incredibly small.
BO: It's like 1 percent of the market. It's not only not cutting into retail, but retail is growing! I look for the Net to play the same role that radio did in the '50s.

The thing people don't understand is that music is a social thing. People do music with other people. They want to hang out with people that are into a given kind of music. It's something they have on in the background of their life. It's like a piece of architecture almost. It's not something where they put their life on hold to concentrate on like a film. It's a very, very different product, and Motown was really aware of that. That and the dancing.

In retrospect, another thing is blatantly obvious, but I don't think anybody really realized it back then. What we called the R&B chart was really the women's chart [laughs]. I think the thing we didn't realize was that beginning with the Beatles, men had become an important component in buying records, and the records we were making largely appealed to women. We weren't all that successful at making records that men were into. That just kind of came crashing home to me recently. It's like our own racism limited us because we thought it was a racial thing, and it probably wasn't. That may be true of the whole industry. Now it's swung back that way again. This last year, women just started buying more records than men for the first time since the Beatles.

I read somewhere that the demographic that buys the most records nowadays is a white woman over 30.
BO: It's the fastest growing group, I know that. I've actually been trying to research that some myself. In our Web mastering project, one of the things that I have been doing is trying to come up with statistics about signal processing and demographics. Unfortunately, most of the research has been done by broadcasters and is extremely proprietary. They paid for it, and they're damned if they're going to have other people knowing what they learned.

I had an exchange with Bob Orban whose Optimode compressor/limiter is at the heart of most radio and TV stations' signal chains and found out a couple of real interesting things. Apparently too much high frequency absolutely kills you with women, but a lot of bass is very important to women. Too much compression kills you with women because it becomes what he calls "intrusive." You want it to be able to be on and in the background all the time. You don't want it pulling your attention away. You still don't want it to be boring and dynamics actually help with that, so it's a fine balance from a station's viewpoint. In order to appeal to women, they have to be less in your face, and the more in your face thing has to do with maybe the first ten seconds that somebody listens to a station before they adjust the volume control.

How do you think we're going to get back to the use of dynamics—because now we're squeezing the life out of everything everywhere along the line?

BO: The usual theory is that nobody will question it as long as it is selling, but I am starting to find signs that a lot of new recordings are not selling. I found out that the average new release is selling something like 800 copies. While you've got these spectacular gross figures and a few titles selling very well, the recordings that are selling millions and millions of copies are not paying for the ones that aren't. Apparently this came up in Soundscan and *Billboard* printed the thing, and a bunch of the majors tried to actually get them to pull that issue off the stands because they didn't want their stockholders seeing that statistic. So there is certainly something going on there.

I have heard that there are some major meetings going on in an attempt to more or less reel production back into the record companies. They are rethinking a lot of stuff because of the dropping percentage of titles that are paying for themselves. It may all come out in the wash because while stuff certainly is going to get squeezed, if people can come up with figures that indicate that overcompression can harm sales, that is definitely the message that can turn it around.

Returns would scare people away from going too far.

BO: You had that same economic with vinyl. But in this case, we can do things beyond anything we were ever able to do before, like turn the signal into a square wave even. The other thing is that people are commonly going too far with compression during mixing so much that an awful lot of mixes can't be helped. I average a couple of mastering jobs a year where I can't do anything to it. If you switch anything in at all, it just absolutely turns to dust. All you can do is hope that the stations that play it won't destroy it too much more.

Do you have a philosophy about mastering?

BO: Well, first, do no harm. To me it's a matter of trying to figure out what people were trying to do, and then do what they would do if they had the listening situation and experience that I have. I sort of try to be them because I see the whole process as a matter of trying to clear the technology out of the way between the artist and the audience. You've got this person on this end who is doing a performance, and you have these people on the other end who are listening to it, so I think it's largely about keeping the technical aspects from distracting from the performance. That's the most basic thing. Then to a certain degree you can enhance things, of course. You can get it so that you can hear more of what they were doing on a wider range of playback systems or playback circumstances.

But the big thing is communication. It's about somebody working some magic in front of a microphone and people having the effect of that magic coming out of a loud-speaker. To me, that is the key to the whole thing. Do everything you can to get the music to happen in front of the mics and everything you can to protect it after it is an electrical signal.

The whole thing is to try to maximize the amount of expertise that you can afford because you don't really want to master your own recordings. For my own recordings, if I can push the budget, I go to Bob Ludwig. I'm frankly more impressed with his work than almost anybody I have heard, and I have taken projects to just about everybody in the business. I think the man deserves his reputation. The unfortunate part of it is that at this point I suspect he gets mostly save jobs. Stuff where you'll never know how bad it really was. And so a lot of the stuff that has his name on it is fairly mediocre and often was probably sent to somebody else, and the label bounced it back and said, "Well, okay. Let's throw the big bucks at this and see if he can save it."

What makes a great mastering engineer as opposed to someone who is just competent?

BO: A willingness to go the extra mile and really dig in and try and make something better. It's a willingness to fix the intro of something that is a little off as opposed to just letting it go.

When you're mastering these days, are you doing it mostly in analog or digital domain?

BO: In my case, I'm doing mostly digital.

In the workstation?

BO: Yes, with some outboard hardware. But for what I'm doing, which is mostly turning parts up, turning parts down, putting different EQ on different parts and trying to get the dynamics so that there are some, it works fine. I'm really trying to make something that somebody got working on a pair of Genelecs work on big systems and little ones but yet somebody at a listening station in a record store won't need to switch the volume control. So it has to be up at the current accepted level and yet I have to try to figure out how to do the least harm to it and still have it be an experience that people want to hear repeatedly. I can't understand the idea of somebody buying a record that they aren't going to want to listen to over and over. To me that is kind of the whole point.

How long does your typical mastering job take?

BO: For independent clients, typically at least six hours. For Hearts of Space, anywhere from two days to a week. That's the reason Stephen built his own mastering studio. He had been going to all the top people and he realized that with a lot of his artists he would be better off putting a lot more time into it than was practical in a regular mastering facility. Like we use ProTools, which takes considerably longer than a Sonic or a SADiE setup. Then of course we go back and forth with the artist to make sure that we haven't driven it into left field from their point of view. It's really a very different model than a commercial mastering facility or the way a lot of the industry works.

So when you're finished, are you sending a CD-R off?

BO: I find I get the best results with a DDP tape. We did a bunch of studies doing different methods of cutting some years ago and we found that our own DDP tapes consistently resulted in pressings that sound like our own CD-Rs. That wasn't necessarily the case if we sent out a CD-R. For a little while we played with making a time code DAT and transferring that to a 1630, but it was too unwieldy and it was debatable whether it got a better result. We tried the DDP and it just worked so well that we decided it made sense to do it that way.

Do you have to add effects at all?

BO: Like reverb? Yes, we do that on some things. We do a lot of compilations where we're starting with wildly different sources and trying to get them to lay together. It can be pretty challenging. We just did a compilation of some Russian choral music where some new recordings had been done in a pretty dry church and it just didn't mix with the stuff that had been done in a cathedral, so I had to add a ton of reverb to that.

What did you use?

BO: Well we have a NuVerb sitting in a spare machine and that appealed to me because you can save the settings. Of course in mastering, a whole lot of what it's about is how do you reproduce it five years later. So I'm very, very anal about archiving source files and settings and even software in some cases so that I can pull it back later. Because as things have progressed, I've found that I can go back and take something I mastered five years ago and do a heck of a lot better job today. So if I can go back to the sources and even just see what my settings were, I can just use newer software.

The software that's made most of this happen is the KS Waves stuff. And both of us, at home and Hearts of Space, have really high-end playback systems so stuff really sticks out if there is a problem.

Are you using just one set of monitors or do you go back and forth?

BO: I don't like multiple monitors in a studio although I'll use the little speaker on a Studer two-track. I also check things out in my car. I find midlevel alternate monitors just confuse things.

Do you listen in mono much?

BO: Yes, because too many decisions are made in mono down the line. We have had occasional problems. We had one artist who decided they liked the effect of the lead vocal 180 degrees out of phase on each side, so when you mixed it to mono it went away. We had to explain to them that you don't really want to know what the limiter at a radio station is going to do on that, because the stations have these correlation switchers that try to switch everything in phase. I understand there are also things that will somewhat monoize a signal because it will reduce the distortion in stereo. So there is a lot of manipulation going on there. They assume a clean, coherent signal going in, so if you give them something that isn't, heaven only knows what will happen.

How do you see mastering changing in the future? What will the mastering facility of the future look like?

BO: I think there is going to be a lot more involvement by the producers and mixers than there has been because if any of the new formats fly, things are going to be a lot more complex. Having three different mixes of voice up, voice down and voice in the middle in a six-channel surround is going to be pretty unwieldy to keep straight. I mean, there are just so many more things that can go wrong that I think a lot of it is very likely to go the way of the film business because that was how they worked out how to deal with all the different theatrical formats. Film mixes are done to stems and then those are mastered to the various surround formats.

Have you done any surround yet?

BO: Only for film. I haven't done much in the way of music. I did some quad back in the '70s, and I've done quite a bit with playing with matrix decoding. In other

The Mastering Engineer's Handbook

words, listening to the mix through a matrix decoder and adjusting it so that it does nice things. That's what we've done with a lot of the ambient stuff. I'm pretty excited about what happens in Circle Surround with a number of the Hearts of Space titles.

You've used circle surround?
BO: Yes. We've decoded it, but we haven't encoded it yet.

Are you using subwoofers?
BO: Not any more. I did at home up until three years ago when I got the Duntech Sovereigns. Before that I had the second M&K subwoofer on the market and was using the BBC LS3/5as for satellites.

What are you using to power those?
BO: For my home Duntechs I'm using a pair of Hafler 9505s, and at Hearts of Space we use big Thiel speakers with the largest stereo Mark Levinson amp. It's real good for digital because it's a very bright, clean system, so it really shows up any artifacts. That's basically what we want it to do. We just want to come up with digital stuff that doesn't bite.

If ever there was Godfather of Mastering, Doug Sax has truly earned the title, as evidenced by the extremely high regard that the industry holds him in. One of the first independent mastering engineers, Doug literally defined the art when he opened his world famous The Mastering Lab in Hollywood in 1967. Since then he has worked his magic with such diverse talents as The Who, Pink Floyd, the Rolling Stones, the Eagles, Kenny Rogers, Barbra Streisand, Neil Diamond, Earth, Wind & Fire, Rod Stewart, Jackson Brown, and many more.

Do you have a philosophy about mastering?

DS: Yes. If it needs nothing, don't do anything. I think that you're not doing a service adding something it doesn't need. Mastering doesn't create the product. I don't make the stew, I season it. And if the stew needs no seasoning, then that's what you have to do. If you add salt when it doesn't need any, you've ruined it. I try to maintain what the engineer did. A lot of times they're not really in the ballpark due to monitoring, so I EQ for clarity more than anything.

When you first run something down, can you hear the final product in your head?

DS: Oh yes. Virtually instantly. Because for the most part I'm working with music that I know what it's supposed to sound like. But once in a while I'll get an album that is so strange to me because of either the music or what the engineer did, that I have no idea what it's supposed to sound like and I often will pass on it. I'll say, "I just don't hear this. Maybe you should go somewhere where they're glued into what you're doing."

But for the most part, I'm fortunate to usually work on things that sound pretty good. I do Bill Schnee's stuff and George Massenburg's and Ed Cherney's and Al Schmitt's, who's the most nominated engineer, you know. I've done his stuff since 1969. These are clients that I'm the one they go to if they have a say in where it's mastered. Every room has its claim to fame, and mine is that I work on more albums nominated for engineering Grammys than any other room, and probably by a factor of three or four to the next closest room.

***How has mastering changed over the years from the time
you started until the way it is now?***

DS: My answer is maybe different than everyone else's. It
hasn't changed at all! In other words, what you're doing is
finessing what some engineer and artist has created into
its best possible form. If an engineer says, "I don't know
what it is, but the vocal always seems to be a little cloudy,"
and I can go in there and keep his mix and make the vocal
not sound cloudy, that's what I did in 1968 and that's still
what I do in 2000. The process is the same; the goal is the
same. I don't master differently for different formats. I
don't master differently for CD than I would for an LP
because you essentially make it sound as proper as you
can, and then you transfer it to the final medium using the
best equipment.

There's a three-CD set which is a lifetime retrospective of
Linda Ronstadt. I had mastered, I would say, 95 percent of
all the originals starting from *Heart Like a Wheel* when she
was on Capitol Records because I've done most of Peter
Asher's work. So in 1999, it gave me a chance to look at this
stuff that I had done in the '70s. Most of these tapes have
the original EQ notes in them. My equalizers are the same
as they've been for 30 years, so I could put on the tape, line
up the tones, and throw up what I had done in '75 or in '78
or in '81. I would make some changes if necessary, but for
the most part, what felt good then feels good now.

What surprised me is I had done a lot of work on my
analog machines since then and some of the tapes sounded
absolutely better than in 1975 or in 1983. I could play them
better today, so I was quite surprised how good some of
those tapes sounded.

***Did that influence any of your decisions then, because the
stuff was coming back cleaner and better?***

DS: No. I just got more enjoyment out of it. Maybe a
couple of times I took a dB of top off because I felt like I
was getting more off the tape than I did then. Or maybe I
felt that it could use a dB more bottom than I had done in
'75. I've read articles in all the trade magazines about how
the mastering engineer had to roll off the bottom to fit it

on the disc, and now that we have CD you don't have to do this. And I think, "Who are they talking about?" I never filtered my low end for an LP, and I cut a very wide stereo. So I was wondering who they were talking about when they said that, now that supposedly you can really hear the full bottom because it didn't have to get all rolled off to fit onto an LP record. I was shocked at that.

Do you think that working on vinyl has helped you in these days of CDs? Would that experience help a mastering engineer?

DS: I don't know if working on vinyl helps. I think having worked on many different types of music over the years helps. In one sense, being from the vinyl days I was used to doing all the moves in real time. I never went down a generation. In other words, a lot of mastering places would make a fade on a tape copy, then they would assemble a copy and cut from that. I never did that. I always cut directly from the master tapes, so if you blew a fade on the fourth cut, you started over again. So the concept of being able to do everything in real time instead of going into a computer probably affects the way I master because I don't look at things as, "Oh, I can put this in and fine-tune this and move this up and down." I look at it as to what I can do in real time.

I find the idea that you have a track for every instrument and you put them all together to have great clarity doesn't work. I think it works the opposite way. The more you separate it, the harder it is to put together and have clarity. So if you're EQing for musical clarity to hear what is down there, that's unchanged today from way back 30 years ago. It's the same process. And the EQ that would make it clear, that would make somebody call up and say, "Wow, I really like it. I can hear everything and yet it's still full," is still as valid today as it was then.

I'll tell you what the biggest difference is today from back then. The biggest thing is dynamics. There is no dynamic range now, and nobody wants dynamic range.

Why do you think it has changed?

DS: I think I know precisely why it's changed. It has to do with the fact that there's an increasing amount of music listening being done in the car, and there's one thing that doesn't work in the car and that's dynamics. Long, sexy fades that ease you out of one song and into another are worthless in the car.

The thing that brought this to mind was when I was working on a critical album for a pretty famous engineer. We had done a couple of changes and he came back and we did a couple more changes. Finally, we got to the point that the last change was made, and he called up in about an hour and said, "I love it. Don't touch a thing. It's done." And I said, "How can you judge? You haven't even been home yet." He says, "Oh, I do all my listening in the car. In fact, my home stereo hasn't even been on in a year." I'm not going to mention his name, but he's a major engineer who wins Grammys for his engineering, so it really brought to mind that I do my own listening in the car. I get stuck in traffic, but for recreation I listen to music that I don't normally work on, which is symphonic music. That's my background. I was a symphonic trumpet player, and you know Bob Ludwig is a trumpet player. And I think Ted Jensen is a trumpet player as well. I don't know what it is, but trumpet players seem to make pretty decent mastering engineers.

What's the hardest thing that you have to do?

DS: I come from a time when an album had a concept to it. The producer worked with one engineer and one studio, the group recorded everything, and there was cohesiveness as to what was put before you. Once you got into where they were going and what they were doing, you sort of had the album done. The multiple producer album to me is the biggest challenge because you might have three mixes from Nashville in different formats, a couple from New York, and two that are really dark and muddy and three are bright and thin. The only good part that I see about this is that you absolutely have to have a mastering engineer. There's no question, the mixes don't go together, and they don't work.

The hard part is to find some middle ground so that the guy that has the bright thin tape is still happy with what he's done and not drive off the road when the dull thick one hits after the bright thin one. So that is the biggest challenge in mastering, making what is really a cafeteria sound feel like a planned meal.

I'm very proud of the fact that I've trained a lot of good mastering engineers, and I'll tell them, "You're not going to learn how to master working on a Massenburg tape. It's pretty well done. If he didn't like it, he wouldn't have sent it. But you get engineers that are not great or you get these multiple engineer things, then you can sort of learn the art of mastering by making these things work using your ears." Otherwise, it's pretty easy.

Were you the first independent mastering engineer, or one of the first?

DS: Absolutely. Independent has to be clarified because if you go back to the late '60s and before, everything was in-house. You were signed to a label. You were given an A&R man. You stayed at the label. You recorded at Capitol. You went down to Capitol's mastering to get your product mastered to lacquer. You went to Capitol's art department and they gave you an artist that designed your cover, and that's the way it was. It was really at the end of the '60s that certain top producers would say, "I love the security, but I would like to work with an artist that's not on this label. I would like to work with Streisand, but she's on Columbia." So they started to break off and really started the process where nobody uses label stuff for anything any more. "If you sign me, I'll use the engineer I want and I'll record and master where I want." That's 30 years of hard-fought independence. So from the standpoint of an independent that is not aligned with a label, just a specialty room that handles mastering, the answer is yes.

I was one of the pioneers when there was no business. We opened up our doors December 27 of 1967 and by '71, '72, you couldn't get into the place. By '72 we were doing 20 percent of the Top 100 chart and there weren't a lot of competitors. There was Artisan in L.A., and Sterling and maybe Masterdisk just starting in New York. That was it. Now there seems to be a thousand because the reality is that it's very easy for someone to go into this business now. You can get a workstation with all the bells and whistles for a song and a dance. A Neumann lathe setup in 1972 was $75,000, and that was just the cutting system. You still needed a room and a console. So there were only a few people doing it and you had to have a big budget. Now you fire it right up.

And don't forget that in the industry for almost ten years there were no tones on an analog tape, so you didn't know how to line up to the machine.

There were no tones?

DS: No tones. I'm one of the instigators in railing on these guys to go back and print the tones so I could at least get my machine to be where your machine was. And there was no such thing as near-field monitoring. It didn't exist. So people used to go to these strange studios with big speakers in the wall, most of which were useless as far as relating to the world, and the engineers never knew that they were out in left field because they had nothing to take home. The cassette was just starting, and only handful of engineers that I can think of actually had a 15 ips tape machine at home that they could take home a mix and find out where they were.

I started the process in the early '70s just in self-defense. I would say, "Look, before you do anything, come in on-the-house with your first mix and find out if you're in trouble. We'll listen to it and get you straight." I just got tired of watching these guy's eyes open the first time they ever heard it out of the studio. "Oh, my God. I couldn't hear any highs in the studio so I kept adding highs. I asked the guy, 'Are these monitors right?' and he said, 'Yes.'" That absolute horrendous reality is the reason really why near-fields came in.

The truth of the matter is that the tools are getting so much better. I hate to say this as a mastering engineer, but used right, the Finalizer can do some awesome things. There was nothing like that three years ago. Digital technology is moving so fast and it's gone from, in my view, absolute garbage to, "Hey, this is pretty good." They're getting better clocks on the computers. They're getting better signal processing and better DSP. What used to be something that was really unmusical to me, if I have to say it, is now getting there.

I look at the Finalizer. A lot of mastering engineers bad-mouth it, and I get a kick out of that because with the Finalizer, you can make your product loud instantly. Mastering engineers don't like that because they used to be the ones that made it loud. But the reality is that everyone's going to have it and as a result everyone can make their CD loud. Once that becomes absolutely no trick at all, then the question becomes, are there things that maybe we should do besides just make it loud? I'm hoping that there's still going to be a business for someone that treats the music with love and respect when they're mastering it. And I think there's going to be a small reversion away from, "I want the loudest CD."

I get people in here new off the street that say, "I want the loudest CD ever made," and I say, "You're in the wrong place." Once in a while they'll pull out a CD and put it on and it's absolutely blazing and I'll say, "Find out where that was mastered and go there and get what you're looking for." But as I say, I still do more Grammy-nominated albums for engineering, so I have to be competitive from the standpoint that you don't want to turn it up a bunch when you put the thing in a CD player.

Your reputation is that you're more of an analog guy…
DS: My partner and I did some of the pioneering work in digital in the late '70s. The classic 3M machines were designed out in Camarillo, and my partner lived in Camarillo and did the original piano tests for them in '78. The very first recordings that were done on the Soundstream machine, before it was even up to a 44.1k sampling rate, we participated in. It was done right down the street at a church here. So when I'm being critical of digital, it is because I really have heard digital from the beginning and I knew that it was not up to the best of analog. But

we're talking about 1980, and there's been 20 years of development since.

I get a lot of 96/24 stuff in. It's cheap, it's here, it's now. So any comments that I make about a Sony 1610 from 1985 that was absolutely just horrible then is true. And when I say that a 96/24 recording done with dB Technology converters sounds terrific, that's also true.

The 96/24 stuff you're getting in, is that coming in as a file on a CD-ROM?

DS: The new Apogee PSX-100 has a bit-splitter in it so you can go into that thing, come out of the bit-splitter onto a DA-88, and you've got 96/24 on ten bucks worth of tape. It's transportable, the tapes play, and it's not a fortune in equipment. So I get some of that. I get some on Genexes. James Guthrie is bringing in his SADiE and it's all 96/24. In fact, he did *The Wall* movie, and he did the whole thing in 96/24.

Which workstation do you use?

DS: I don't have one in my room yet. I have a Sonic and I have the new HD Sonic that I'm evaluating. It'll be between that or the SADiE.

There's absolutely no point in buying anything that's not high density because that's coming sooner than later. The industry has always been interested in starting the mastering process with the best tapes they can make. If they came in with a half-inch 30 ips in 1980, they knew that they were only going to get a certain amount of it onto an LP, but they still wanted to come in with the best that they could. High density is pretty damn good, so to buy a new workstation and not be able to edit 96/24 is crazy.

What is the ratio of analog tape to DAT that you are getting?

DS: That's a good question. I have to clarify the answer. If it's a budget product, I'm going to get a DAT. So I like to look at the product where the budget is sufficient that the format is picked by merit and not by cost. So of the albums that have a meaningful budget, it's probably 70 percent half-inch analog from my room. Overall, I'd have to say 55/45, maybe leaning toward digital if you add all the DATs and the high-resolution stuff. It's moving quicker that way because guys that would never come in with a DAT will now come in with high-resolution digital.

What are you delivering to the replicator then?

DS: It's really what they want. I don't do a DDP, but with my new workstation I'll be able to. Without question, the best results are still from a 1630. It's the least amount of transfer. You don't have to go into computer because you can assemble right to it. It's one generation from the source and you can cut glass from it. So for the most part I either do 1630 or PMCD.

Describe your signal chain, or is that proprietary?

DS: No, it's not proprietary. As a point of interest, whether the source is analog or digital, if it needs EQ, I EQ it as an analog. That makes sense because if you come in with 96/24, I just look at it as good sounding analog. I do what I want with it, then I'll get it down to 44.1 and 16-bit in the best way possible. So whether it's half-inch or quarter-inch analog or digital, it goes into good converters and comes up as analog. Then the EQ is passive with the same equalizer I've had since 1968. The limiters are all tubes, and they're transformerless. Ninety-nine percent of what I do is done between those two devices.

What do you use for monitors?

DS: I use my own. They're two 15s with a midrange horn and a tweeter, and they've been here since 1968. I have no near-fields.

That's fantastic that what you have has weathered the test of time.

DS: Yes. It's the same concept that I have about mastering. I don't master any differently today than I did in 1968. The speakers allow me to put the right stuff on, and if they steer me wrong, then they're worthless.

Noted veteran engineer Eddy Schreyer opened Oasis Mastering in 1996 after mastering stints at Capital, MCA, and Future Disc. His work spans various musical genres with chart-topping clients such as Babyface, Eric Clapton, Christina Aguilera, Fiona Apple, Hootie and the Blowfish, Tracy Chapman, Offspring, Take 6, and Tupac, as well as soundtracks of movies like *Phenomena*, *Pleasantville*, and Howard Stern's *Private Parts*, Eddy's work is heard and respected world wide.

Do you have a philosophy about mastering?

ES: Yes, I do. I would say the philosophy is to create a sonic product that gives the song balance and competes with the current market in terms of sonic quality and level.

What do you mean by balance?

ES: Frequency balance—not too much bottom, not too many mids, and not too much top. Balance is making adjustments with compression, EQ, and such so that it maintains the integrity of the mix, yet achieves balance in the highs, mids, and low frequencies. I go for a balance that it is pleasing in any playback medium that the program may be heard in. And obviously I try to make the program as loud as I can. That still always applies.

But all mixes can't be cut as loud as others, so there're many limiting factors as to how loud something can go, and there are also limiting factors on what balance can be achieved. Some mixes just cannot be forced at the mastering stage because of certain ingredients in a mix. If something is a little bottom-light, you may not be able to get the bottom to where you would really like it. You have to leave it alone so it remains thinner because it distorts too easily.

There are a lot of people that are complaining that things are so squashed these days, and it's because of everyone trying to get their competitive level up.

ES: What I am hearing is that various houses are really over-compressing, trying to get more apparent level. The trade-off with excessive compression to me is the blurring of not only the stereo image, but blurring the highs, too. An overcompressed program sounds pretty muddy to me. In the quest to get the level, they end up EQing the heck out of these tracks, which of course induces even more distortion between the EQ and the compression. I am hearing things that are very, very loud, but in my opinion not a very good sound. I am hearing a program that is just way over-EQed because they're trying to get back what the compressor has taken away.

How do you determine what's going to work and what isn't?

ES: By listening. You go as loud as you can and you begin listening for digital clipping, analog grittiness, and things that begin to happen as you start to exceed the thresholds of what that mix will allow you to do, in terms of level. Again, just spanking as much gain as you can, be it in the analog or digital world, doesn't matter. You go for the level and properly control it with compression, then you start to EQ to achieve this balance. Of course, it all depends on the type of mix, how it was mixed, the kind of equipment that was used, how many tracks, the number of instruments, and the arrangement. Just the number of instruments can be a very limiting factor on level also. For example, a 96-track mix may not go as loud as a 24-track mix because there is too much signal to be processed.

You don't seem to compress things a lot—a dB and a half at the most. Is that typical?

ES: It's very typical of what I do with all my stuff, but I compress more than people are aware. I can compress in different stages so hopefully you are not even really hearing it. You are not actually seeing the compression, either analog or digital, that I'm doing. But I do go a little lighter than a lot of other mastering houses.

Do you use multiple stages of compression then?

ES: Yes. I do use analog and digital compression and sometimes digital limiting. Sometimes I digitally limit, I digitally compress, and I analog compress. Very rarely do I use analog limiting, though. I use whatever is needed to control the program. In other words, when a program is mixed a little heavy on the snare for example, I can use a digital limiter that will sort of clip the peak off that so that I can back off the dynamics of that particular instrument in the mix without EQing it out. Because if I go for the snare with EQ, I'm going to be pulling down the vocals and possibly the guitars as well. Likewise with the bass. If I go for a kick that's mixed too hot, adjusting 80, 60, 40 cycles or something to pull a kick down, it will really sacrifice the bottom quite a bit, so I'll tend to use digital limiting to peak-limit excessive dynamics in those particular cases. And then there's de-essing for sibilance on vocals and cymbals. That's all in trying to achieve balance again.

Do you use multiband limiting or multiband compression at all?

ES: Like in a TC? No. I have yet to hear one that is really happening in terms of side chains and things.

Do you think there is a difference in the way people master from city to city or coast to coast?

ES: Maybe slightly. And that only comes into play on the East Coast, for example. Certainly I think there is competition on both coasts, but the East Coast might be a little more aggressive because of the competition between the mastering houses to be the king of the hill, so to speak.

So the sound is more aggressive.

ES: Absolutely. Whereas I think West Coast houses might be spread out a little more so they are a little less aggressive with the style and type of mastering that's done. Which gets back primarily to level. It seems to me that the East Coast has gone a little overboard in the level game.

What do you think makes a great mastering engineer as opposed to somebody that's just good?

ES: Probably the ability to hand-pick various pieces of equipment that maintain a sound. When I say maintain a sound, I mean keep the stereo separation strong. Also, the ability to use taste and know how far mastering can and can't go. Put it this way: a lot of times less is better.

EDDY SCHREYER

Then you have the environmental issue. You can't make a move or create a fix if you can't hear it, so obviously the mastering environment is extremely important. Then the ability to know just how far to push the creative envelope is important.

For example, I enjoy the creative editing possibilities when using Sonic Solutions in helping an album maintain some continuity and flow. If I hear something that will make a good crossfade, I'll mention it to the client. It may or may not fly, but we'll always try it. So I definitely like the creative part of Sonic, as it has created a great situation for mastering engineers to step forward and have a little more say in terms of the flow of the album with edits, spread times and things like that. It's all part of the big picture, if you will, to keep the flow of an album happening.

What do you think makes for a great facility? And is it possible to have a great mastering engineer and a mediocre facility?
ES: A great facility to me means both client services and a comfortable place that's able to facilitate both large and small sessions. I am assuming my studio is somewhat the norm. I can seat about five to six people in my room very comfortably, and I believe that is probably somewhat common. I think a mastering room that's too small is not a good thing. At times there are more than two or three people who want to show up at a mastering session, so that part of the client relationship is very important to me. So the facility sort of dictates what your goal is in terms of the client/engineer relationship and just how comfortable you want these people to be. The client distractions are also one of the most important, yet simplest things—be it games or a nice kitchen where people can sit down and relax. Obviously, staff is very important as well in terms of helping clients, whether it be receiving a phone call or setting them up in a lounge to hear playback of various material. All of that, to me, represents a good facility.

Regarding the back end of that question, I've always felt, as a pretty good mastering engineer, that I've worked in some pretty lousy places. I'm one of those guys that might have been in lesser facilities until I got the chance to build my own. To some degree, you can certainly have the ability and be hampered by budgetary concerns where equipment that you need is not being purchased. Or it could be just the physical limitations of the room, the size of the room, the type of monitors, or the sound of the room, which is certainly the most important thing. If the room is not there, I really believe you are in trouble. So some of the best guys have been locked down, I think, in lesser rooms.

Can you hear the final product in your head when you first do a run-through?

ES: Usually, yes I do. Typically when I first put up a mix, the first thing I do is just go for the level without touching EQs unless there is something blatantly wrong. So I pretty much do get a picture in my head. The extreme is that a good mix is sometimes even more difficult to master in some respects than something that has a blatant problem, so I have got to be very careful because sometimes less is better.

Sometimes you throw up a mix and it's so kick-heavy with an 808, for example, that it is absolutely distorting from the get go, so then you're tweaking right from the beginning. You immediately start to drop the bottom and try to get that balance going so you can dial out some of the kick, then the level starts increasing. I've mastered records where I pulled 4, 5, 6, 7, 8dB out of the bottom and all of a sudden I'm able to get 4dB more overall program level. So when something is not balanced, it can really create big problems.

I do love the fact that vinyl is still hanging around because ultimately, when a lot of these projects are cut to vinyl, that's what really susses engineers out. If they're distorting and mastered to the improper side of loud, it certainly doesn't go to vinyl well. Just the process of cutting vinyl is probably adding 15 percent distortion or more. The good news here at Oasis is that we're hearing that our vinyl sounds better than anybody in the world at this point and I'm very proud of that.

I know you cut vinyl for a long time, but you don't now. Do you miss it?

ES: Not terribly, no. It is a tedious process. I'm glad that I did cut vinyl, because again, that gets back to that big word "balance." The best sonic and the most properly mastered products always cut real well. The worst mastering jobs and the worst mixes mastered really badly. So I'm referring to this smoke and mirrors black art of balance, if you will, that's the toughest game, and cutting vinyl has probably been the biggest help in my entire career. Trying to get the audio balanced so that it would cut well was a huge help because a bad mastering job would cut just horribly. As you started balancing projects out properly, they would cut that much better.

Unfortunately, you can probably count the lacquer houses on one hand now in this country, so the new generation of mastering engineers have not had that training. As a result, it's a little tougher to get to that final stage of mastering something well. Just like anything else, you can't have too much experience. I'm still learning every day because mastering is a constant learning experience. That's the good news, frustratingly so. The vinyl is just totally unforgiving, whereas the digital medium allows you to slam anything into it that you want, clipped or not, because it's not going to skip. In other words, you can almost do anything to a CD and get away with it. Left-right balance can be totally wrong, image can be totally wrong; it just doesn't matter because that CD will not skip. So basically the taste factor becomes the limiting issue.

What's the hardest thing that you have to do? Do you get projects that are more difficult because of the way they're prepared or treated?

ES: I'd say one of the most difficult types of project is the one with source mismatches where some of it's on DAT and some is on half-inch. I still find half-inch, properly aligned on good tape and a good machine, to be a deeper, wider sound. And I still enjoy listening to analog more than I do a lot of the DATs. But cutting an album with source mismatches is quite difficult because the DATs always sonically shrink to me. No matter what I do, that

DAT is just going to sound a little thinner and a little less deep than the half-inch, so trying to create and maintain an album with flow and continuity in terms of sonics becomes difficult.

Soundtrack albums are probably the singly most difficult type of project for me to do, especially if a score is involved. Sequencing is terribly important if score is coming behind a big rockin' song. It's very difficult because the score is dynamically wide with levels from maybe –20 to +3. The low-level score is never loud enough. I think it's always best to help maintain good continuity and flow with good song sequencing. So maintaining some sort of sonic equality, if you will, on a soundtrack album is very difficult, especially if you're sequencing material that's maybe 10 or 15 years old and then current stuff. So probably the most difficult stuff outside of mismatching of sources would be the soundtrack album, but I enjoy doing them, and I think I do them pretty well.

What makes your job easier? Is there something that a client can do to make everything go faster or smoother?

ES: Having some common sense like being organized and obviously having a sequence in mind helps. In general, I'd always prefer to have the best mixes first. But if several studios were used for mixdown, I'd rather keep all the mixes from each studio together. So, if four or five different studios were used, I would start with all the tracks from studio number one. I don't care if it's song number 1, 3, 10, or 12; I would rather master those as a unit and then move on to the next studio to keep some sort of continuity.

What's the thing that you enjoy most about mastering?

ES: The thing I enjoy most is taking a project to another level. And obviously, it's the greatest feeling in the world when Fiona Apple or Christina Aguilara or Offspring ends up being really outstanding sonically and then also achieves the sales that they do. It makes everybody involved with the project pretty happy.

What's the ratio of half-inch to DAT that you get in these days?

ES: It's about 75 percent digital to 25 percent analog. It's getting worse. If you asked me that question about a year ago, it would have said about 70/30, but I think it's creeped up a bit.

Of that 75 percent digital, how much is bit-split?

ES: Boy, 1 percent. It's still pretty rare.

I've seen you get a couple of the 24-bit Tascams in, too.

ES: Right. That's now coming with a little more regularity. In fact, I would suspect that this year there'll be far more dumping to 24-bit. It's a big improvement over 44.1/16-bit. We've gotten in a couple in at 88.2kHz that were very happening. The 88.2kHz through some good converters is as close to analog as I've heard, as a matter of fact. Yeah, the higher sampling rate is just really, really superb.

What are you mostly delivering to the replicator these days?

ES: PMCDs are probably still the most common. 1630s are dwindling. Exabyte DDPs, maybe 5 percent. But PMCDs are really taking over now.

On a typical project, what kind of parts do you normally make?

ES: Usually one to two PMCD masters and obviously a couple of CD refs. But in terms of production parts to go to the plants, I'd say one to two PMCDs as far as the album goes. Maybe a cassette master too, which is done typically to DAT with a 15-second gap between sides one and two.

Do you do all of your equalization and compression and limiting before you hit the workstation?

ES: Oh, absolutely. If the source is analog, it's the best of all worlds because then you're making just one digital conversion into the workstation, so that's the ultimate. I think it's silly to make an A/D conversion, process digitally and then go back into the workstation. The less signal jacking, the better, in my opinion. There are cases where DATs come in, and they must be left in the digital domain so basically there is no additional signal jacking, just the digital processing of a DAT. But ultimately, I will always master the music then dump into the workstation.

So you don't use any plug-ins?
ES: I do some after-the-fact processing in Sonics, but primarily I use the computer EQ just for cutting frequencies. I just did a Fiona Apple cut that is a good example because I could get the exact frequencies that I needed in Sonics, in tenths of a dB with variable Q to the tenth. So it's extremely accurate. There is a definite need to process in the workstation sometimes, but I do as much as I can going in first.

I've noticed that you use a lot of little bits of EQ. Is that typical of most mastering guys?
ES: To tell you the truth, I don't really know how a lot of guys master their projects. I would suspect that I'm somewhat similar to a lot of guys though. I tend to build sound versus stabbing things pretty strongly in one spot. That's about the easiest way as I can say it. I have digital and analog EQ, and upon listening the decision is made which should receive the bulk of the work.

How did you come by that method?
ES: Probably from tuning rooms using third-octave EQs

How often do you have to add effects?
ES: Very rarely. I mean, it might happen twice a year in this room. We don't tend to get those sorts of problems.

Do you get people who premaster things where they'll maybe cut intros off or cut fades off or something like that?
ES: Yes, sometimes for the worse. Usually they think they are saving time, but they might create more problems than if they left it alone in the first place. I've had some projects where they clipped intros, and I've had to grab beats from other places and put them on the top, so I prefer it if you don't cut the program too tight. If there is a lot of very deliberate editing to be done and you want to save time and money offsite, then I understand it. But it better be right.

How important is mono to you? Do you listen in mono a lot?

ES: No, but I believe MTV uses a fold-in process, so there is certainly a consideration to be made for that. Depending on the mix, it's possible that certain instruments will disappear on the fold-in. So pure mono is really not a consideration at all, but if you're thinking of MTV at all, it is definitely a good idea to maybe narrow the spread just to maintain a little better match between a slight fold-in and pure stereo.

How did you go about choosing your monitors?

ES: I've been using Tannoys since about 1984 or '85. I'm just a big fan of the dual-concentrics. I think the phase coherency is just unsurpassed. Once you get used to listening to these boxes, it's very difficult to listen to spread drivers again. In this particular case, my Dual 15s have been custom modified for the room to some degree, and using them is just a great treat. I think they are one of the easier speakers to listen to since they certainly don't sound like the big brash monitor that they possibly might look to be. A typical comment made about the monitors here at Oasis is that they sound like the best big stereo system they've ever heard, which is a terrifically flattering compliment. I also have some little Tannoy System 600s for near-fields, and now I've added some dual 15 subs to the mains. Sonically speaking, I have been in quite a few rooms, and I have yet to hear a system that rivals this, so I am very happy with it.

Tell me about the subwoofers. What was the reason for getting them and why did you get two as opposed to one?

ES: My mains, the Dual 15s, are definitely light from say, 30Hz down, so I wanted to fill in the extreme lows more accurately because of the amount of R&B that I do. Darren Cavanaugh and Aria came up with a design that I just absolutely love. I feel I have a little bit better control with the pair than with a single sub in terms of where they sit. Whereas with one, you are pretty much locked down positionally, with the two you actually have a little more flexibility.

Now that you had some experience with surround sound, how do you feel about that as opposed to stereo?

ES: Oh, I am loving it, but it's a difficult medium to work in. It's not something you just throw up and do. To some degree you'd think it would be easier because you have five speakers to fill up instead of cramming all this information in two speakers, but it is not. The balance of the monitor system is extremely important, and the adjustment of levels of the drivers and then interfacing the sub is extremely critical on the mix. I find that the stereo image between the left and right, left and left surround, right and right surround in the crisscross from the left to the right surround is very, very tricky. I do hear some unusual low-frequency phase characteristics that I'm not real happy with, depending on the mix. I've also heard some very, very good mixes, so it can definitely work. It is a difficult medium at best to really make sound good, but so is a really great stereo mix. 5.1 is just so new to all of us that it's much more difficult at this point, but when something is nailed, it's just awesome.

What's your favorite piece of gear?

ES: That is tough because the digital Weiss desk that I have certainly is still unsurpassed at this point. The Manley LimCom [Vari-Mu compressor] is definitely one of the best units I have in terms of analog. I really don't have a piece of gear in here that I dislike, so between Tube Tech and Manley and Avalon, Waves L-2 and Junger, it is all my favorite stuff, to be honest with you. Sonically, it just doesn't let me down.

When you get handed a project, what are the steps? What do you actually go through on a whole project? Describe a whole project like Christina Aguilara, for example.

ES: Christina is an extreme example because of the complexity of the album. In other words, that particular album was mastered over the course of six to eight weeks, maybe longer. Songs were being remixed and getting swapped, so it was a little longer process than normal. Not that it was bad because, if anything, I didn't have to deal with the typical 12 or 13 songs in one day and nail them all with one mastering session. An average album rolls in where I am doing that in five to six hours though.

Basically, a project starts out whereby a client comes in, hands me tapes and gives me a song sequence. I just take it song by song and dump it into my Sonic and then offload refs. The procedure can be relatively simple, outside of interludes and any special little musical pieces that may interface with the album in terms of spreads in-between songs.

But Christina was unusual, as I say, because it was done over quite a period of time. That was actually great because as the sequence changed and songs came and went, my perspective on the sound of the album remained consistent because I was always given the time I needed.

Is it harder for you to do something like that over the course of a week or two than it is to do all at once?

ES: It really depends. Sometimes I would say yes, but sometimes it gets crushingly difficult when a project just strings on and on and on because you can lose a bit of your objectivity.

I truly find that the R&B-type pop records are a little easier than rock records. Rock records get a little trickier because the balances are so critical. It just seems that a well arranged R&B pop track is pretty simple for me to hear, whereas rock seems to need more sonic continuity than R&B tracks. It just feels better when they are seemingly coming from a similar place. Whereas R&B pop records can have much more extremes involved and it just plays out fine.

How does Latin stack up?

ES: It's similar. The only catch becomes, just as in my Japanese projects, it's a little trickier to dissect vocal balances if they are not sung in English. I'll often turn to a client and ask about a word in Spanish or Japanese. "Was that okay? Was that discernable?" Because the Japanese market tends to go for a little higher vocal level because it is tough to hear the lyrics in the language. Ultimately, though, balance is still the key.

Glossary

1630—A first generation two-track digital tape machine utilizing a separate digital processor and a 3/4-inch U-matic video tape machine for storage. 1630s were the primary master tape delivered to the pressing plant since the inception of CDs and are still used to this day, although less and less every year. A model 1610 predated this machine.

5.1—A speaker system which uses three speakers across the front and two stereo speakers in the rear, along with a subwoofer.

Acetate—A single-sided vinyl check disc, sometimes called a ref. Due to the extreme softness of the vinyl, an acetate has a limited number of plays (five or six) before it wears out. (See also **Ref.**)

AIFF—Audio Interchange File Format (also known as Apple Interchange File Format) is the most used audio file format used in the Apple Macintosh operating system. An AIFF file contains the raw audio data, channel information (monophonic or stereophonic), bit depth, sample rate, and application-specific data areas. The application-specific data areas let different applications add information to the file header that remains there even if the file is opened and processed by another application. For example, a file could retain information about selected regions of the audio data used for recalling zoom levels not used by other applications.

A/D—Analog-to-digital converter. This device converts the analog waveform into the digital form of digital 1s and 0s.

Asset—A multimedia element, either sound, picture, graphic, or text.

Attack—The first part of a sound. On a compressor/limiter, a control that affects how that device will respond to the attack of a sound.

Attenuation—A decrease in level.

Automation—A system that memorizes, then plays back the position of all faders and mutes on a console.

Bandwidth—The number of frequencies that a device will pass before the signal degrades. A human being can supposedly hear from 20Hz to 20kHz, so the bandwidth of the human ear is 20 to 20kHz.

Bass Management—A circuit which utilizes the subwoofer in a 5.1 system to provide bass extension for the five main speakers. The bass manager steers all frequencies below 80Hz into the subwoofer along with the LFE source signal.

Bass Redirection—Another term for **Bass Management.**

Bit Rate—The transmission rate of a digital system.

Bit-splitter—In order to record a signal with a 20- or 24-bit word length onto a recorder that is only 16-bit, the digital word is "split" across two tracks instead of one.

BLER—Block error rate. A measurement of how many errors a disc contains. A BLER rate of 220 per second or above will cause the disc to be rejected, although the acceptable rate is usually far lower.

Buss—A signal pathway.

Chamber (reverb)—A method of creating artificial reverberation by sending a signal to a speaker in a tiled room that is picked up by several microphones placed in the room.

Chorus—A type of signal processor that mixes a detuned copy with the original signal, which creates a fatter sound.

Clone—A copy of a tape that is bit-for-bit accurate with the original source.

Comb Filter—A distortion produced by combining an electronic or acoustic signal with a delayed copy of itself. The result is peaks and dips introduced into the frequency response. This is what happens when a signal is flanged (see **Flanging**).

Cut—To decrease, attenuate, or make less.

Cutter Head—The assembly on a lathe that holds the cutting stylus between a set of drive coils powered by very high-powered (typically 1000- to 3500-watt) amplifiers.

D/A—Digital-to-analog converter. This device converts the digital 1s and 0s back to an analog waveform.

DAT—Digital audio tape. An inexpensive digital audio format using 4mm wide tape. This format was originally intended for the consumer market but has found widespread use in professional circles due to its small size and low cost.

Data Compression—Achieved through an encoder, which is a device that takes multiple digital data streams (as in six-channel surround sound) and compresses them into a single data stream for more efficient storage and transmission. A decoder performs the opposite function and takes a single encoded bitstream and breaks it into multiple data streams.

DataDAT—A 4mm, two-reel tape cartridge used for computer data backup. (See also **DDS**.)

DAW—Digital audio workstation. A computer with the appropriate hardware and software needed to digitize and edit audio.

DDP—Disc description protocol. A proprietary format developed by Doug Carson Associates using an 8mm Exabyte tape that allows for high-speed glass master cutting.

DDS—Digital data storage. A 4mm, two-reel tape cartridge, sometimes known as a dataDAT, used for computer data backup.

Decay—The time it takes for a signal to fall below audibility.

Delay—A type of signal processor that produces distinct repeats (echoes) of a signal.

Digital Domain—When a signal source is digitized or converted into a series of electronic pulses represented by 1s and 0s, the signal is then in the digital domain.

Dipole—A loudspeaker having a figure 8 directional pattern and often used for reproducing the surround channels of a multichannel audio system by placing the listening area in the null of the figure 8. Dipoles are often found to be better than a direct radiator at reproducing enveloping sounds such as reverberation and ambience and poorer at localizing. Also, dipoles simulate an array of loudspeakers in theaters when used in the home.

Direct Radiator—A loudspeaker where the principal output is directed at the listening area. Universally used for the front channels in a multichannel sound system and widely used for the surround channels, direct radiators are often found to be better than dipole radiator for localization and poorer for diffuse-field reproduction such as for reverberation and ambience.

Dither—A low-level noise signal used to gradually reduce the length of a digital word.

DLT—Digital linear tape. A high-speed, large-capacity format for data backup. Also used as the standard master for DVD delivery to the replicator.

Dolby Digital®—A data compression method, otherwise known as AC-3, that uses psychoacoustic principles to reduce the number of bits required to represent the signal.

Bit rates for 5.1 channels range from 320kbps for sound on film to 384kbps for digital television and up to 640kbps for audio use on DVD. AC-3 is also a lossy compressor (see **Lossy Compression**), which relies on psychoacoustic modeling of frequency and temporal masking effects to reduce bits by eliminating those parts of the signal thought to be inaudible. The bit rate reduction achieved at a nominal 384kbps is about 10:1.

Dolby Prologic®—An active matrix decoder that extracts four signals from two-channel Dolby Surround–encoded material. The four channels are left, center, right front, and a single bandwidth-limited mono surround channel. The amplitude-phase matrix decoder uses level difference between the two source channels, called Lt and Rt, to steer across left-center-right, and the phase difference to steer from front to surround.

Dolby Surround®—A digital encoding system that combines four channels (left, center, right and a limited bandwidth surround channel) into two channels. These two channels can be summed together for mono playback, or played back as normal stereo. When the two channels are fed into the active Dolby Pro Logic decoder, the matrix is unfolded back into four channels again. The limited bandwidth surround channel is reproduced through the left surround and right surround speakers. If the matrix is fed into a passive decoder, then only the stereo signal plus the surround channel is unfolded.

Downmix—To automatically extract a stereo or mono mix from an encoded surround mix.

DSP—Digital signal processing. Processing within the digital domain, usually by dedicated microprocessors.

DTS®—A data compression method, developed by Digital Theater Systems using waveform coding techniques, which takes six channels of audio (5.1) and folds them into a single digital bitstream. This differs from Dolby Digital in that the data rate is a somewhat higher 1.4Mbs, which represents a compression ratio of about 4:1. DTS is also what's known as a lossy compression (see **Lossy Compression**).

DTV—Digital television.

Element—A component or ingredient of the mix.

Elliptical EQ—A special equalizer built especially for vinyl disc mastering that takes excessive bass energy from either side of a stereo signal and directs it to the center. This prevents excessive low-frequency energy from cutting through the groove wall and destroying the master lacquer.

Equalizer—A tone control that can vary in sophistication from very simple to very complex (see **Parametric Equalizer**).

Exciter—An outboard effects device that uses phase manipulation and harmonic distortion to produce high-frequency enhancement of a signal.

Feather—Rather than applying a large amount of equalization at a single frequency, small amounts are added at the frequencies adjoining the one of principle concern.

Flanging—The process of mixing a copy of the signal back with itself, gradually and randomly slowing the copy down to cause the sound to "whoosh" as if it were in a wind tunnel. This was originally done by holding a finger against a tape flange (the metal part that holds the tape on the reel), hence the name.

Fletcher-Munson Curves—A set of measurements that describes how the frequency response of the ear changes at different sound pressure levels. For instance, we generally hear very high and very low frequencies much better as the overall sound pressure level is increased.

Glass Master—The first and most important step in CD replication from which the stampers are eventually made.

HDCD—High Definition Compatible Digital. A process by Pacific Microsonics that encodes 20 bits of information onto a standard 16-bit CD while still remaining compatible with standard CD players.

I/O—Input/output.

Jitter—The AES/EBU waveform should have particular transitions at precise intervals. Jitter is a measure of the instability of this timing. Timing errors result in frequency modulation of the audio signal which in extreme cases can be detected as side bands either side of a constant tone.

Lacquer—The vinyl master, which is a single-sided 14-inch disc made of aluminum substrate covered with a soft cellulose nitrate. A separate lacquer is required for each side of a record. Since the lacquer can never be played, a ref or acetate is made to check the disc (see **Ref** and **Acetate**).

LBR—Laser beam recorder. The device that cuts the glass master from which the CD stampers are made.

LFE—Low frequency effects channel. This is a special channel of 5 to 120Hz information primarily intended for special effects such as explosions in movies. The LFE has an additional 10dB of headroom in order to accommodate the required level.

Lossy Compression—A compression format that cannot recover all of its original data from the compressed version. Supposedly, some of what is normally recorded before compression is imperceptible, with the louder sounds masking the softer ones. As a result, some data can be eliminated since it's not heard anyway. This selective approach, determined by extensive psychoacoustic research, is the basis for lossy compression. It is debatable, however, how much data can actually be thrown away (or compressed) without an audible sacrifice. Dolby AC-3 and DTS are lossy compression schemes.

Lossless Compression—A compression format that recovers all the original data from the compressed version. MLP is a lossless compression scheme.

LPCM—Linear pulse code modulation. The most common method of digital encoding of audio used today; the same digital encoding method used by current audio CDs. In LPCM, the analog waveform is measured at discrete points in time and converted into a digital representation.

Make-up Gain—A control on a compressor/limiter that applies additional gain to the signal. This is required since the signal is automatically decreased when the compressor is working. Make-up gain *makes up* the gain and brings it back to where it was prior to being compressed.

MDM—Modular digital multitrack. A low-cost eight-track digital recorder that can be grouped together to configure however many tracks that are needed. The Tascam DA-88 and Alesis ADAT are the most popular MDMs.

MLP—Meridian lossless packing. A data compression technique designed specifically for high quality (96kHz/24-bit) sonic data. MLP differs from other data compression techniques in that no significant data is thrown away, thus the "lossless" moniker. MLP is also a standard for the 96kHz/24-bit portion of the new DVD-Audio disc, and will be licensed by Dolby Labs.

MO—Magneto-optical. A writable method of digital storage utilizing an optical disc. Each disc stores from 250MB to 4.3GB and may be double-sided. Its widespread use has been limited due to its slow disc access time.

Modulate—The process of adding a control voltage to a signal source in order to change its character. For example, modulating a short slap delay with a .5Hz signal will produce chorusing (see **Chorus**).

Mother—In either vinyl or CD manufacturing, the intermediate step from which a stamper is made.

Mute—An on/off switch. To mute something means to turn it off.

Parametric Equalizer—A tone control where the gain, frequency, and bandwidth are all variable.

Parts—The different masters sent to the pressing plant. A mastering house may make different parts/masters for CD, cassette, and vinyl, or send additional parts to pressing plants around the world.

Phantom Image—In a stereo system, if the signal is of equal strength in the left and right channels, the resultant sound appears to come from in between them. This is a phantom image.

Phase Shift—The process during which some frequencies (usually those below 100Hz) are slowed down ever so slightly as they pass through a device. This is usually exaggerated by excessive use of equalization and is highly undesirable.

Pitch—On a record, the velocity of the cutter head. Measured in the number of lines (grooves) per inch.

Plate Reverb—A method to create artificial reverberation using a large steel plate with a speaker and several transducers connected to it.

PMCD—Premastered CD. A disc similar to a CD-R except that it has PQ codes written on the lead-out of the disc to expedite replication.

PQ Codes—Subcodes included along with the main data channel as a means of placing control data like start IDs and table of contents on a CD.

Predelay—A variable length of time before the onset of reverberation. Predelay is often used to separate the source from the reverberation so the source can be heard more clearly.

Pultec—An equalizer sold during the '50s and '60s by Western Electric that is highly prized today for its smooth sound.

Q—Bandwidth of a filter or equalizer.

Range—On a gate or expander, a control that adjusts the amount of attenuation that will occur to the signal when the gate is closed.

Ratio—A parameter control on a compressor/limiter that determines how much compression or limiting will occur when the signal exceeds threshold.

Recall—A system that memorizes the position of all pots and switches on a console. The engineer must still physically reset the pots and switches back to their previous positions as indicated on a video monitor.

Red Book—The prerecorded CD audio standard that you find in music stores today. Because of this standard, any CD will play in any audio compact disc player. Specified are the sample rate (44.1kHz), bit depth (16), type of error detection and correction, and how the data is stored on the disc, among other things.

Ref—Short for "reference record," a ref is a single-sided vinyl check disc, sometimes called an acetate. Due to the extreme softness of the vinyl, a ref has a limited number of plays (five or six) before it wears out. (See also **Acetate**.)

Reference Level—This is the sound pressure level at which a sound system is aligned.

Release—The last part of a sound. On a compressor/limiter, a control that affects how that device will respond to the release of a sound.

Reverb—A type of signal processor that reproduces the spatial sound of an environment (i.e., the sound of a closet or locker room or inside an oil tanker).

RIAA Curve—An equalization curve instituted by the Record Industry Association of America (the RIAA) in 1953 that narrowed the grooves, thereby allowing more of them to be cut on the record, which increased the playing time and decreased the noise. This was accomplished by boosting the high frequencies by about 17dB at 15kHz and cutting the lows by 17dB at 50Hz when the record was cut. The opposite curve is then applied during playback.

Pumping—When the level of a mix increases, then decreases noticeably. Pumping is caused by the improper setting of the attack and release times on a compressor.

Punchy—A description for a quality of sound that infers good reproduction of dynamics with a strong impact. Sometimes means emphasis in the 200Hz and 5kHz areas.

Return—Inputs on a recording console especially dedicated for effects devices such as reverbs and delays. The return inputs are usually not as sophisticated as normal channel inputs on a console.

Scalability—A feature of DVD-A that allows the producer to select from various sample rates (44.1, 48, 88.2, 96, 176.4, or 192kHz) and word lengths (16, 20, or 24). It is also possible for the producer to assign different sample rates and word lengths to different channel families, such as 96/24 to the front speakers and 48/16 to the surrounds.

SDDS—Sony Dynamic Digital Sound. Sony's digital delivery system for the cinema. This 7.1 system features five speakers across the front, stereo speakers on the sides, and a subwoofer.

Sibilance—A rise in the frequency response in a vocal where there's an excessive amount of 5kHz, resulting in the "S" sounds being overemphasized.

Signal Jacking—When a signal is moved from the digital domain to the analog domain and back again, or vice versa. This is usually an undesirable, but sometimes necessary, operation.

SMART Content—System Management Audio Resource Technique. This feature allows the producer to control the way the multichannel audio is played back in stereo by saving one of 16 mixdown coefficients as control information to a data channel on the DVD-A.

Source Tape—An original master tape that is not a copy or a clone.

SPL—Sound pressure level.

SRC—Sample rate conversion.

Stamper—In either vinyl or CD manufacturing, a negative copy bolted into the presser to actually stamp out records or CDs.

Stems—Mixes that have their major elements broken out separately for individual adjustment at a later time.

Sub—Short for subwoofer

Subwoofer—A low-frequency speaker with a frequency response from about 25Hz to 120Hz.

Synchronization—When two devices, usually storage devices such as tape machines, DAWs or sequencers, are locked together in respect to time.

Threshold—The point at which an effect takes place. On a compressor/limiter, for instance, the threshold control adjusts the point at which compression will take place.

Tripole—A surround speaker (trademarked by M&K) that combines both a direct radiator and a dipole in the same cabinet (see **Direct Radiator** and **Dipole**).

TV Mix—A mix without the vocals so the artist can sing live to the back tracks during a television appearance.

UDF—Universal Disc Format. The file system used by DVD that eliminates much of the confusion that CD-ROM had due to the many different file formats used. All DVD formats use UDF and as a result have some level of compatibility with all DVD players as well as with computers using DOS, OS/2, Windows, Mac, and Unix operating systems.

U-Matic—An industrial video machine utilizing a cassette storing 3/4-inch tape. The U-matic is the primary storage device for the 1630 digital processor.

Variable Pitch—On a record, varying the number of grooves per inch depending upon the program material.

Vinylite—The vinyl used to make records actually comes in a granulated form called vinylite. Before being pressed, it is heated into the form of modeling clay and colored with pigment.

WAVE—An audio data file developed by the IBM and Microsoft corporations and is the PC equivalent of an AIFF file. It is identified by the file extension ".wav".

About the Author

One of the first people to delve into surround sound music mixing, Bobby Owsinski has worked on a variety of surround projects and DVD productions for such diverse acts as Jimi Hendrix, The Who, Iron Maiden, Eddie Money, Christopher Cross, Firesign Theater, Pat Benetar, Tangerine Dream, Yanni, and George Winston, among many others. A principal in the industry-leading DVD production house Surround Associates, he has also penned several hundred audio-related articles for many popular industry trade publications and authored the recently published MixBooks title *The Mixing Engineer's Handbook*.

Thanks to:

Evanna Manley at Manley Labs

Mike Rivers

KS Waves

Karen Childs

Karl Winkler at Neumann

Clete Baker

Index